D0626418

be liked tempered by a genuine concern to engage with a terrible past – are all in this book.' *Guardian*

'Sophisticated and often insightful.' *Time Out*

'Oltermann deftly intersperses his own experience of Britain

with other "encounters" between Britons and Germans – Margaret Thatcher and Helmut Kohl, William Cobbett and Heinrich Heine, A. J. Ayer and Theodor Adorno, and so on – to explore the different attitudes of the two countries to everything from language and politics to sex and sport.' *Observer*

Keeping Up with the Germans

A History of Anglo-German Encounters

PHILIP OLTERMANN

faber and faber

First published in 2012
by Faber and Faber Limited
Bloomsbury House,
74–77 Great Russell Street,
London WC1B 3DA

This paperback edition published in 2013

Typeset by Faber and Faber Ltd
Printed in the UK by CPI Group (UK) Ltd, Croydon CR0 4YY

A CIP record for this book
is available from the British Library

ISBN 978-0-571-24019-7

FSC
www.fsc.org
MIX
Paper from
responsible sources
FSC® C101712

2 4 6 8 10 9 7 5 3 1

Für meine Eltern

Contents

Contents

Preface

'Du bist sehr schön, but we haven't been introduced.'

Blur, 'Girls and Boys'

It was 26 June 1996. Germany were playing England in the semi-final of the European championship tournament at Wembley Stadium. I was sat on the blue sofa in our living room in Norderstedt, a suburb of Hamburg. My parents sat either side of me. On the table in front of us were three glasses filled with carbonated water. You could hear the bubbles popping. About five minutes ago my father had told me that he had been offered a position in the London office of his company, and that he had accepted their offer. He and my mother would start looking for a flat in the next few weeks. I was fifteen: it was obvious that I was too young to live on my own, but also too old to move in with my grand-mother.

'You're so mature for your age, so we thought we could talk about this like grown-ups . . .'

'I know you've got a lot of friends here, but . . .'

'Did you hear about Lena in the year above you? She went to America for a year, and now she's top of her class . . .'

'How about this: you spend a year at an English school, and if you don't like it, we'll be back here in a year?'

It was only when the players gathered around the centre circle that I realised my parents were still waiting for my answer. The score at the top of the screen read 1:1. I should explain straight away that I had never been particularly interested in football as a child – in fact, I had been uninterested in the sport to the extent of actively shunning it. Yet that night, I saw the drama unfolding on the screen in a new way. England had scored early in the match through Alan Shearer, but Germany had managed to equalise before half time through Kaiserslautern's box-shaped striker Stefan Kuntz. In the second half Kuntz had a second goal disallowed for an apparent foul, and in extra time Paul Gascoigne had missed an easy tap-in by an agonising inch. As the match was still undecided after 120 minutes, the commentator explained, there would be a penalty shoot-out.

We each took a sip of fizzy water. I had a closer look at the players gathering around the centre circle. The English team wore a dull grey kit. There was a curious washed denim effect on the shirts on their bodies, and tense expressions on their faces. When they managed to get the ball into the back of the net, their expressions contorted with joy to an absurd degree. Stuart Pearce, a defender with a menacing stare and a blond tangle of hair, gave the crowd a winking smile and an exaggerated thumbs-up gesture when he scored, as if he had just stepped on stage at a West End comedy club. Paul Gascoigne did a thing where he punched his fists in a downward motion and then jutted out his chest.

The faces of the German players, by contrast, expressed neither excessive joy nor undue concern. Thomas Hässler struck low to the left, Thomas Strunz hammered his shot in the top left corner, Stefan Kuntz scored high to the right, and both Stefan Reuter and Christian Ziege lofted the ball to the right of David Seaman's palm: all taking their penalties with the utmost urgency and precision, like a team of scientists trying to finish an important experiment.

Gareth Southgate was next for England. Was there a frown on his face as he placed the ball on the spot? 'A relative newcomer to this team,' commentator Gerd Rubenbauer said on German TV. 'The most soft-hearted defender in England, even according to his coach,' adding, as Southgate started to run, 'He has to be tough now.' The German keeper blocked Southgate's shot. It was now up to Germany to decide the match. On German TV, Rubenbauer finally started to show nerves. 'If Möller now scores, Germany could be in the final. Möller, of all people!'

Let me briefly introduce Andi Möller. Andi Möller was a fast, dribbling midfielder, who was disliked intensely by the German press and went by the moniker 'Weepy Susie' in the tabloids because he had once cried in a post-match interview. Throughout the 1980s and 1990s, Möller played football for Eintracht Frankfurt, Juventus Turin, Borussia Dortmund and Schalke 04; on that night, he was leading the German team as captain. He had curly brown hair and a mullet –

a haircut that continued to be popular with German football players as late as the mid-1990s, when Gascoigne and co. were already modelling aerodynamic short back and sides. On 26 June 1996, around 10 p.m., Andi Möller thwacked a penalty – an unstoppable, fierce, near-perfect penalty – under the roof of David Seaman's goal inside Wembley Stadium. Möller's penalty knocked England out of their own tournament and Germany into the final. And yet I wasn't feeling particularly excited or happy. The knot in my stomach had tightened rather than loosened. The reason for this was Andi Möller's goal celebration.

Goal celebrations are a curious feature of international sport, and football in particular. Going by footage of football tournaments before 1990, goalscorers used to celebrate by running back into their own half and hugging their teammates. On the occasional extravagant whim, they might have jumped into the air and waved their arms about. Whenever Kevin Keegan scored, for example, he used to merely stand on one spot and push both his fists into the air until his spine bent backwards, like an inverted letter C. It looked like an authentic expression of joy: he was celebrating for himself, not for the people around him.

In modern football, things are different: the movement is outward rather than inward – towards the fanblocks by the corner flags or the cameras on the touchlines – and the performances are self-consciously theatrical. The Euro '96 tournament had already scaled new heights in on-pitch theatrics with Paul Gascoigne's 'dentist chair' celebration: after the winning goal in a first-round game against Scotland, the team had huddled around the scorer to re-enact the by now infamous drinking game, with a plastic water bottle in place of the vodka. As unlikely as it may sound, the German celebration was much, much worse than that.

With the ball safely in the back of the net, Andi Möller ran to the right-hand corner flag, by the German block. Next to the flag, he stopped abruptly, puffed up his chest and struck his arms into his sides to form the shape of perfectly triangular wings: he looked like a flamboyant cockerel at a prize show. It was the one of the campest, most bizarre goal celebrations the world had ever seen. Linguistic fluency wasn't required to grasp that Andi Möller hadn't improved my chances of making new friends in England, though with a better knowledge of the English tongue I might have gleaned that the Germans on the pitch that night had managed to go from being total Kuntz to acting like complete cocks.

*

I sometimes wonder if Germany in my lifetime has been hated with more passion than it ever was in the 1910s or 1940s. This might sound wilfully polemical. But if you take the world of sport as a screen that allows us to glimpse international relations as they really are, without the false formality of diplomacy, then the evidence is hard to ignore. The French hated us because in the 1982 World Cup, our goalkeeper, Harald 'Toni' Schumacher, had knocked out their defender Patrick Battiston with a bodycheck that would have left seasoned WWF wrestlers in tears. As Battiston lay unconscious in a pool of blood and broken teeth, and millions of TV viewers around the world feared for the Frenchman's life, the German stood casually propped against the goalpost, chewing gum with undisguised disdain. Schumacher was one in a long line of German goalkeepers prone to volcanic temper, all worthy successors to Kaiser Wilhelm in the 'madman of Europe' category. The Algerians hated us too, not because of our goalkeepers, but because we had knocked them out of the same World Cup with an unsporting 1:0 against Austria, whose passage to the next round was guaranteed with the result – a match which has gone down in sporting history as the *Anschluss* match of 1982. The Argentinians hated us because we had beaten them in the 1990 final. The Hungarians hated us because they thought we were on drugs when we beat them in the 1954 final. The Spanish? The Spanish actually secretly admired our success at sport but they hated us too, mainly because they could (I once came across an old issue of *El País* in which a photograph of two German footballers was captioned, in a very matter-of-fact way, 'Paul Breitner and Uli Stielike, two ugly Germans'). The Dutch? The Dutch hated us more openly than anyone else: so much, in fact, that one Dutch player found himself spitting in the curly mullet of a German player on live television, not once, but twice in one match. So much that when one German player offered to swap his shirt with his Dutch opponent after a game in 1988, the Dutchman grabbed the white Adidas top and pretended to wipe his bottom with it as he walked away. By the 1990s, this development had come to its logical conclusion: hating the

German team at football was just *what you did*. To sympath-
ise with the Germans would have been like crying when the
Death Star blows up at the end of *Star Wars*: not just unlikely, but quite unnatural.

The English initially hated us with more reserve, though
this would eventually ebb away during the 1990s. A con-
ciliatory tone had determined proceedings at the first big
encounter after the end of the Second World War, the 1966
World Cup final at Wembley: German papers noted the 'fair
play attitude' of the English fans, and there wasn't the booing
of the German national anthem that later became custom-
ary; only the *Daily Mail* wanted to remark that 'if Germany
beat us at Wembley this afternoon at our national sport, we
can always point out to them that we have recently beaten
them twice at theirs'. Forward thirty years to the same loc-
ation, and the mood was notably less friendly. The *Mirror*'s
front page has gone down in Fleet Street folklore: 'Achtung!
Surrender!' next to Photoshopped portraits of Paul
Gascoigne and Stuart Pearce wearing stormtrooper helmets.
The *Daily Star* gave it 'Watch out Krauts. England are going
to bomb you to bits'; the *Sun* chipped in with 'Let's Blitz
Fritz'.

It might be unfair to take these kind of headlines too literally, to ignore the tradition of wordplay in the British press,
and its egalitarian nobody-is-spared approach. Yet neither
context nor excuses do much to explain what happened after
Andi Möller had despatched his penalty. On the night of
26/27 June 1996, acts of anti-German violence led to more
than two hundred arrests across the UK. In London, sixty-

six people were injured in a riot in Trafalgar Square; a man in his thirties had his throat slashed with a broken bottle. In Exmouth, Devon, a Volkswagen was wrecked by a group of young men who were heard shouting 'Look, a German car'. The windows of a BMW dealership in Birmingham were smashed. In a park in Hove, Sussex, a teenage boy – roughly the same age as me at the time – was stabbed five times in the neck and face for being German. It later turned out that he was Russian.

You could blame it all on football, with its crowd-enforced tribalism and toxic cocktail of endorphins and disappointment. But that wouldn't explain why even among men and women in grey suits, the 1990s witnessed an all-time low in Anglo-German relations. The unification of East and West Germany in 1989–90 would certainly have been a factor. Welcomed by most politicians on the European mainland, and even more so in Eastern Europe, it was viewed with scepticism from Westminster. At a lunchtime meeting between Margaret Thatcher and Mikhail Gorbachev on 23 September 1989 – weeks before joyous Berliners from East and West would dance together on the crumbling wall – the prime minister told the spiritual father of perestroika that 'Britain and Western Europe are not interested in the unification of Germany'. As a result, the British ambassador to Germany reported that his home country was viewed as the least positive of the three Western allies, and the least important. Britain's image, he informed Whitehall on 22 February 1990, 'was at its lowest for years'. Germany's image in Britain, likewise, was sinking fast. In the

British press, the expulsion from the European Exchange Rate Mechanism after the 'Black Wednesday' of 16 September 1992 was widely blamed on the German Bundesbank. If only 23 per cent had worried about a resurgence of German National Socialism in a 1977 survey, in 1992 53 per cent of the British public were concerned that the reunited country might again pose a threat.

More specifically, there was a growing fear that when the Nazis came back, they would be wrapped in the star-sprinkled flag of the European Union: a fantasy which might seem far-fetched, but which became increasingly powerful in British minds over the course of the 1990s. There was never any shortage of respectable political figures queuing up to add contours to this paranoid vision. In March 1990, Margaret Thatcher brought together Britain's leading historians at Chequers in order to give her a crash course in German history. A memo, leaked to the press, concluded that 'typical' German qualities included 'angst, aggressiveness, assertiveness, bullying, egotism, inferiority complexes and sentimentality'. In July 1990 the Conservative secretary of state for trade and industry, Nicholas Ridley, described the European Monetary Union in a *Spectator* article as 'a German racket designed to take over the whole of Europe'. On 26 June 1996, on the day of the football semi-final at Wembley, an op-ed by John Redwood urged readers of *The Times* to 'think again about the problem of Germany', because Helmut Kohl had suggested the UK take a more active role in the EU. The concluding sentence of that article would have made a nice slogan for a war bond poster in

1939: 'Stand up to Germany, on and off the field'. With German victories at Wembley and Wimbledon (between 1985 and 1996 there were no fewer than fourteen German champions at the most traditional of tennis tournaments), the British prime minister had become noticeably irritable. 'If Boris Becker wins again this year,' one of her cabinet ministers confided to a journalist in 1990, 'Margaret will be hell in cabinet the next day.'

Perhaps blaming Margaret Thatcher for all this is a little too obvious. Because the thing about Germany in the 1990s wasn't just that all our European neighbours hated us. As the American poet C. K. Williams put it, writing in *Die Zeit* in 2002, Germany had become a 'symbolic nation': a blank canvas on which nations from around the globe were able to project their disgust with the world. In fact, Germany made such a good symbolic villain that even we Germans had started to hate Germany. If you ever cross the railway bridge at Berlin's Warschauer Strasse train station, and if you have a minute before the next S-Bahn arrives – turn around and look north. Miles away, yet clearly visible across the barren industrial landscape, someone has written *Deutschland verrecke!* across the roofs of a row of houses, letters the size of barn doors. Somehow I can't imagine the words 'Die, England, die!' on display in a similarly public place in central London. The monarchy, the government, no problem: everyone remembers the Sex Pistols and that green grass mohican given to Winston Churchill's statue in Parliament Square. But 'Fuck England'? The whole shop? Cream teas *and* fry-ups? Elgar *and* the Smiths? Enid Blyton *and* Harold

Pinter? Britishness is a broad church, broad enough to en-
compass official as well as alternative accounts of its own
history. There are different Britains – radical, multicultural urban Britain; genteel Middle England Britain – you can
choose to feel patriotic about. Growing up in Germany, the
choice was much simpler: you were either for Germany, or
you were against it. I have seen that graffiti every time I have
been to Berlin in the last ten years. *Deutschland verrecke!*
Clearly, no one feels strongly enough to scrub it off.

At the start of the 1990s it was not just the Iron Lady
who worried about a revival of the German far right, but the
Germans too. In the summer and autumn months of 1992, a
series of attacks on migrant minorities seized the country: in
a suburb of Rostock in the east a group of young men set fire
to a hostel that housed about 150 Vietnamese immigrants,
and continued to riot for several nights; there were similar
attacks in Schleswig-Holstein and North Rhine-Westphalia.
The images in the news haunted the Federal Republic like
flashbacks of a bad dream. One photograph in particular
was printed over and over again: a bystander in a Germany
football shirt, one hand hanging limp down the side of his
urine-stained tracksuit bottoms, the other raised in a *Sieg
Heil* salute. To me, the pictures from Rostock were shocking
mainly because they seemed so far removed from my own
situation. My older sister had recently started seeing a man
from Peru, whom I revered; my brother had moved in with
his German-Japanese girlfriend. Even without an interest in
football, I had gleaned that none of my classmates were supporting Germany at international matches. One evening in

the winter of 1992, my parents, my sisters and I went on a protest march around the Alster Lake in the centre of Hamburg, carrying a candle. We were five of nearly one million people who made a stand against racism and xenophobia that night, forming a *Lichterkette* or 'chain of light' in German cities. I knew that we weren't part of the ugly Germany. I was convinced that the man in the tracksuit bottoms had nothing, nothing at all, to do with me, my friends and my family. I remember people handing out stickers that said 'Foreigners, don't leave us alone with the Germans'. In the decade in which Germans were hated more than ever, we were also more eager than ever to be loved.

The prospect of more money had certainly motivated my father's decision to accept the job in London. But there might well have been a psychological motivation too: a secret desire to become more than just 'a German', a longing to escape that restrictive villain role and dive straight into a London which, more than any other city in Europe, seemed to embody a dream of personal freedom and intercultural harmony. It felt to me like every second friend or relative I knew had decided to leave the country at that time, or was considering it. My parents certainly weren't the only Germans who weighed up a move abroad in 1996. In 1997, the German-born population of the United Kingdom swelled to a high of 227,900, making us the third largest foreign-born group on the island, well ahead of the Pakistanis, the Poles, the Jamaicans, the Ghanaians, the Australians and the Americans (even though an unspecified percentage of that number would have been born in Germany because their British fathers were stationed there).

My parents and I were three of those 227,900. Because after Andi Möller had scored his penalty, after Paul Gascoigne had given the crying Gareth Southgate a hug and after thousands of England fans had left the pub in search of German cars, I eventually answered my parents' question: yes, I would give England a go. As long as it was only for a year. If I didn't like it, we had to go back – that was the deal. We shook hands and clinked our glasses of fizzy water.

*

After beating England on penalties at Wembley, the German football team went on to beat the Czech Republic in the final. After the final whistle, Jürgen Klinsmann, Germany's blond mop-topped captain, walked up to the royal box and received the trophy from the hands of her majesty the queen. This should have been a promising sign, because Klinsmann, a former Tottenham Hotspur striker and the first foreign player to win the Premier League's player of the year award, symbolised a different, less straight-faced Germany – summed up by the celebration he had performed after scoring his first goal, a bellyflop on the wet turf at Hillsborough, a knowing reference to his reputation as a 'diver'. But I wasn't convinced that my new schoolmates would notice such subtle differences. When I was introduced as a German, wouldn't they think of arrogant Andi Möller and the man in the tracksuit bottoms?

In social situations, Germans can come across as coolly

distant or uncomfortably frank, with their eternal insistence on the firm, businesslike handshake when saying hello and goodbye, even among close friends (an old schoolfriend was left with veritable trauma after an English girlfriend of mine had greeted him with a peck on the cheek). Deep down, however, the German attitude to friendship is unashamedly romantic. *Ein Freund* is not just a mate, but an ideological category, a 'sacred German concept', as Christopher Isherwood once called it. A friend is an unwavering comrade for life, a soulmate. '*Ein Freund, ein guter Freund, das ist das Schönste was es gibt auf der Welt*', goes a popular song from the 1930s: a good friend is the most beautiful thing in the world. No German goes through their teens without reading Karl May's series of paperback Westerns about the friendship between two 'blood brothers', the red Indian Winnetou and the cowboy Old Shatterhand. The German football league trophy has an engraving that reads *Elf Freunde müsst ihr sein, wenn ihr Siege wollt erringen*: if you want to win, you have to be eleven friends. The organising principle of English football is the notion of 'fair play': the idea that every player on the pitch should be treated with the same amount of respect, whether he is a teammate or an opponent. The central idea of German football, on the other hand, is *Mannschaft*: the many as one. It assumes a much tighter emotional bond. I was an utter German in this respect, and my thoughts about moving to England were dominated by one theme. Would I be able to make friends in England?

It is said that some time in the build-up to the fall of the Berlin Wall, the German chancellor had invited the British prime minister to his favourite pub in his native Rhineland-Palatine. Helmut Kohl – a rare example of a politician whose ego was matched by his body mass, whose gargantuan waistline and curious head shape had earned him the nickname 'The Pear' – was keen to get on good terms with Britain's famously combative leader. Personally selected gifts had failed to leave a lasting impression at recent meetings, so this time Kohl had chosen to up the ante and give Maggie Thatcher an exclusive tour deep into the dark heart of Germanic cuisine. Kohl seated himself and wrapped a napkin around his waist. Thatcher teasingly asked if the napkin was a sign of surrender. Then the meal arrived. The party fell silent. From a national menu famed for its over-reliance on boiled meats, potatoes and cabbages, Kohl (a man whose name literally translates as 'cabbage') had chosen a meal meatier and heavier than all others. *Saumagen*, or pig's stomach, is the ultimate embodiment of the German adjective *deftig*, meaning plain but emotionally comforting: sausage-meat and boiled potato, wrapped in pig's intestines and served with boiled carrots and sauerkraut. According to Thatcher's chief foreign policy adviser Charles Powell, the prime minister pushed the contents around her plate until it looked as if she had eaten some.

After the meal, Kohl took Thatcher to Speyer cathedral, a marvellous Romanesque church which houses the tombs of those pioneers of a united Europe, the early Holy Roman Emperors: a highly symbolic place, or so Kohl thought. As Thatcher wandered around the cathedral, the German chancellor pulled Powell behind a pillar and said: 'Now that she has seen me in my home territory, right here, in the heart of Europe, close to France, she will surely realise that I am not so much German, I am European.' Soon after, the two politicians parted ways, and Thatcher's car drove her to Frankfurt airport. Thatcher climbed up the steps of her chartered plane, threw herself into her seat, kicked off her heels and said to her adviser: 'Charles, that man is *so* German.'

*

I love this story because it hints at that German desperation to be liked, but also because it tells us more about the subtle factors at play when people of different nationalities meet. To Kohl, serving Thatcher his favourite meal must have felt like a warrior king dropping his armour in front of his opponent in battle, like Othello's 'Rude am I in my speech/ And little blest with the soft phrase of peace': a glimpse of his own weakness offered in order to create some political chemistry. For Thatcher, the pile of carbohydrates was merely a symbol of Germany's monstrous appetite: would it gobble up Britain for dessert?

I have been fascinated with anecdotes of meetings like these ever since I came to England. They promise to give a more subtle and nuanced picture of Anglo-German relations through the ages than surveys or statistics ever could. When two people from different cultures meet, two national stereotypes are held up to the light and tested. Sometimes, the cliches are exposed as just that: as prejudices, preconceived ideas based on films and books. Sometimes, as when Helmut Kohl met Margaret Thatcher, or when Germany met England at Wembley, the stereotypes are reaffirmed and hardened.

I wanted to try to explore what it means to be English or to be German through a series of meetings, chosen to give a glimpse of the changing attitudes and ideas over the decades. Some of these meetings are public events or state affairs, like the ones mentioned in this preface. Many of them are less spectacular than that: chance encounters, people brushing past each other in the hallways of history, meetings that should have happened but never quite did. Some of them are successful, others are failures. Some of them are instructive, some of them aren't. Few of them, you might notice, deal directly with the two world wars, because more intimate contacts between the countries were severed than made during those periods: before and after that grim forty-year interlude, the traffic of ideas, goods and people has been much higher than we tend to admit.

Some of the meetings in this book even involve me. The reason for this is that the things you read about in history books sometimes merely confirm something you've already experienced in person. Long before I first came across Helmut Kohl and Margaret Thatcher's meeting over *Saumagen*, for example, I had already learnt that food is one area in which German and English people can agree about very little.

1

Heinrich Heine Can't Bear William Cobbett's Swearing

I don't remember much about the day we arrived in England. I don't remember whether we arrived in the morning or the evening, whether it was rainy or sunny, whether it was cold or hot, whether we took the train from the airport into town or a taxi. I do, however, know that I was in a bad mood, and that we arrived on a Sunday, because that same evening one of my father's new colleagues had invited us for a welcoming meal which she announced as 'a Sunday roast' when we stepped into her house. We had barely taken off our jackets when our host – all wavy coiffured hair and buck teeth – hugged us emphatically and tried to kiss me on my cheeks. She had accompanied the words 'Sunday roast' with a showy movement of the hands, like a butler lifting a silver dish cover, conveying an impression of ceremony and theatre. A Sunday roast, this hand movement tried to say, was not like any other meal.

We sat down at the dinner table and tried to converse politely in broken English. I was confused when the meal eventually arrived. The contents of my plate looked something like this: three thin, very well done slices of beef, four stems of broccoli, eight roast potatoes, all collapsed on top of each other like weary travellers at the end of a long journey. Spread around the plate, a pool of very thin brown sauce. Copying our hosts, we had dropped generous spoonfuls of horseradish sauce and bright yellow mustard onto either side of the plate. Mixing these pastes (they called them 'condiments') with the main meal, however, was a bad idea, as my father found out the hard way. His eyes were watery and bloodshot when he eventually stopped coughing. Paradoxically, the fact that the condiments were spicy didn't actually mean that the meal itself was very flavoursome. In fact, the further you worked your way to the heart of the dish, the blander the flavours seemed to become – by the end, I found myself gnawing on an extremely stringy, dry morsel of beef. This appeared to have been a deliberate choice on behalf of the cook in charge, because no attempt had been made to trap the natural flavours of the meat by sealing it. Nor had the vegetables' natural crunch been maintained. The sauce or 'gravy' was so bland as to not really be a sauce at all, but a further attempt to water down the flavours contained in the food. The whole thing reminded me of a picture painted with watercolours, or a song played on an unplugged keyboard.

Our hosts tucked into the roast as if it was manna from heaven. 'Yummy yummy in my tummy', the son of the family said after he had put the first forkful in his mouth. As he threw himself with glee into the pile of limp flesh on his plate, I noticed that the boy's face looked both bloated and slightly bloodless. Was this what English cuisine did to you?

I turned to look at his father. The corrosive effects of the national diet were visible here too, for the man had a red, bloodshot nose and a rapidly receding hairline, as well as crooked, yellowing teeth. I was also distracted by his table manners. In Germany, my parents had always insisted that I held my cutlery in the correct manner: using the knife in my right hand as the brush to the dustpan of the fork in my left. The English, however, used the fork as a kind of stabbing device, with the knife then being used to jam more food into a mini-kebab of roast beef, potato and broccoli. The English ate angrily and with no apparent enjoyment of the process of consumption, washing down barely chewed mouthfuls with hasty gulps of liquid.

Back at home, we usually had our dinner with *Apfelschorle* (tart apple juice diluted just enough with fizzy water) or, on special occasions, *Spezi* (Coca-Cola mixed with Fanta). Here, our hosts served our food with a drink that increasingly manifested itself to me as a potent symbol of the English national character: a lukewarm glass of tap water.

*

Through the ages, a number of abstract concepts have been associated with Britain and England in the German mind: democracy, independence, originality, eccentricity. They are loose associations, which will vary between regions; the distinction between 'England' and 'Britain', for one, has never been particularly consistent among Germans. On the whole, though, they used to be positive qualities: at various stages in history we have looked up to the English as pioneers in politics, industry or culture, or even just revered them as beacons of moral conduct. But these days 'bad food' is always at the top of these lists, and it is still surprising how few English people are aware of this. They have a vague notion that the French might not rate English cuisine very highly, but the Germans? Land of sausage and sauerkraut? Food is reliably the German's first concern when you mention that you live in England. 'You poor thing!' 'Is the food really that bad?' 'No wonder you look so skinny.'

German food, like English, traditionally consists of a diet of boiled meats, potatoes and conserved veg, but conceptually speaking, the approach is very different. German sausages have a bad reputation abroad, mainly because their poorest specimen, the frankfurter, is also the most widely known. Yet the frankfurter's more adventurous cousins, the Nürnberger, Thüringer or Krakauer, can be a veritable feast for the tastebuds: be they smoked, roasted or infused with herbs. The *Currywurst*, a sausage doused in spicy curry ketchup which is finally becoming recognised as the country's true national dish, speaks of a deep yearning for exotic spice and oriental heat. Even more traditional German cuisine is full of good intentions and surprisingly bold flavours. You can get cumin-spiced bread in every bakery, liquorice-and-chocolate lollipops in many cornershops and pepper-flavoured biscuits every Christmas. The classic German Christmas *Stollen* is still an archetype of how a good meal should be constructed: a firm yet not too sweet cake dusted with icing sugar, whose taste intensifies as you chew your way to the core, with your teeth eventually sinking into a rich goo of marzipan, candied fruit, pistachio and poppy-seed. Flavour awaits you at the centre, that is the key.

Other regional fare attests to a maverick streak in German cooking: traditional north German meals include a bacon, bean and pear stew, black sausage with potato mash and apple puree, or one of my all-time favourites: a revolting-looking salt beef and potato mush with pickled beetroot and fried egg called *Labskaus*. I got very excited when my father told me once that *Labskaus* was the traditional comfort food of seamen like his father, and that its culinary tradition had been kept alive only in elite seafaring hubs. In Liverpool in the north of England an entire people were apparently named after the dish. Yet when I tried my first English 'scouse' years later, I was left with the same under-whelmed and undernourished feeling I had after my first English roast.

*

My parents wouldn't have any of this. As we drove to our hotel after dinner, they could not stop going on about the moreish crunch of the potatoes and the fantastic zing of the horseradish. '*Ganz köstlich!*' Criticism of the roast was *verboten*.

Like many northern Europeans, they were already closet Anglophiles before we made our move. It had taken a mere scratch to the surface for them to break out in a positive Anglomania. Over the next few days, bags of salt-and-vinegar crisps appeared in the cupboards of our self-catering apartment and cans of bitter invaded the fridge overnight.

In the mornings I would wake up to the smell of fried bacon and baked beans. Everything authentically English had to be tried at least once: shepherd's pie, toad in the hole, even the unique delicacy that is Marmite spread on a toasted slice of mass-produced white bread – yet another example of the inability to synthesise extreme flavour and extreme blandness into a coherent culinary experience.

Perhaps what irritated me wasn't the food at all, but the fuss that my parents made about it. Until we moved to England, 'making a fuss' was not really something I had thought my parents capable of. My childhood was marked by a near-complete absence of open conflict or raised voices, in part because I was the youngest of four children and my parents were already well equipped for the traumas and tantrums of adolescence by the time I reached my teens. In other families I knew there were constant complaints about the behaviour of an unruly brother or a bossy sister, yet in our household relations were rarely too hot or too cold, but always perfectly adjusted to a pleasant room temperature. Moving to England threatened to change this delicate balance. The plan was that we would spend the first week visiting a number of schools within the London commuter belt and look at flats in the same area. In the interim, my father's company provided us with a small flat near Mortlake in west London: a soulless place that not only smelled of grandparents but was also extremely small. For the first time in my life, I was spending large periods of time with my parents on my own, and without my older sisters and brother as a buffer, I began to worry that the atmosphere might soon turn toxic.

My mother and father had been born in adjacent villages on the stretch of land along the river Elbe known as *das Alte Land*, the old land. Yet in spite of the proximity of their birthplaces, their natural characters could hardly have been further apart. My mother was born into a family of seven children and had trained as a kindergarten teacher before she had my older brother. A deep sense of empathy determined her interaction with others: 'seeing the other side of the story' was a moral duty. My father's father was a river pilot on the Elbe, who would join large container ships at a pick-up point a couple of miles from the city and help them navigate the shallows in the river. His son, my father, was one of the first in a line of Oltermanns who hadn't gone to sea, and the first child in his family to go to university, but that sense of knowing the correct route and sticking to it had been passed through the family. Working in big business came naturally. Here in London my parents' contrasting personality traits were merging into something strange and new: a laissez-faire tolerance towards English eccentricities, coupled with a dogged determination to adopt these eccentricities into our own lifestyle.

I was approaching my seventeenth birthday at the time. In that phase of your teens, a number of things feel very important: hanging out with cool people, listening to cool music, wearing cool clothes, meeting girls who were impressed with your cool friends and your cool clothes and your cool taste in music. Spending more time with my parents wasn't exactly a top priority, and the thought of being holed up in a small flat did enough to cause discomfort.

After we had survived the adventure of our first English meal on the Sunday, we decided to play it safe. The next evening we visited the curry house a few steps from our hotel, a living-room-sized place with irritating background muzak and a withered old waiter, who took a lifetime to come to our table. As my father launched into a detailed discussion about the differences between the 'winderloo' and the 'yarlfretzi', I rolled my eyes with embarrassment and turned away to the wall on my right. I stared straight at my own eyes: the walls of the restaurant were mirrored. The picture in front of me made for a dispiriting sight: a German couple in their mid-fifties, an elderly Bangladeshi waiter and an awkwardly lanky teenager in a typical teenage huff.

*

Far from being unusual, my parents' love of all things English is a common phenomenon in northern Europe. And there are few parts of Europe more Anglophile than the area where I had grown up. Hamburg is Germany's second largest city. Located on the banks of the river Elbe, about sixty miles from the North Sea, its harbour is the city's sole source of pride: 'Gateway to the World' is how Hamburgers describe their hometown in moments of grandeur. The Reeperbahn, the city's red-light district, runs from the port into the city centre in a straight line, like a red carpet laid out for thirsty sailors, and once a year the city's population gathers at the bottom of that road to celebrate the birthday of the harbour with a firework display. When my friends and I first started taking girls on dates, we took them to the Strandperle in

Othmarschen, a ramshackle beach hut where you could order a pretzel and a bitter Jever lager while overlooking the birdlike cranes unloading container ships on the other side of the port. To a Hamburger, the industrial panorama of the docks is the most romantic thing in the world.

Hamburg's maritime heritage also means inhabitants of the city have traditionally felt a stronger kinship with English tradesmanship than with German agrarian (and later industrial) self-reliance. In the thirteenth century, the city became one of the founding members of the Hanseatic League and developed strong commercial ties with trading partners in Bruges, Amsterdam and London. As the Royal Navy rose to world dominance in the seventeenth century, Hamburg's merchants looked on in fawning admiration. At the height of the Napoleonic wars, Hamburg managed to get on the Little Corporal's wrong side by trusting its pro-British instincts and handing over a group of Irish revolutionaries who had sought exile in the city. In 1806 the Grande Armée invaded the city, burning all British goods, banning all trade with France's greatest enemy and effectively bankrupting Hamburg in the process. Only after Napoleon's defeat, when British traders returned to the city, did Hamburg achieve prosperity once more.

That memory must have stuck, because when people talked about Britain or England in my youth, it was usually done with an air of reverence, as if one was referring to ancestors rather than competitors. England tended to have a stronger appeal to conservative souls: one would talk of *die feine englische Art* or *der gute englische Stil* without specifically meaning English style or English manners, but meaning proper civilised conduct in general. Britain, on the other hand, resonated with the more rebellious aspect of the German psyche – something that was borne out by the enthusiastic reception of Britpop. With the dawn of New Labour, Britain had taught itself to re-embrace the kind of blatant patriotic gestures that had been so unfashionable during the 1980s. Blur played songs about such icons of national life such as rural estates ('Country House'), Radio 4's Shipping Forecast ('This is a Low') and the white cliffs of Dover ('Clover over Dover'), while Oasis glorified the banalities of everyday English patter ('Do You Know What I Mean?') to the sound of crashing guitars. In 1996, there were Union Jacks everywhere: on cars, on guitars, on miniskirts. But in Germany 'Cool Britannia' was at least as cool as in Britain, if not cooler. The German edition of *Rolling Stone*, which I read every month, was full of gushing, pages-long profiles of Blur, Paul Weller and the Gallagher brothers, written by beardy fifty-something Germans who lapped up every inanity like they had wangled an exclusive interview with the Messiah. Even ageing British pop-rockers who had long faded from the limelight in the UK were still received with open arms in Germany. Phil Collins always played on heavy rotation on Radio Hamburg. Eric Clapton still filled stadiums. Joe Cocker brought the house down when he appeared on German talkshows. We treated them like old masters in the pop canon: Cocker, Collins, Clapton were England's answer to Bach, Beethoven and Brahms.

There was similar reverence in the way films were treated. Foreign programmes on TV were always dubbed into German – only English comedies got a special subtitle treatment. Monty Python was so revered that the group had to record two German-language specials for Westdeutscher Rundfunk in the early 1970s, called *Monty Python's Fliegender Zirkus*. When my school in Hamburg held a large-scale charity raffle, the top prize was a free ride in an authentic black cab. Even the bad food was forgivable: the English couldn't cook, but at least they really couldn't cook at all. English food was the archetype of bad food in the same way England provided the archetype of good manners and good taste. Last but not least, there was my own name. Handing out traditional German names was unfashionable among my parents' generation of awkward anti-nationalists, and my classmates weren't called Otto or Karl-Heinz but Marco, Vincent, Dennis or Patrick. Yet 'Philip' still sounded so English to German ears that my grandmother shook her head in disbelief when she first heard it.

Growing up in northern Germany in the 1980s, it was hard not to find some truth in the words of the Austrian architect Adolf Loos who had in 1898 described the English as '*unsere Hellenen*': 'The English, those engineers, are our ancient Greeks.'

What makes this Anglomania all the more remarkable is that the citizens of Hamburg would be perfectly entitled to feel some coolness towards their English neighbours, if not downright resentment. In the summer of 1943, British and American planes had pounded the city with over nine thousand tons of incendiaries in the space of ten days – more than were dropped over London during the entire Blitz – creating an enormous firestorm. An estimated fifty thousand civilians were killed during 'Operation Gomorrah', roughly equalling Britain's entire civilian losses by air bombing up to that point in the war. The *Feuersturm* has a distinct place in local folklore. There is a stark, expressionistic monument to the victims of the attack near Dammtor station in the centre of the city. But the memory of the disaster is practically disconnected from the men in the planes who dropped the bombs: it's remembered as a punishment from the heavens rather than an Allied war crime.

One reason the aerial assault on Hamburg left only minor mental scars might be that the Second World War never defined the German view of Britain in the same way it defined the British view of Germany. Germany's formative period in this respect was arguably not the years 1939 to 1945, but the first few decades of the nineteenth century. Napoleon's final defeat at Waterloo in 1815 had left Germans in a muddle. On one side was France, whose liberation from autocratic rule still looked like a potential blueprint for the formation of a German republic. On the other side was Britain, successfully allied to General Blücher's Prussian troops at the battle of Waterloo, and potentially a more realistic political guide for the years to come. And it is important to bear in mind that in 1815 Germany was not 'Germany', but only a loosely bound patchwork of semi-disconnected German states. France had undergone a political revolution, and England was in the middle of an industrial revolution. Germany, however, was still a land of feudal landowners and farmers, which beheld the rapid developments in its neighbouring countries with wonder and no little admiration. The industrial pioneers, the Krupps and the Siemens, were all ardent Anglophiles who anglicised their first names and headed off for London or Manchester at the first opportunity.

Germany *did* have a philosophical revolution, whose impact was much harder to measure. Immanuel Kant, Friedrich Schiller and Johann Wolfgang von Goethe were revered across Europe, and German philosophers enjoyed a favourable reputation in England, mainly thanks to Thomas Carlyle and George Eliot, who both read and translated German literature enthusiastically. Carlyle's *Sartor Resartus* and Eliot's *Middlemarch*, two of the most important novels of the Georgian era, were brimming with German philosophy. But even that particular brand of Germanness was in part indebted to the English. Goethe's mentor Johann Gottfried Herder had been convinced that in order to find their proper voice, German writers had to first look to the British isles: *Schäkespear*, as he called him, was destined to 'create us Germans'. If French dramatists looked to the Greeks for inspiration, Germany's first *Dichter und Denker* saw their idol in the British Bard.

For the generation who laid the foundations of German culture, there was no way around the English playwright. Wieland and Schlegel were considerably more famous for their Shakespeare translations than for their own writing in their lifetime. Schiller adored *Othello* at school and died trying to put on his own version of the play. Goethe felt a deep inferiority complex when faced with the Shakespearean annihilation of classical stage conventions: 'I am often ashamed before Shakespeare, for it often happens that at first glance I think: *I* would have done that differently; but soon I realise that I'm a poor sinner, that nature prophesies through Shakespeare, and that my characters are soap-bubbles blown from romantic fancies.'

In particular, a certain prince of Denmark acquired a special place in the German imagination. 'Hamlet and his monologues are ghosts that haunt all young German souls,' wrote Goethe. 'Everyone knows them by heart and everybody believes that they could be as melancholy as the prince of Denmark.' Why Hamlet? Perhaps the clue can be found in Act V, scene i of the play, where the protagonist is described as a 'boy, thirty years'. Nineteenth-century Germany might have been old in years, and burdened with responsibility, but it was politically and economically immature: a well-read but volatile and impressionable teenager, desperately in need of a strong role model.

*

In April 1827, a young man took a boat to London to find out a little more about Germany's more mature North Sea neighbours. The 'satirist and poet Heinrich Heine', as the *Morning Herald* announced him in a brief notice of his arrival, had a complicated relationship with England, as he did with most things. Even though he is commonly regarded as a member of the Young Germany movement of romantic patriots, Heine is more famous for the fun he poked at those who tried to summon a spirit of communal Germanness:

> When I think of Germany at night
> Thoughts of sleep are put to flight

is the most frequently cited line, along with the prophetic 'Where they burn books, they'll end up burning people too', from his 1821 play *Almansor*. 'Everything German makes me want to throw up,' he told his fellow student Christian Sethe the same year. 'The German language makes my ears explode. My own poems disgust me when I see that they are written in German.'

Born into a Jewish family from Düsseldorf, Heine had grown up with a deep respect for the way Napoleon had defended the emancipation of the Jews during the French occupation of the Rhineland – in later life he revered Bonaparte to such an extent that he lied to his own biographer about the year he was born; not 1797, but 1799, the year of the *coup d'état* of 18 Brumaire which marked Napoleon's ascent to power. But for Hamburg-raised Heine, England was in many ways a more obvious source of inspiration. After all, the name on his birth certificate had been 'Harry' Heine, after one of his father's trading partners from Manchester (he didn't officially change his name to Heinrich until 1825). Like all other artistic Germans of his generation, the young Harry Heine adored the works of Shakespeare and idolised Lord Byron: his first works were either translations of the English proto-dandy or one-act tragedies in the Byronic style. The intriguing thing about the English was that they had a distinct national character – 'a secret consensus ruling over the hustle and bustle of life' – at a time when Germany's national identity was still vague.

Above all, what fuelled Heine's interest in England was the country's reputation as the motherland of democracy: a place where parliamentarians could discuss what they wanted and newspapers could write what they liked without the ruling elite being able to do anything about it. Spying the green banks of the Thames from the upper deck of his ferry in 1827, he called out: 'Land of freedom, I salute you!' and managed to convince himself that unlike in the land of Gothic church spires he has left behind, the people of England worship only freedom, 'the new religion of our times'. The English love of freedom might not match the French flaming passion for liberty, he concedes, being more like a relationship between 'a husband and his long-term wife' in which excitement had given way to routine and awkward silences over breakfast. But at least the English were nothing like the Germans, 'who love freedom like an old grandmother'.

On his arrival Heine made his way down to the Crown and Anchor Tavern on Arundel Street, just off the Strand: a grand hall with candelabra framing the entrance, known as a hothouse of political radicalism. In 1789, the Crown had been one of the few places where people raised a glass to cheer the fall of the Bastille. Heine was going to a lunch party in celebration of the reformist politician Sir Francis Burdett's thirtieth year in parliament, though Burdett was only a figure of minor interest to him. Instead, the German poet was eager to meet William Cobbett: rambler, pamph-leteer and campaigning journalist *extraordinaire*.

Cobbett's journalism in particular fascinated the German: he had been avidly reading the *Weekly Political Register*, the newspaper Cobbett had founded after returning from the US in 1800. In his lifetime, Cobbett had moved from being a staunch Tory via supporting the liberal Whigs to aligning himself with the proto-socialist group of political figures that were merely known as 'radicals'. The *Political Register*, likewise, had moved from a pro-monarchy and anti-French stance to becoming the voice of British anti-government protest. A newspaper which openly criticised the government? This was quite unheard of in Germany. In Britain, the first law to stop censorship had been introduced as early as 1695, as a result of impassioned appeals by John Milton and John Locke. In Germany, on the other hand, writers continued to suffer at the hands of the censors until 1854; the Carlsbad Decrees of 1819 meant that writers of the 1820s had to be particularly careful. Heine's *Book Le Grand* had been banned in Prussia shortly before he travelled to England, on the grounds that it would 'offend serious Prussians'. Out of frustration he would occasionally take to censoring himself. As he writes at the start of Chapter XII of *Book Le Grand*:

The German censors — — — — — — — — — — —
— — — — — — — — — — — — — — — — — —
— — — — — — — — — — — — — — — — — —
— — — — — — — — — — — — — — — — — —

— — — — — — — — — — — — — — — — — —
— — — — — — — — — — — — — — — — — —
— — — — — — — — — — — — idiots — —
— — — — — — — — — — — — — — — — — —
— — — — — — — — —

Cobbett's *Political Register* had no need for such games. Stylistically, it pioneered the use of the 'leading article': a subjective opinion or argument that was distinct from the objective reporting of news. By the 1820s, Cobbett had become of one of England's leading radicals, and the *Political Register* the most widely read voice of the disaffected working classes. The targets of his ire were wide-ranging and plentiful. Cobbett believed in social hierarchy, but he complained bitterly about poverty, 'real insufficiency of the food and raiment and lodging necessary to health and decency'. Land reform was an imperative in his view, as 'the land, the trees, the fruit, the herbage, the roots are, by the law of nature, the common possession of all the people'. Britain's empire in the East? 'A terrible evil', Cobbett thought. Stockmarket manipulators? 'Swarms of locusts, who, without stirring ten miles from the capital, devour three fourths of the produce of the whole land'.

A recent issue of the *Political Register* had caught Heine's eye. Cobbett had here presented the following thesis: the French Revolution had threatened to strip aristocracy and the church of its privileges. So in order to distract the people of England from the massive social change that was unfolding across the pond, England had started a war with

France. Wars cost a lot of money, but as the king didn't have any money, the state had to borrow, which led to crushingly high taxation. This made the poor poorer and the rich richer than they had been before the war. In short: Cobbett was Heine's sort of Englishman, and there was no reason to assume that Heine wouldn't also be Cobbett's kind of German.

On a good day, William Cobbett could be 'affable, clear-headed, simple and mild in his manner, deliberate and un-ruffled in his speech', as William Hazlitt once described him. The day Heine went to visit Cobbett in the Crown and Anchor was not a good day. A few minutes into dinner, Cobbett attacked Burdett for his complaisance towards the recently sworn-in interim prime minister George Canning. The rest of the party, all friends of the host, tried to ignore Cobbett. Cobbett got angrier and started to swear. His face, beneath forward-combed hair, was now bright red. A few minutes later Heine stormed out of the premises. A year later, when he sat down to write his account of the meeting, it sounds like he is still trembling with a confused mixture of hatred and empathy.

Poor old Cobbett! Dog of England! I have no love for you, for every vulgar nature my soul abhors; but you touch me to the inmost soul with pity, as I see how you strain in vain to break loose and to get at those thieves who make off with their booty before your very eyes, and mock at your fruitless springs and your impotent howling.

It's unclear what exactly it was that upset the German poet so much, though several accounts of the evening suggest that Cobbett's swearing was obscene. He was certainly a creative user of the English language when it came to dishing out abuse, having once laid into the yeomanry as 'loan-mongers, tax-gatherers, dead-weight people, stock-jobbers, shag-bag attorneys, bailiffs (most Scotch), toad-eating shop-keepers'. In Cobbett's book Cambridge and Oxford were 'dens of dunces', Scottish thinkers were 'Scotch feelosofers' and newspaper editors were merely 'mercenary villains'. A duchess could be 'an old eat' and a bishop 'a dirty dog'. The quiet and unassuming were usually attacked with the same force as the high and mighty, so that even choirs, people eating potatoes and drinking tea were subject to abuse (the latter 'a destroyer of health, an enfeebler of the frame, an engenderer of effeminacy and laziness, a debaucher of youth and maker of misery for old age'). G. K. Chesterton wrote that 'the strongest quality of Cobbett as a stylist is in the use he made of a certain kind of language; the sort of use commonly called abuse'.

Rude words alone can't account for the failed meeting between Heine and Cobbett. Even though they both idolised freedom, their ideas of what freedom actually looked like were quite different. To Heine, it was not just the escape from the religious authorities of the past, but a new belief system: 'freedom is a new kind of religion, the religion of our time'. To watch Cobbett reduce this sacred ideal to the status of mere rabble-rousing, 'impotent howling', must have felt to Heine like a new kind of heresy. To Cobbett, on the other hand, freedom was not abstract but material: the right to farm and walk on your own land, to speak the words you wanted, even if they were rude. Freedom as a concept was barely worth remarking upon: 'The words rights, liberty, freedom, and the like, the mere words, are not worth a straw', he wrote in 1831, 'and frequently they serve as a cheat.'

Heine's idea of freedom is much like a schoolboy's view of members of the opposite sex: a romantic ideal based on the imagination rather than actual experience, easily contradicted by the inconvenient truths of the real world. And there is undoubtedly something of a teenage strop in the way he couldn't just let matters be, and agree to disagree with the mad dog of Britain.

Not just the man, but the whole country suddenly dropped in Heine's estimation after their meeting. Any mention of England post-1827 comes with a bitter aftertaste. Here's Heinrich Heine on English music: 'These people have no ear, neither for the beat nor indeed for music in any form, and their unnatural passion for piano-playing and singing is all the more disgusting.' On English art: 'They neither have accurate . . . sense of colour, and sometimes I am befallen by the suspicion that their sense of smell may be equally dull and rheumy; it is quite possible that they cannot distinguish horse-apples from oranges by the smell alone.' The English: 'a grey, yawning monster of a people, whose breath smells of deathly boredom', 'the most repulsive people God has ever created in his anger'. England: 'a country which would have been swallowed up by the sea long ago, were it not for the fear that it might turn the sea's stomach upside down'. No more 'land of freedom' – England is now 'the island of the damned'. Occasionally his diatribe against England sounds like a perfect reversal of more modern prejudices: 'Don't send poets to London! This bare-faced seriousness of all things, this colossal uniformity, this machine-like move-ment, this moroseness even in joy; all-exaggerating London will crush your imagination and tear your heart to pieces.'

A year after his trip to England, Heine travels to the village of Spinetta Marengo in Piedmont, where Napoleon sealed the success of his Italian campaign. 'Let us praise the French!' he finally concludes in a thinly disguised dig at Bonaparte's vanquishers. 'They addressed two of the greatest needs of human society: good food and the equality of its citizens.'

*

Back in twentieth-century London, one week in Mortlake became two, and two weeks became three. Day after day was spent inspecting apartments and calling schools to request an appointment with the headmaster. Inevitably, the only appointments we could get would be on the same day but on opposite sides of the city, which meant that we had to get from one place to the next in a mad rush. More than once, we would board the wrong train and find ourselves faced with a carriage full of commuters who were either unable or unwilling to tell us if we were going in the right direction. Our pleas for help were met with blank stares.

When we eventually arrived at a school, I was usually met by the head of the sixth form who would start by taking me on a tour of the school. Most English schools had been built in a similar way, whether they were old Victorian buildings or more recent constructions. Right in the centre of each school was usually a large 'assembly hall', in which students apparently had to meet before their first class, something that struck me as more appropriate for army barracks than an educational establishment. I was also mildly disturbed by the young people in identical school uniforms who streamed past us in the school corridors: an army of English gentleman robots in matching ties, mini Frankenstein's monsters whose exchanges with the teacher who was taking me on a tour of the premises were as short and hollow as army protocol. 'Yes, sir,' 'Thank you, sir,' 'Of course, sir.' They had manners, for sure, but did they have a soul?

At the last school we visited, I was horrified when we walked past a milky-faced boy in camouflage gear who was guarding the school entrance brandishing what looked like a real rifle. This, the headmaster explained, was the usual drill for Armistice Day. I didn't know whether to laugh at the suggestion that carrying a gun into a school was an appropriate way of paying tribute to the armistice, or to cry at the blank expression on the boy's face.

After the interview, we drove back to Heathrow to board a flight home to Hamburg. My head pressed against the car window as we drove past rows and rows of suburban houses. Each house had a little path covered in Victorian tiles leading to the front porch, stucco on the front and a little bay window, through which you could peek straight into the lounge. There was even a little tray on each doorstep, with six empty pint-sized milk bottles. The only variation was the front doors painted in different colours. We stopped at a zebra crossing and waited for a group of schoolboys to cross, all wearing identical duffel coats and short trousers. They looked as if they had stepped straight out of an Enid Blyton story. In fact, everything looked exactly like I had seen it portrayed in books and films about England. Did things ever change in this country?

Back in Hamburg, while we were waiting to hear whether or not the schools had accepted me, I returned my copy of Heine's *English Fragments* to the local library and picked up a collection of essays by the novelist and poet Theodor Fontane, a former London correspondent for the Prussian intelligence agency and a prolific translator of Shakespeare. Much like Heine, Fontane came to England enamoured with the English ideal, but was soon underwhelmed by what met his eye. He was baffled by English people's enthusiasm for song and dance, and their evident lack of artistic talent: 'Music, as many have pointed out, is England's Achilles' heel.' In particular, Fontane managed to grasp the profound boredom that resulted from the uniformity of English life. 'England and Germany', his diagnosis ran, 'relate to one another like form and content, like seeming and being.' The most perfect expression of this overwhelming tedium was what he called 'the English Sunday': 'The great tyrants have all died, only in England one lives on – the Sunday.' Far from being a country which worshipped only freedom, England turned out to be a country of pious churchgoers. The English Sunday was to the rest of the week what the Sunday roast was to the main meal: something insufferably dull in a place where you expected romance and entertainment. Fontane invites his readers to imagine an evening full of wine, song and beautiful women, and then the next morning, when the first rays of sunshine reveal a burnt-down candle and broken glass: '*That's* a Sunday in London.'

But not everything that Fontane had to say was negative. If the English were by nature grey and dull, London was the opposite: majestic and tranquil when viewed by boat from the river, sprawling and messy in the City, fairytale-like in the lit-up West End. London had green parks, heaving bars, churches made of marble and palaces made of glass, and more nightguards than the whole of Saxony had soldiers. England's capital, Fontane eventually confesses, is 'awesome and incomparable'.

To me, all this sounded promising: London would be the antithesis of the Sunday roast, an exotic and exciting centre, framed by circles of ever-increasing suburban blandness. When a bunch of envelopes with English stamps arrived at our Hamburg home a week later, I felt for the first time something like excitement. The envelopes contained four rejections and one letter of acceptance, from the place with the boy automata. My parents replied instantly to accept. There was no way back now.

*

Heinrich Heine's lofty ideal of freedom not only proved incompatible with English politics, it also proved hard to put into practice in his motherland. By 1830, heavy taxation and political censorship had spread unrest around the country. Diplomatic relations with Denmark in the north and France in the west were tense. Nationalist sentiment was on the rise, inspiring visions of a united Germany, as expressed in a popular song which would eventually become the country's anthem: '*Deutschland, Deutschland über alles*', 'Germany, Germany above everything else'. Two great thinkers died – Georg Wilhelm Friedrich Hegel in 1831 and Goethe in 1832 – leaving many with a sense that an era of Hamlet-like introspection was coming to an end. In 1848 feelings eventually boiled over. In February, public unrest led to the abdication of Prince Louis Philippe of France, inspiring similar uprisings across the German provinces. On 31 March the first pan-German assembly, a kind of proto-parliament, was held at Frankfurt's St Paul's church. The outcome of the Frankfurt assembly was a constitutional monarchy not unlike the English model, with the king of Prussia acting as the head of state within the parameters of a constitution. But as with the English civil war, the intended outcome and the actual outcome were not to be the same thing.

Four years before, the poet Ferdinand Freiligrath had written a poem in which he questioned the German Hamlet's ability to revive the ghost of freedom. This particular teenager, he concluded, had already spent far too much time in bed reading and lacked the resolve for concerted revolutionary action: 'Thinking is his acting'. Freiligrath was proved right. Parliament dithered while liberal advances were rolled back across the provinces. By the end of 1848, King Friedrich Wilhelm of Prussia had been swayed by a conservative group of advisors influenced by the anti-revolutionary Otto von Bismarck, and in June 1849 Germany's first parliament was dismissed.

While German interest in England as a political model might have been on the wane, London now became of practical interest. King Louis Philippe of France, Prince Wilhelm of Prussia, Count Klemens von Metternich: they had all jumped on the first boat to London in 1848. But just as England had played host to continental aristocrats on the run when the revolution had erupted, it also provided shelter to liberals who fled their countries when the revolution ran out of steam. Karl Marx moved to England in 1849, Friedrich Engels in 1850. In 1800 there had been around six thousand Germans in London. By 1861 the figure had doubled, with Germans outnumbering the French two to one. By the end of the century, the number had risen to almost thirty thousand, by far the largest foreign community from western Europe. 'Little Germanies' sprang up in Whitechapel, Stepney and Mile End; a German Hospital opened in Hackney in 1845; a German Gymnasts' Society was founded in King's Cross in 1861. An East End music hall called the Sugar Loaf catered especially for the German sugar refiners who made up a large group of the émigré community, and there was even a German-language newspaper called *Hermann*. Apart from the baking industry, English Germans worked mainly in the service sector – so many that one German migrant complained that the English 'regard us as a nation of waiters and hairdressers'.

In Germany, 1848 is remembered as a revolution that

didn't change anything. But if nothing else, it crucially changed the way the English thought of the Germans. Until 1848, the typical German had been brainy but largely apolitical, and therefore harmless. The influx of German migrants after 1848 put a stop to that. In Arthur Conan Doyle's *A Study in Scarlet*, from 1887, the first murder mystery in the Sherlock Holmes series, the plot centres on a grim find in a filthy apartment off the Brixton Road: the dead body of a man whose face is distorted into 'an expression of horror … such as I have never seen upon human features'. On the wall opposite, Holmes discovers 'R-A-C-H-E' on a bare stretch of plaster in blood-red letters. The police officer in attendance concludes that a woman called Rachel must have played some part in the crime. Holmes corrects him, explaining that *Rache* is in fact the German word for revenge. A further twist to the tale is revealed only after Holmes and Dr Watson have left the premises. The writing, the master detective tells his confused assistant, was not done by a German: 'The A, if you noticed, was printed somewhat after the German fashion. Now, a real German invariably prints in the Latin character, so that we may safely say that this was not written by one, but by a clumsy imitator who overdid his part.' The scarlet letters, then, were really a red herring, 'a blind intended to put the police upon a wrong track, by suggesting Socialism and secret societies'.

This short passage merely hints at the fact that by 1887, the old stereotypes that had seemed glaringly obvious to Heine and Fontane were already on their way out. New national characteristics were taking shape. The English weren't all as straight-faced and prosaic as Inspector Lestrade and his policemen, but also Holmes-like, which is to say with a sharp mind and eccentric quirks beneath the surface. The adjective 'German', on the other hand, was no longer just a shorthand for romantic dreaminess, but also for irrational behaviour and general hot-headedness: the term *furor Teutonicus*, originally coined by Lucan to describe the fierce temper of the Germanic tribes of the Roman period, entered the English lexicon. The late developer in the European family was growing into an intemperate and impulsive teenager, a troublesome black sheep who was shaping up for a major fallout with the European family.

2

Christopher Isherwood Listens to Marlene Dietrich

The last weeks of the summer of 1997 were almost unbearably hot. Covered in a permanent membrane of sweat, I spent my days under the sweltering timber roof of a wonky Tudor building in Bury St Edmunds. Having moved our belongings to the rented flat in Mortlake, my parents had insisted that I take an intensive language course before the start of the school year, something I considered an utter waste of their financial resources and my precious time. Every day from nine until twelve I worked my way mindlessly through preposition tables and endless lists of irregular verbs. Eat – ate – eaten. Forgive – forgave – forgiven. Shake – shook – shaken. Take – took – taken. English grammar was a bit odd (spell – spelt – spelt?), but not that complicated. It struck me as nothing but an inevitability when I breezed through the grammar test we had to take at the start of the course.

After the test our tutor Will – a recent Cambridge graduate with a Hugh Grant-esque flop of hair and a packet of Marlboro reds permanently lodged in his shirt pocket – asked me to come to the staffroom. He was pleased to see me do well in the test, he said, but might I consider showing a little more humility in class? If I thought that correct grammar was all there was to speaking good English, then I was missing the point. *Good* English, he said – and at this point he pulled out a well-thumbed copy of a Penguin edition of *Hamlet* from his leather satchel – was not spoken by those who were content with learning sentence structures, verb constructions and comma rules. Those who spoke really good English broke those rules and made the language malleable again.

Did I want to learn how real people spoke English?

I nodded enthusiastically. Where better to start than Shakespeare, that patron saint of German poets and thinkers?

To my confusion, the book disappeared into the satchel again, where it stayed for the rest of the course. It emerged that the gateway to the English language wasn't to be found in Hamlet's soliloquies, but in a taped episode of a TV programme called *Blind Date* from the early 1990s. In one part of the show in particular, our tutor paused and rewound the tape again and again. A man in his twenties read out a question: 'What would you say if I tried to kiss you on our first date?' One of the three women on the other side of the wall, a curly brunette, replied: 'You'll be pulling the HMS *Belfast* out into the open sea before you'll manage to pull me, mate.' Teacher Will explained that this was a typical example of the British fondness for wordplay. The beauty of the English language was its potential for euphemism. A toilet was a toilet, but also a lavatory, a lav, a restroom, a loo, a bog, a john, a water closet, a WC, the Gents, the Ladies, and so on. The

English language, he said, was the most creative language in the world.

I am not sure I had really understood Will's point at the time, but by the end of the course I got a brief glimpse of what he had been getting at. I had waved goodbye to my teachers and my parents were driving me back from Suffolk to Surrey. It was the first day of September. We had stopped at a petrol station on the outskirts of London and I was staring through the car window, when I noticed the mock handwriting on a battered *Evening Standard* poster. 'Dodi and Di Dead', it read. As we rejoined the Lower Mortlake Road, I rearranged the syllables in my head: Do-Di. Di-Do. Di-Die. The tragic message of that headline was only one small tweak away from sounding comic: 'Dodi and Di Die'. At that moment, I was convinced that I had reached a deep insight into English as it was understood by natives: this was a language that could not resist wordplay even at the most inopportune moment. In the extended family of languages, English was the embarrassing uncle who told dirty jokes at a funeral reception. Did the tragedy of Prince Hamlet not revolve around the skull of court jester Yorick, 'a fellow of infinite jest'? Perhaps the English weren't as glum and robot-like as the books had told me after all. Dodi and Di Dead as a Dodo! I was cracking the secret codes of Englishness at breakneck speed. Who was to say that I wouldn't manage to fit in here?

In the first week of September, temperatures suddenly dropped and rainclouds hugged the sky like a permanent frown. In Britain, September 1997 is commonly remembered as a month of communal mourning and awkward royal inertia, but for me it turned out to be a time of blissful isolation and bustling industry. For days on end, I would get up early in the morning to sift through my newspapers, magazines and novels with a red marker pen, dutifully highlighting words I didn't know, looking them up in the dictionary and jotting down translations in a little black notebook. Some words that I had grown up thinking were English had actually fallen out of usage long ago. Most people wore 'jumpers' instead of 'pullovers'. Our word for a mobile phone, *handy*, was actually an adjective meaning 'useful'. In British English a 'beamer' was an affectionate term for one's BMW, but almost certainly not a kind of film projection equipment, as it was in Germany. Others sounded deceptively German but meant something completely different. I learnt that a 'preserve' was jam and not a *Präser* or condom, that a 'puff' was not a bordello but a ball of smoke. The English word for *Miete* was 'rent' and not 'meet'; the word for *Rente* was 'pension' and not 'rent', and the word for *Pension* was 'guesthouse' and not 'pension'. 'To wink' didn't mean to wave, and 'to wank' definitely didn't mean to walk unstably.

Luckily, false friends were outweighed by some extremely satisfying similarities. At the start of the holidays I had received a letter from my school listing a number of books which would be taught in the first term, including an anthology of twentieth-century poetry. Flicking through that book one day, I came across a poem called 'The Pity of It', in which Thomas Hardy put a finger on the linguistic kinship between English and German. Walking in rural Hampshire, 'afar from rail-track and from highway', Hardy detects the Germanic heritage of the English language in the local dialect, still audible in

> many an ancient word
> Of local lineage like 'Thu bist', 'Er war',
> 'Ich woll', 'Er sholl' . . .

The First World War struck Hardy as a conflict between peoples of a joint background, rather than a clash of cultures:

> Whosoever they be
> At root and bottom of this, who flung this flame
> Between kin folk kin tongued even as are we,
> Sinister, ugly, lurid, be their fame.

I was reminded of my grandmother, who spoke fluent *Platt* or Low German and used to say *Buddel* rather than *Flasche* for a bottle and *Water* instead of *Wasser* for water. Even the English word 'love' had a not-so-distant cousin in the German *Liebe*, their family tree stretching from the Gothic *lubo* via the Old High German *luba* and the Old Frisian *luve* to the Old English *lufu*.

By the start of term I was brimming with confidence. On the day itself, I got up at six thirty, which is 'half six' in English, and not *halb sieben* or 'half seven' as it would be in German. I slipped into my brand new chinos, buttoned up my navy-blue shirt, tied the laces of my black leather shoes and put on my father's old pinstriped jacket: 'suited and booted', as they say. Next up was the tie – a much better, more self-explanatory word for something you tie around your neck than the German word for the same garment, *Schlips* (the word *Schlips*, incidentally, is not to be confused with the word *Slip*, which has nothing to do with what English people call 'slippers' and everything to do with undergarments which were also sometimes called 'knickers'. In English, you could get your knickers 'in a twist', you could twist your lip into a 'slip of the tongue', and that was one thing that would not happen to Philip Oltermann on his first day at English school, thank you very much). My father dropped me off at the school gates and I confidently joined the stream of suited young gentlemen rushing into the main building.

The first lesson of the day was A-level English literature. Our teacher, Mr P, introduced himself and explained that he was meant to be teaching us Shakespeare's *Hamlet* this term. Mr P, I noticed, wore what German people called *ein Pullunder* and English people called a 'tank top', tank being the English word for *Panzer*. Sadly, Mr P continued, our copies of the Arden *Hamlet* hadn't turned up yet. Instead we would spend today reading poems from the anthology on our syllabus. Stapled photocopies were passed around the classroom. Poetry, Mr P announced, had to be read aloud to be really understood. Did the tall young man in the front row want to start us off?

Twenty-five pairs of eyes focused on me. I scanned the page. The poem, by Wendy Cope, was called 'The Uncertainty of a Poet'. The first three stanzas read like this:

I am a poet,
I am very fond of bananas.

I am bananas,
I am very fond of a poet.

I am a poet of bananas.
I am very fond.

George Bernard Shaw once complained about the unreliable nature of English spelling by pointing out that the word 'fish' could feasibly be spelt 'ghoti': the 'gh' pronounced as in 'tou*gh*', 'o' as in 'w*o*men', and 'ti' as in 'na*ti*on'. 'Banana', like Shaw's slippery fish, struck me as a veritable banana skin of a word. I knew what it meant, of course, but how did you pronounce it? Was the letter 'a' stretched wide like the 'a' in 'father', or short and cut off like the 'a' in 'hat'? Was it more of an 'ay' sound like in 'able', or a straight 'ah' as in 'umbrella'?

'Would you like to start reading now?'

I decided to hedge my bets. 'I am fond of bawnanners', 'I am bannannahs', 'A poet of baynanis', 'Very barnarners'. . . I felt my face turn bright red as each banana boomeranged straight back at me, my confidence oozing to the classroom floor as waves of giggles rippled around the banks of desks. 'That's fine, you don't have to finish.' For the rest of the class, I kept my head down and my gaze fixed to the desk in front of me.

I didn't even look up when another boy read out a poem by Sylvia Plath, daughter of an American mother and a German father. 'The tongue stuck in my jaw,' it went. 'It stuck in a barb wire snare. / Ich, ich, ich, ich' – (the boy made it sound like 'ick, ick, ick, ick') –

> I could hardly speak.
> I thought every German was you.
> And the language obscene
> An engine, an engine
> Chuffing me off like a Jew.

*

Until I came to England, it had never occurred to me that it wasn't just the Germans who were perceived as ugly, but also their language. Now, I was reminded at every opportunity. On the bus home, I sat behind boys who read each other words from their German textbooks as if they described acts of unspeakable sexual degradation: *Botschaft* (which sounded like 'bot shaft'), *Wunderbar* (which sounded a bit like 'wonderbra'), *Brustwarze* ('breast warts' for nipples!), *Schmetterling* (a butterfly is a poetic *papillon* in French, a muted *mariposa* in Spanish, a fluttering *flutur* in Albanian, or a whispered *chou chou* in Japanese – only German could render it as, literally, a 'little smasher').

Two features of the German language in particular provoked much hilarity. On the one hand there was the harsh, throat-clearing sound of the 'ch', on the other the over-abundance of softer 'sh' and 'f' sounds. The boys in the seat in front of me knew a million examples: *Flaschenpfand*, *Schadenfreude*, *Faschismus*, *Arschloch*. Where in English there was 'camp', in German there was *Kampf*. The English 'damp' became the German *Dampf*, 'steam'. The German language created an impression of a people always on the verge of boiling over with rage, as the multilingual diplomat Salvador de Madariaga once said: 'No German can make P explode neatly without letting off after it the surplus pressure of the steam in his soul.' One of the boys got off the bus at Twickenham. As the bus pulled out of the stop, he pointed an air machine gun at his friend, while shouting *'Ich liebe Dich, Schweinehund!'* – the joke being that 'I love you' in German sounded like it really meant 'I want to kill you!'

It wasn't just the noise of the German tongue that people seemed to hate. The chafing-chuffing apart, the thing that caused most annoyance was its capacity for generating seemingly never-ending word torrents. The common complaint among the boys taking A-level German was that the language created page-long sentences with subclauses and parentheses that left a reader literally breathless – a side effect of the rule whereby German verbs are placed at the end of a sentence. Mark Twain, who had a love–hate relationship with 'the awful German language', once remarked that whenever a literary German dived into a sentence, 'that is the last you're going to see of him till he emerges on the other side of his Atlantic with a verb in his mouth'. The length of the average German sentence seemed to betray a wasteful sluggishness at the intellectual level. This was a language jammed with verbal detritus and positively clogged with so-called 'modal particles': unnecessary filler words like *halt*, *eben*, *nun*, *mal*, *schon*, *doch*, *eh*, *ja* or *irgendwie*, ever further complicating the grammatical structure of a sentence without clarifying its meaning. If the German language was a kind of road, it was a long, winding one, with sleeping policemen and traffic lights at every corner, and a speed limit on the bits in between.

By contrast, English seemed to resemble a flyover on which speeding was not just tolerated, but actively encouraged. On my first day at school, I was amazed to overhear one of the boys from my English class complain that his mum had forgotten to pack his 'sarnies'. 'Sandwich' already struck me as an elegant improvement on the German *Butterbrot*, yet the English were evidently keen to squash up their language even further: 'sarnie' becoming a flatpack version of 'sandwich' in the way that a sandwich itself was a flatpack version of a proper lunch. Had the boy's mother remembered to pack his sarnies, so I learnt later, he would have not declared the snack delicious, but 'delish'. The sofas in our sixth-form common room weren't comfortable, but 'comfy'. Like some expensive Formula One sports car, English was constantly in the lab, experimented on in order to improve its speed and manoeuvrability – a conclusion that was merely confirmed when I watched English television outside school hours. Anyone who has ever watched a German talkshow will be familiar with the sing-song in which Germans speak when they want to sound intelligent: a slow-motion pile-up of subclauses and modal particles. German talkshow hosts will rarely interrupt their guests – it's as if the sentences themselves are unbreakable. English talkshows, in comparison, were a chaotic tug of war, in which word-streams were constantly being cut off, interrupted and teed up for a restart.

English teacher Mr P might have made a good talkshow host in a different life. Born in London's East End and educated at Oxford, he had a habit of occasionally dropping his Ts and aitches ('Wha's 'amlet's mo'ivation in this scene?') while simultaneously affecting a peculiar verbal tic whereby he would repeat the word 'the' in rapid succession ('Hamlet believes that nothing is real apart from in the-the-the the mind of the individual'). The 'Oxford stutter', as I later learnt to call it, struck me as the equivalent of racing drivers revving their engines: it gave Mr P thinking time without actually interrupting the flow of words. When in full swing, he was practically unstoppable, the accelerator pedal pushed to the floor in spite of the English language's evident slipperiness. We learnt about the importance of Hamlet's speech ('the rest is silence') and 'Pinteresque pauses', though silences and pauses seemed completely counter-intuitive to Mr P's mode of speech. So thick and fast was the verbal torrent that you were led to assume that his wages were calculated by an hourly word count. Did I understand what he was talking about? That was another matter. Mr P had an extraordinary talent for 'deep reading', the art of exploring the intricacies of a piece of writing from unexpected angles, and he could spend hours debating a small detail, such as whether the phrase 'moss'd cottage-trees' in Keats' 'To Autumn' was more like the sound of biting into a crunchy Braeburn or a succulent Cox. He once likened his method to that of a diver who had managed to fill a Renaissance cathedral with water and was exploring the frescoes up close. By the end of the first term, we hadn't progressed beyond Act I, scene ii of *Hamlet*.

'Rambling on' is a phenomenon that does not quite exist in the same way in German. Even when Germans go on at length about some irrelevant detail, there is still something about the structure of the language which will lend their words an appearance of purpose and direction. The German word for 'term' is *Begriff*, from the verb *greifen*, meaning to grapple, to grab or to hold: one of its outstanding features is the ability to get a very firm hold on specific meanings. The English 'to put' translates as *stellen*, but the German can be adapted to be more specific than that: *einstellen* ('to put into'), *vorstellen* ('to put in front', also 'to introduce'), *wegstellen* ('to put away'), *hinstellen* ('to put into a place'), *abstellen* ('to put down'), *durchstellen* ('to put through') and so on. The impression is of a wheel with an extremely tight grip on the road. And there is also something in the construction of a sentence that lends comfort and encouragement to native speakers. If, say, a cat is the grammatical subject of a German sentence I might not know immediately if that cat is going to catch a mouse, knock over a bottle of milk or get run over by a car, but at least I know something is definitely going to happen to the cat at the end of the sentence.

By the time the Christmas holidays arrived, I had admitted defeat. It was evident to me that I would never be able to fully master the English language in the way my peers could. I might be able to build up my vocabulary to the extent that I would have a thousand different words for toilets, beers, dinners or kisses; I might even be able to teach myself a half-decent Oxford stutter, yet there would always be some verbal banana skin plotting my downfall. German brains were too sluggish for English words, English sentences too flexible for German souls longing for the comfort of precision and predictability. English had elegance, and wit, and playfulness, but it didn't do a very good job of making me feel like I knew where I was going.

*

Historically speaking, the sense of determination and direction that manifests itself in German grammar took some time to rub off on its politics. Germany's otherness, which had caused such discomfort throughout the 1800s, continued to haunt the country after the turn of the century. Under the arch-reactionary Prussian chancellor Bismarck, Germany had paradoxically become a more progressive country in many ways. Liberals had been invited back into Bismarck's parliament, a basic version of the welfare state had been established, and in 1871 Germany had eventually become a unified nation state. Aided by unification, the economy had grown too, even if German industry paled in comparison to superpower Britain, with its trade networks wrapping themselves around the globe and a vast navy to protect its empire. Mentally, however, Germany was still provincial and inward-looking, content in its splendid isolation and clumsy in matters of diplomacy. In 1908 Kaiser Wilhelm gave an interview to the *Daily Telegraph* in which he intended to supply sweet soundbites on the nature of

Anglo-German friendship, but managed to alienate not just the entire British reading public but also his own political advisers ('You English are mad, mad, mad as March hares,' went one memorable quote). The German Hamlet was evidently a slow learner.

Some thought that otherness should be turned into a virtue. In 1914, shortly before the start of the First World War, several German intellectuals tried to put a positive spin on the notion of a German *Sonderweg* or 'special path'. One theory was that Germany was somehow more thoughtful and philosophical than other countries: it was a 'culture', and not a 'civilisation' like France or Italy, thought the novelist Thomas Mann. Another argument proposed that German society worked differently from those of other European countries. Germans lived in provincial communities, not urban conglomerations: a *Gemeinschaft* rather than a *Gesellschaft*, as the sociologist Friedrich Tönnies put it, a tight-knit 'community' rather than a more open-minded 'society'. Others thought the difference was more instinctive: Germany was a deeply idealistic nation of 'heroes' and 'dreamers', claimed the theorist Werner Sombart – as opposed to England's market-minded nation of traders and shopkeepers. Paradoxically, the consensus seemed to be that Germany was mentally adrift from its neighbours while at the same time geographically boxed in between capitalist England and France on the one side and Tsarist Russia on the other – making it uniquely predisposed to claustrophobia or *Platzangst*. Whatever the precise nature of German otherness, most agreed that these unique circumstances justified a military conflict.

When that war was lost, the natural thing would have been for Germany to go back to Hamlet-like soul-searching. Instead, something interesting happened. After nearly a hundred years of inwardness, Germany became interested in rebuilding bridges with its neighbours. There was the new constitution, signed on 31 July 1919 in the Thuringian town of Weimar: a document brimming with the ambition to get Germany on a par with other democratic states in Europe, if not ahead. Germany got a host of human rights, a centralised tax law, its first ministry of finance, and female suffrage (nine years before Britain). Germany re-entered the League of Nations, naturalised thousands of immigrants and established new trade links with Hungary, Romania and Bulgaria. There was the aptly titled weekly newspaper *Die Weltbühne* ('The World Stage'), edited by the campaigning journalist Carl von Ossietzky and the satirist Kurt Tucholsky, which called for international dialogue and exchange. 'You can imagine a Frenchman speaking English,' Tucholsky lamented under the pseudonym Peter Panter on 24 November 1924. 'At a push you can even imagine an Englishman speaking French. Heavens, you can even imagine an Eskimo singing Italian arias. But a black man speaking with a Saxony dialect: that's still hard to imagine.' In the arts, there were the poems and paintings of German expressionists, with their cult of *Mensch* – the human in its primal, super-national form.

The most telling relic of German cosmopolitanism in the

1920s is neither treaty nor newspaper, poem nor painting, but a film: Josef von Sternberg's *The Blue Angel*, produced by Berlin's legendary UFA studios and released when the Golden Twenties were almost over, on April Fool's Day 1930. Von Sternberg's film was designated UFA's first truly international picture. Envy played a large role in its inception: in 1927, America's Warner Bros studios had released *The Jazz Singer*, the first sound movie to enjoy major success at the box office. From then on, 'talkies' were all the rage. French cinema followed suit with René Clair's *Sous les toits de Paris*, and British International Pictures raised the bar with Alfred Hitchcock's taut thriller *Blackmail*, released in 1929. UFA, having led the pack when it came to production and set design throughout the 1920s, and having been bought by the proud nationalist Alfred Hugenberg in 1927, was feeling the pressure.

If you look at the credits alone, *The Blue Angel* could easily have been produced in the US. Von Sternberg, the director, was originally from Vienna but had moved to America when he was two, and he had made his name with a number of well-received gangster films. Emil Jannings, the male lead, was German but worked in Hollywood, where he had won the inaugural Best Actor Oscar for his roles in *The Way of All Flesh* and *The Last Command* in 1928. The soundtrack was provided by a jazz band, the sound of the metropolis and still a distinctly 'un-German' musical style. The novel on which the film was based – *Professor Unrat* by Heinrich Mann, brother of Thomas – was German, but the thematic parallels with the French and the German box-office smashes are hard to ignore. *The Jazz Singer* told the story of a Jewish musician who breaks away from his strict orthodox family to become a beer-hall pianist. *Sous le toits de Paris* is a musical comedy about a street singer who falls in love with a Romanian girl called Pola. *The Blue Angel* then, by sheer coincidence, is the story of a strict, disciplinarian teacher, Professor Immanuel Rath (called '*Unrat*', 'rubbish', by students behind his back), who one night pursues a wayward group of his students to a beer hall and falls in love with the woman he sees on the stage, a jazz singer called Lola Lola. Von Sternberg's film had deliberately obscured its place-specific setting in Lübeck: this was supposed to be a film located in the dark subconscious of a universal imagination, rather than a recognisably German place. Large chunks of Mann's novel are rendered in thick north German dialect – another feature purged from the screenplay. In fact, the way this talkie talked was the most extraordinary thing about it. To underline its international ambition, von Sternberg recorded every scene twice, effectively producing two films along the way: *Der Blaue Engel* spoke German, *The Blue Angel* talked to you in English.

The great irony of *The Blue Angel* is that in spite of its overt cosmopolitanism, you cannot help thinking what an incredibly German movie it is once the film unreels. Unlike *The Jazz Singer* or *Sous le toits de Paris*, the romance between Emil Jannings's Professor Rath and Marlene Dietrich's Lola Lola doesn't have a happy ending: as soon as the teacher relaxes his Prussian discipline, he fatally turns slave to his emotions. A few years after their engagement, we see Rath as a member of Lola Lola's ensemble: shock-haired, wild-eyed and insane with jealousy for his extravagant wife, who is about to embark on an affair with a circus strongman. *The Blue Angel* ends – unusually, for a sound film – in silence, with Professor Immanuel Rath suffering a mental break-down in his old classroom and dying underneath the blackboard.

To a 1930s audience, the film would have had more than a faint resemblance to recent German history. In the final throes of the First World War, Germany's cash-strapped Supreme Command had decided to go out with all guns blazing, seeking a climactic battle against the British Royal Navy in the English Channel. But in the naval ports of Kiel and Wilhelmshaven, sailors refused to follow military orders. Mutiny spread across the land, leading to the declaration of the German republic and the abdication of Kaiser Wilhelm. If the arch-conservative teacher Rath symbolised Wilhelmine Germany, his uppity young students more than resembled the revolutionary agitators around Rosa Luxemburg and Karl Liebknecht, the 'Spartacus League' which had temporarily driven the uprisings. But the film's take on all this looks overwhelmingly reactionary: it concludes bleakly that there was no way that Germany could be brought into the new world without death and bloodshed – a sceptical gloss on the Weimar Republic's political experiment. Mix old and new, the film seemed to be saying, and you'll have to deal with the consequences.

More German character traits: for a film about the underground world of a nightclub, *The Blue Angel* is incredibly mannered. In 1930, the Marx Brothers made *Animal Crackers*, a film which featured Groucho Marx being carried into a ballroom by a group of African tribesmen and Harpo Marx shooting at a cuckoo clock with a rifle, wearing underwear, braces and a top hat. Four years later, Jean Vigo would make *L'Atalante*, a film which involved three actors on a barge, clowning around among a small army of stray cats. *The Blue Angel* never manages to celebrate on-screen anarchy in the way those films did.

Siegfried Kracauer, a critic and arts editor for the liberal *Frankfurter Zeitung*, went one step further. Writing in 1947, he suggested that von Sternberg's film wasn't just nostalgically attached to Germany's old order, it already bore the marks of Hitler's Third Reich. Populated with characters who revelled in the suffering of others, *The Blue Angel* laid bare a sadistic streak in the German psyche. As Kracauer saw it, Dietrich's Lola Lola paired 'callous egoism and cool insolence'; the students 'were born Hitler Youths'.

The most German thing about *The Blue Angel* is also the most famous: its sound. The moment in which Professor Rath becomes hopelessly infatuated with his backroom beauty is marked by a song whose refrain starts with that jarring, grating 'ich' sound –

> Ich bin von Kopf bis Fuss
> Auf Liebe eingestellt . . .

– and keeps returning to it at the end of every verse like a hand scratching a scab:

> ... Denn das ist meine Welt,
> Und sonst gar nichts ...
>
> Männer umschwirr'n mich
> Wie Motten um das Licht,
> Und wenn sie verbrennen,
> Ja dafür kann ich nichts.

The tongue sticks in a barb wire snare.

If the German *Blue Angel* sounded threatening to English ears, the English version was unintentionally comical. This was a talkie crying out for the invention of the dubbing track. 'Men cluster to me', Dietrich sings, 'like moffs around a flame/ and if their weengs burn/ I know I'm not to blaym.' The scene is hard to take seriously, though not as downright puzzling as the one in which the professor admonishes his students in a German accent for not being able to read *Hamlet* with the proper English accent. 'To be or not to be,' says the student, 'zat is ze . . .' Rath interrupts him: 'Halt, rong. You are effidentally diss-satisfied with the akcepted pro-noun-see-ation of ze word "the".' This, perhaps, was the way in which *The Blue Angel* was most emblematic of Germany in the 1920s: its attempt to present itself as worldly-wise and cosmopolitan, and its ultimate failure to do so.

*

Like everyone who has grown up in Germany, I knew the melody to 'Falling in Love Again' by heart and had seen *that* picture from the film's poster a million times. *Die Dietrich* in stockings and suspenders, one leg pulled up to her body in order to bare a pale flash of thigh, a white top hat balancing on her head at a waggish angle, a visual shorthand for that decade's curious mix of self-discipline and self-abandon. Like most people, I had also never actually seen the film. Now, in England, without any friends with whom to spend my evenings and weekends, I had plenty of time to catch up. I went to the video shop at the bottom of our road, where the ponytailed man behind the counter told me that *The Blue Angel* was currently out on loan, but that I should just get *Cabaret* instead, which was 'basically the same thing'. He handed me a grubby VHS box. The cover looked almost identical, apart from the fact that the woman in suspenders was wearing a black bowler instead of a white top hat.

Cabaret, it turned out, was a story about a coy, well-mannered Englishman, played by Michael York, who moves to Berlin to work as an English teacher and befriends a fellow Anglophone expat and cabaret performer called Sally Bowles, played by Liza Minnelli. The story of their friendship is interspersed with musical numbers that seem to fall into two categories: songs performed by Sally Bowles, in an overblown American stage-musical style with a life-affirming message, or songs performed by the German contingent in the troupe. The latter would invariably contain men and women with pale faces, darkened eyes and red cupid's-bow lips, and an excessive use of sexual innuendo.

Cabaret and *The Blue Angel* aren't 'the same thing', but the link between them isn't entirely arbitrary either. Bob Fosse's film was based on a Broadway musical, which was based on a play, called *I Am a Camera*, which was based on a book by the English writer Christopher Isherwood, which was based on his own experiences in Berlin. Isherwood had lived on and off in the city from November 1929 until May 1933, and one of the things he rated most about the German capital was the wide variety of German films showing at Berlin's 5,600 movie houses, including – *quod erat demonstrandum* – *The Blue Angel*, which premiered five months after his arrival.

While Germans were keen to draw the world's attention to their growing political maturity and cosmopolitan openness, English observers noticed one thing, and one thing only. *Cabaret* and the stories in Isherwood's *Goodbye to Berlin* share the common assumption that Weimar Germany is the fatherland of sexual experimentation, and Berlin – in the painter Wyndham Lewis's words – 'the Pervert's Paradise'. Sex is by far the dominant theme in English writing about Germany in the 1920s. Some registered it with a sense of disgust: writing about his first visit to Berlin, the Anglophile Sicilian Giuseppe di Lampedusa is overwhelmed by the city's 'indecency', its 'innumerable trollops' and 'overly elegant and overly shaven lads'. Others were positively enchanted by the people and their language. When Christopher Isherwood's friend, the poet Stephen Spender, arrived in Hamburg in July 1929, he wrote in his diary: 'Now I shall begin to live.' Another mutual friend, W. H. Auden, even wrote a series of love poems in that terrible German language, in the summer of 1930, while feeling lovesick for Gerhart, a sailor from Hamburg ('The balls on him are beauties/ His cock's a beauty too/ When we're in bed together/ We find plenty to do').

Isherwood's own position lay somewhere between the two. On the one hand, he liked to complain about the corruption of the nineteenth-century 'Germany of the mind' and the kitsch trivialisation of Romantic poetry he found in cabaret lyrics like Dietrich's: 'The word *Liebe*, soaring from the Goethe standard, was no longer worth a whore's kiss,' he writes in one of his stories. 'Spring, moonlight, youth, roses, girl, darlings, heart, May: such was the miserable devalued currency dealt in by the authors of those tangoes, waltzes, and foxtrots which advocated the private escape.' (This, one should note, from a man who could barely ask for a stamp at a German post office.)

But to the former public schoolboy Isherwood, Berlin also meant liberation from the strict sex codes of upper-middle-class Britain. In Blighty, class always played a role in the bedroom – behind the heavy leather curtains of the Cosy Corner and the Adonis Klause it didn't, or so it seemed to a non-fluent foreigner like Isherwood. Writing about his experiences in the third person in 'Christopher and His Kind', he says that 'Christopher was suffering from an inhibition, then not unusual among upper-class homosexuals; he couldn't relax sexually with a member of his own class or nation.' In the company of German boys, however, 'he who had hinted and stammered in English, could now ask straight out in German for what he wanted. His limited knowledge of the language forced him to be blunt and he wasn't embarrassed to utter the foreign sex words, since they had no associations with his life in England.'

Germans, in Isherwood's Berlin stories, are always overtly physical, their bodies constantly on the verge of spilling over into their surroundings. In 'A Berlin Diary', the previous lodgers in his flat have left their marks all over the apartment: there's the stain where Herr Noeske was sick after his birthday party ('What in the world can he have been eating, to make a mess like that?'), the coffee stains on the wallpaper, from that time Herr Rittmeister 'got a bit excited in his feelings', or the inkspots from Professor Koch's ejaculating fountain pen. His next-door neighbour, Fräulein Mayr, is a music-hall *jodlerin* whose 'nude fleshy arms ripple unappetisingly', and even his landlady, Fräulein Schroeder, confides that she is unhappy with the volume of her bursting bosom. The English, by contrast, are pale and bloodless: Sally Bowles's hands are 'nervous, veined and very thin – the hands of a middle-aged woman'. Isherwood himself is so lightly sketched, he is nigh invisible. 'I am a camera with its shutter open,' he writes in the much-quoted opening to the story, 'quite passive, recording, not thinking. Recording the man shaving at the window opposite and the woman in the kimono washing her hair.' The convenient thing about cameramen is that they are never in the picture themselves. At one point in the story, one of his students – a 'fat pretty girl' with a 'self-indulgent laugh and a well-formed bust' called Fräulein Hippi – asks Isherwood, with eyebrows raised in comic surprise: 'And tell me please, do you find German girls different than English girls?' Isherwood blushes and evades the question with a typically English instinct. Trying to counter his nervousness about sex with his confidence in matters linguistic, he corrects her grammar. The only problem is that he is so flustered that he can't remember 'whether one says *different from* or *different to*'. Fräulein Hippi persists: 'Do you find German girls different than English girls?' To Isherwood's relief, the doorbell rings and he is let off.

*

What is the difference between the German and the English approaches to sex? This was almost as popular a subject on my school bus as the German language, particularly after some of the boys had returned from a school trip to Wuppertal. German girls weren't necessarily more attractive, one of them announced, but they were definitely more 'up for it'. There were whole beaches in Germany where no one wore any clothes. They also showed porn on primetime TV over there, and in the shops you could buy a magazine called *Bravo*, which was basically pornography for teenagers. 'And they all had hairy pits and hairy muffs.'

'What, did you get some action, then?'

'I meant the girls in the magazines.'

'I know. And I meant: did you get some action then?'

'Oh, yeah, of course. Of course I did.' The boy suddenly took a keen interest in the comic lying in his lap.

'So I heard this story', said a third boy, 'that one of the boys on that trip was asked to join his host family in the sauna and then ...'

'Yeah, we've all heard that.'

'Uh, OK.'

For the rest of the journey, the group sat in silence.

I wasn't so sure that German girls were very different from English girls. In retrospect, I find it hard to tell if the really rabid phase of teenage puberty merely kicked in a bit later at my old school, after I had left, or (which is more likely) that I lived through it without really noticing. German girls certainly didn't spend quite as much time talking about 'pulling' as the boys at my new school. They merely allowed us to kiss them at some point, without much fuss and tribulation. It's perhaps telling that the first memory I have of my parents 'having a word' with me about sex is the time my mother told me that I should make sure not to flush used condoms down the toilet.

One simple explanation for all this is that single-sex schools are rare in Germany – there are barely ten boys-only schools in the whole country. One of the most commonly cited arguments in favour of single-sex education is that it is less likely to distract students. Yet in England I learnt that nothing could be further from the truth. Male interest in the female anatomy, it seemed, ran in inverse proportion to a schoolboy's proximity to live specimens, and girls were discussed with inexhaustible vigour and never-ending fascination, drawing on an infinitesimal arsenal of rude hand gestures to discuss depraved details. The ubiquitous 'cock-and-balls' drawing, a staple of public-toilet doors and the margins of exercise books, is a unique product of the English single-sex school system, which I never came across in ten years of German schooling. Before school assembly each Monday morning, the conquests of the weekend were discussed in graphic detail: who had kissed whom, and who had been allowed to touch whom where. A good-looking girl was a 'fittie', I learnt, which had usually very little to do with her actual physical fitness. I also learnt that 'to pull' didn't mean to flirt, but to French-kiss. The German term for pulling was *mit jemandem abstürzen*, to fall with someone, implying a biblical fall from grace, or at least a loss of face. 'Pulling', on the other hand, implied physical achievement – appropriate for the manner in which the weekend's conquests were recounted on a Monday morning.

In the middle of the spring term, I had a minor breakthrough with my schoolmates. One day after Mr P's English class, one of the tall, athletic boys walked over to my desk and handed me an invite to his eighteenth birthday party. Perhaps he did it out of politeness, perhaps out of sheer embarrassment. Still, I couldn't possibly have been more excited. The party was going to be held on a Saturday at the local rugby club and had a 'fancy dress' theme. This struck me as slightly odd for an eighteenth birthday party, given that in Germany my friends had stopped having costume parties when we were about eight. But I also knew that Germans were famously unimaginative when it came to dressing up, as anyone who has ever seen the endless variations on the clown, cowboy and Red Indian at a German carnival procession can testify. The English could undoubtedly do better. When Saturday came, I spent most of the day preparing a beetle costume out of old cardboard boxes and pipecleaners.

Arriving at the venue, my costume was greeted by pitiful smirks. The English interpretation of 'fancy dress' was evidently less about disguising than disrobing. A large percentage of the girls from the single-sex school at the end of the road had dressed up as the 'sexy devil' you would otherwise only see in Ann Summers' window displays. Many of these were prim and proper middle-class girls who played lacrosse and took Higher Maths A levels – yet here they were, in minier-than-mini miniskirts with breasts bulging out of their boob tubes like flesh-coloured toothpaste. I don't think I had ever seen a girl my age in a short skirt before – the girls at my German school always wore jeans, even at parties. Many of the boys had dressed up in women's clothing too, particularly the tall, muscular jocks who played rugby. By the end of the night, some of the girls had taken to flashing their breasts at pedestrians passing by outside, to which a group of young men on the other side of the window responded by pulling down their trousers and baring their behinds. And Germans were meant to be obsessed with nudity?

The Russian critic Mikhail Bakhtin pioneered the use of the term 'carnivalesque' to denote a phase of misrule in which the dominant values and codes in a society are ritually inverted. In England, carnivalesque misrule was not so much an occasional occurrence as a social constant. It was as if over the years carnival had become a monthly event, then a weekly celebration, and now something you would revel in on a Thursday evening as well as a Friday and a Saturday and a Sunday lunchtime. Historians talk of 'merrie

England' as if it was a historical period in which the English were more sexually liberated and less socially inhibited, when in actual fact merrie England wasn't all that different from the England of today. I remember being confused by the way in which English people talked about Christmas: when winter came, newspapers were filled with articles about 'drunken snogs' at 'office parties', illustrated with pictures of people wearing garish shirts and silly paper hats. In Germany, I associated Christmas with sombre music and candlelit rooms, with 'Silent Night' instead of 'Ding Dong Merrily on High'.

The idea of the English as no-sex-please-we're-British prudes will never die out, but it is, in truth, a big fat lie. There are, to my knowledge, no other people on this planet who are so passionately and so privately devoted to exploring the wondrous connectivities of the male and female organs.

*

The German attitude to sex is both more straightforward and more complicated than the English. I only fully realised this years later, when I finally got my hands on *The Blue Angel*. Two things jumped out at me. First: unlike Liza Minnelli, Marlene Dietrich doesn't really sing her songs. She half speaks, half sing-songs them. The melody of 'Falling in Love Again' isn't really the melody of a song you hear in a musical, but the melody of a wind-up music box. It starts, and then it slows down until you think it has stopped, and then it starts again. Her voice is squeaky-high in the first couple of numbers in the film; here, it suddenly drops an octave midway through the number. The impression is of a woman singing a duet with herself. Second: Lola Lola isn't really sexy. Or at least she isn't a sex kitten or a 'sexy devil'. The odd thing about her song is that even though we can see that Rath is meant to be romantically enchanted by it, the lyrics of 'Falling in Love Again' actually say the opposite. The imagery is that of mechanical exchange. In the German, Lola Lola isn't even falling in love, she is 'adjusted to love, from head to toe'. To her, love is not something that happens in her heart, but something her body has been programmed to do: 'I can only make love, and nothing else'. Kenneth Tynan once described Marlene Dietrich as 'sex without gender', and that seems to come pretty close. This particular German angel certainly wasn't that blue at all.

The German attitude to sex is more straightforward because it is almost entirely non-ironic, and more complicated because one can't fully understand it unless one also gets one's head around the German attitude to language. Perhaps the oddest thing about German grammar – and the feature that is most infuriating to non-native speakers – is neither the modal article nor the split infinitive, but the use of gender articles. In English, we have a definite and an indefinite article, but neither 'the' or 'a' has a gender in its own right. To ask if a table is male or female would be absurd, and rightly so. The absence of gender articles places English at one extreme of the spectrum, as most world languages tend to have at least a male and a female gender article: *un* and *une* in French, *el* and *la* in Spanish, and so on. German, however, has not just one gender article, but three: male (*der*), female (*die*) and neutral (*das*). Frustratingly, these three articles are assigned to different nouns by a seemingly arbitrary law. A person's mouth, neck, bosom, elbows, fingers, nails, feet, and body are always of the male sex, whether their owner is a man or a woman. A woman's head, for example, is male, yet her hands, lips, nose, eyebrows, shoulders and toes are female; her hair, ears, eyes, chin, knees and heart don't have any sex at all. Mark Twain exposed the absurd side effects of such a system: 'In German, a young lady has no sex, while a turnip has. Think what overwrought reverence that shows for the turnip, and what callous disrespect for the girl.' Gender confusion, in other words, is already hardwired into the German language.

Twain's comments were published as part of his non-fiction travelogue *A Tramp Abroad* in 1880 and translated into German in 1892. It's unlikely that this essay on its own did much to sting German self-confidence, but by the turn of the century, and with the rise of English as a global lingua franca, the pre-eminence of German and French on the European mainland was increasingly felt to be under threat. Particularly in German-speaking countries this translated into an acute philosophical anxiety about what language as a whole could and couldn't do. This phenomenon is also known as the *Sprachkrise*, and the best example of the supposed crisis of language is a letter published in the Berlin literary magazine *Der Tag* in October 1902. Simply titled 'A Letter', it purports to be a despatch by a young English poet called Philipp, Lord Chandos, to his mentor, the philosopher Francis Bacon. In fact, it was written by Hugo von Hofmannsthal, a young Viennese writer who had recently befriended the influential German poet Stefan George and his circle. In the letter, 'Chandos' writes that he has lost his faith in language: words he used to speak with 'unhesitating fluency' now disintegrate in his mouth 'like rotten mushrooms'. It started with abstract words, like 'spirit', 'soul' or 'body', but now he can't even speak to his four-year-old daughter without having 'to make an effort to sputter to the end of my sentence, as if I had fallen ill' – the words of the letter, in fact, are the first he has managed to get down on paper in almost two years. The crisis of language, Chandos writes, is 'like spreading rust'.

A flipside of this distrust in words, he goes on to reveal, is a growing obsession with mute objects. Chandos compares himself to the great Roman orator Lucius Licinius Crassus, who in old age fell increasingly silent and became infatuated with a tame eel. Everything around him seems to mean something:

> a dog, a beetle, a stunted apple tree, a cart path winding over the hill, a moss-covered stone mean more to me than the most beautiful, most abandoned lover ever did on the happiest night. These mute and sometimes inanimate beings rise up before me with such plenitude, such a presence of love that my joyful eye finds nothing dead anywhere.

Even his own limbs seem to speak to him: 'It is as if my body consisted entirely of coded messages revealing everything to me.'

One should take von Hofmannsthal's Chandos letter with a pinch of salt: it would be naïve to conclude that the German language somehow went broke at the start of the twentieth century. If anything, the letter itself is proof of the fact that it still works perfectly well. But it would be equally foolish to dismiss the *Sprachkrise* as something that mattered only to a literary circle, or to philosophers in ivory towers. By the time that Christopher Isherwood's train arrived in Berlin in 1929, the cult of the mute body had already seeped into popular culture. German nudism's first manifestos were written at this time, such as Hans Surén's *Der Mensch und die Sonne* ('Man and Sun'), which went through an incredible sixty-one printings in one year and sold 250,000 copies. German dance, ballet and pantomime flourished. UFA produced *The Cabinet of Dr Caligari*, *Metropolis* and *The Last Laugh*: would German silent cinema have led the way if there hadn't been a sense that bodies could convey emotion better than words could? Even *The Blue Angel*, as a talkie, is Chandos-esque in its instincts: this, after all, is the story of a man who abandons the world of letters for the unrestrained pleasures of the body. Professor Rath's fall from grace is marked by a screeching, painful crowing sound: it tells you something about his demented state of mind that words never could.

If the naked body was sinful in Catholic countries, and embarrassing in Puritan England, then in Germany it had by now become something positive and worth celebrating.

By the same logic, in the Chandos worldview the most honourable profession there is is that of the prostitute: someone who is completely in tune with the human body and the messages it conveys. While von Sternberg's film leaves it open whether Lola Lola is prepared to sell her body or whether she just sings about it, other films and plays were less ambiguous. In Bertolt Brecht's *The Threepenny Opera* the gangster king Macheath ends up on the scaffold because he cannot resist stopping off at his favourite brothel when he should really be on the run from the police. In Frank Wedekind's Lulu plays *The Earth Spirit* and *Pandora's Box* – turned into a silent film by G. W. Pabst in 1929 – the eponymous central character has affairs with a string of men and women and eventually ends up working as a prostitute in London, where she is murdered by Jack the Ripper. Wedekind describes her as 'the true animal, the wild, beautiful animal' and a 'primal form of woman'.

These plays were written nearly a hundred years ago, but they sum up an attitude to matters sexual that you can still find in Germany today. Naked bodies are more casually on display in Germany than in England – on the beaches, in the parks, not hidden away on page 3 of the tabloids but always on *Bild*'s front page – not just because of sex, but precisely because nude bodies here are always more than just sex. In 2008, the English-born German TV presenter Charlotte Roche published a semi-autobiographical novel called *Feuchtgebiete*, which is also a manifesto against genital hygiene. 'I wanted to write a book about the ugly parts of the human body,' Roche said in an interview shortly before her book appeared in Britain in 2009. 'The smelly bits. The juices of the female body. Smegma.' In Britain, *Wetlands* made for good 'clit-lit' headlines and a couple of laboured 'is it porn or is it art?' debates. In Germany the book went straight to the top of the bestseller charts and stayed there for seven months, selling more than a million copies in the process. And if it's acceptable to move from 'respectable' television into pornography, it's equally common for people to move from smut to showbiz. A large percentage of German actors who came to fame in the *Heimatfilme* of the 1980s – Sascha Hehn, Heiner Lauterbach or Ingrid Steeger – had their breakthrough in Bavarian soft-porn movies like *Beim Jodeln juckt die Lederhose* or the interminable *Schulmädchen-Report* series in the 1970s. More recently, actresses like Sibel Kekilli and Tyra Misoux have transferred from hardcore to arthouse with ease. The role of prostitutes in German society is still enigmatic. The practising prostitute Domenica Niehoff, for example, became a major celebrity in Germany in the late 1970s: the poet Wolf Wondratschek wrote poems about her, she played roles in the theatre and took part in art installations, and when she died in 2009, there was a fawning obituary even in the arch-conservative daily *Die Welt* ('She had a great big heart for everyone'). It's hard to imagine even an upper-class callgirl like Christine Keeler ever receiving similar eulogies.

The *Sprachkrise*, likewise, lives on, not least in the form of a permanent German anxiety over the way words are spelt. In 1996, German authorities decreed a spelling reform concerning the use of caps in phrases like *recht haben* ('to be in the right', now *Recht haben*), and the use of the sharp German 's' sound, the *Eszett* or ß (now commonly replaced with 'ss'). In other countries, this might well have been a minor issue for a select group of academics. Yet in Germany spelling reform was aggressively debated in all the news magazines and TV stations, and continues to divide the country. Some of the federal states use it, others don't. Most newspapers, including *Der Spiegel*, the *Frankfurter Allgemeine Zeitung* and the *Rheinischer Merkur*, initially adopted the new spelling rules only to return to the old system later. It's hard to imagine England's laissez-faire linguists going through an equally painful process – even though English might actually benefit from it more than German (for instance, a consistent take on the use of 'ie' or 'ei' could save generations from misspelling the word 'weird'). It's tempting to put this down to a German love of rules and authority, but what makes the German spelling reform uniquely German is that it has left everyone even more confused as to how we spell or pronounce words properly. France and Italy have centralised bodies which control their languages – the Académie française and the Accademia della Crusca – Germany doesn't.

*

The political reforms of Weimar Germany barely survived longer than the linguistic reforms of the 1990s. On 3 October 1929, Chancellor Gustav Stresemann, whose currency reform in 1923 had paved the way for the cultural flourishing of the Golden Twenties, died of a stroke. Marlene Dietrich left Berlin for New York on 1 April 1930, straight after *The Blue Angel*'s premiere at Berlin's Gloria-Palast cinema – von Sternberg had managed to negotiate a two-movie deal with Paramount Pictures, who were looking for a European star to rival the pulling power of MGM's Greta Garbo. In the opening fifteen minutes of her first American film, *Morocco* (1930), there is a scene that now looks like a symbol of Germany's decade to come: banished from home, stuck on the crowded deck of a small steamer that appears to be all at sea, lost in fog somewhere off a foreign coast. A woman emerges, pushing her way past the silent onlookers. She drops her suitcase, which bursts open and its contents are scattered over the floor. An American man comes to her assistance. 'Your first trip to Morocco?' he asks, and then: 'I make the trip quite often. Perhaps I can be of some service? I'd be happy to help you.'

More than any other country, it was America that was to become a home and shelter for the creatives and intellectuals who had made 1920s Germany such an interesting place. The Wall Street stock-market crash, which had rocked the global economy, triggered something dark and sinister in Germany, but in America it inspired a new kind of optimism, which found its best embodiment in the community-spirited New Deal. Where Germany was increasingly repressive and monocultural, America was liberal and multicultural, to the extent that even a German movie actress could become a national hero.

In *Morocco*, the German woman responds to the American's offer of help by saying, 'I won't need any help.' That, at least, 'was what was put in', wrote von Sternberg in his autobiography later, 'but that was not what came out.' Dietrich, like most Germans, had a tendency to substitute 'v' for 'w', 'w' for 'v', 'ch' for 'j', 'b' for 'p', and 'z' for 's'. 'Help' came out as 'helubh', even after the director had stopped filming and taken the actress to one side. The German tongue 'had dealt a deathblow to her charm', and for a while it looked like Dietrich's career in Hollywood had ended before it had even begun. The fact that it didn't was due to von Sternberg's persistence, but also Dietrich's realisation that even Germans can learn to improvise. After forty-eight takes, she tried to pronounce the sentence phonetically, as if it was written in German, and the scene was a wrap. A year later, she was nominated for an Oscar. During the war, she helped raise money for war bonds and performed a version of 'Lili Marlene' for US troops, for which she was awarded the Presidential Medal of Freedom. Her Hollywood Walk of Fame plaque, at 6400 Hollywood Boulevard, is testimony to America's ability to embrace external influences, to encourage people to invent and reinvent themselves, to make them realise that cultural identity is a performance rather than something fixed.

America appealed to sexually repressed Englishmen as much as to culturally repressed German women: in May 1933 Christopher Isherwood emigrated to California too, though his and Dietrich's paths did not directly cross for another thirty-five years. In May 1968, Isherwood – now sixty-two years old – went to a concert at Los Angeles's Ahmanson Theatre. The voice of the singer performing that evening, he noted in his diary, 'was uneven and often spoiled by her mannerisms and too often repeated tricks'. And yet Isherwood found himself strangely roused by the intimacy of the performance: 'We were carried out of ourselves because we were moved, and moved because we were carried out of ourselves.' The applause, he wrote, 'was like a thunderstorm which was always in the air throughout the performance and kept exploding and even interrupting the beginnings and ends of songs'. Enraptured, he rushed backstage to meet the singer at the end of the show, only to be pushed out of the way by a reporter from *Time* magazine, who pressed the singer for a quote for the 'People' section of the magazine. 'Don't you want to be in "People"?' he asked. Marlene Dietrich replied, with a perfectly formed 'pl' sound popping on her lips: 'I am *not* People!' The door shut in the two men's faces.

3

Theodor Adorno Doesn't Do the Jitterbug with A. J. Ayer

In the porter's lodge at Merton College, Oxford, there is a stack of leather-bound black A4 notebooks with marbled endpapers in which students have, over the decades, left their comments on the less elevated aspects of academic life. The book covering the years 1932 to 1937 records the 'crying need' for a new ping-pong table, the 'great door knocking mystery' of December 1934, 'females' making themselves seen and heard in the college bar ('Is this necessary?') and a poem on the subject of undergraduates throwing up on lavatory seats:

> Pray, what is a rear for,
> And why do we find ours
> So often bedewed by vomition?
> Behind a door bolted
> I've twice been revolted
> By the 'Grand Old Oxford Tradition'.

In February 1935, a more mature voice suddenly rises from the mayhem of student juvenilia. Th. Wiesengrund-Adorno writes: 'Sir, may I suggest that we get further supply of those cards with the Merton blazon crest. They seemed to me to be much nicer than the present ones.' On 11 November, by the same author: 'Sir, it was awfully kind of you to arrange a new supply of the cards with the crest. But they have disappeared at once! Is it proof of their popularity – or due to a general ressentiment against them?' A year later, on 29 July 1936: 'What do you think of writing paper with a crest, like the cards you got again in such a kind way after my suggestion on the subject?' Mr Wiesengrund-Adorno's insatiable desire for stationery emblazoned with Mertonian blue and yellow evidently didn't go unnoticed. On 26 November, at 10.15 p.m., some joker scrawled the following entry: 'Oh vere, oh vere, mein lieber Herr, are our leetle envelopes gone?'

The name 'Wiesengrund-Adorno' disappears from the comment book soon after. A delve into the college records might tell you that the student had joined Merton College in 1934, aided by a personal recommendation from the economist John Maynard Keynes, who thought the young man 'of rather unusual talent, combining philosophy, primarily the theory of aesthetics, with exceptional musical gifts'. It might tell you that Wiesengrund-Adorno was a German Jew, and that he had little chance of gaining employment in a German state that was now run by an anti-Semitic National Socialist regime. It might also tell you that the German enrolled as an 'advanced student' in spite of being thirty, and having already completed a PhD aged twenty-one. And it would tell you that Wiesengrund-Adorno didn't stay in England for very long: in 1937 he abandoned his degree in

Oxford and moved to California, as Dietrich and Isherwood had done before him.

The name Wiesengrund-Adorno manages to conjure up a slightly fractured, somewhat bipolar character. *Wiesen-grund*, 'lawn-ground', evokes quintessential Germanness – allotments, cross-hatched fences and garden gnomes – while 'Adorno' has more than a hint of southern European *joie de vivre. Je t'adore!* It sounds like a name invented by his friend Thomas Mann, a novelist drawn to characters who carried indicators of their internal division on their passport, such *Death in Venice*'s Gustav 'Ash-brook' Aschenbach. With a name like that, perhaps it is only natural that Theodor Wiesengrund-Adorno decided to follow American naming convention as soon as he was naturalised as a citizen of the US in 1942. 'The Authoritarian Personality', the 1950 essay that garnered him an international reputation, appears in university catalogues under 'Theodor W. Adorno': a beauti-fully symmetrical name, with those two wheel-shaped 'o's in each word, which rolls off the tongue like a Matchbox car. In my youth, it was nothing less than a household name.

'Household name' sounds right when talking about movie stars or brands of washing powder, so it's odd to hear it used about Theodor Adorno, because Adorno was a philosopher. And yet to my younger self 'Theodor Adorno' had been just that: a name that you picked up if you stayed up long enough to watch the news review show *Tagesthemen* or when you overheard older students having a discussion in the lunch queue. 'Adorno says . . .' 'Well, you will find that Adorno argues that . . .' 'Adorno would disagree with you.'

To an entire postwar generation, Adorno was what Germans call *eine moralische Instanz*, a moral authority of such high standing that merely quoting a line could put a stop to a complicated debate.

What did Adorno actually have to say? This is a more difficult question. Because even though I know that Adorno belonged to a group of philosophers known as the Frankfurt School, even though I know that Adorno's most famous book was *Dialectic of Enlightenment*, co-authored with Max Horkheimer, first published in America in 1944, republished in Germany in 1969, even though I know exactly what Adorno looked like – a pair of heavily framed glasses supported by a pale, moonish face and a round body in a grey suit – I didn't really know what Adorno was *about*. Growing up in Germany, Adorno was less someone whose ideas you had understood than a sound you recognised – in the same way that you might recognise a song by your favourite band on the radio. At the time I first heard the 'Adorno sound' I was into the shambolic guitar-rock played by bands such as Nirvana, Pearl Jam and Sonic Youth, known as grunge. In many ways the 'Adorno sound' and grunge were similar. Like the feedback of Kurt Cobain's electric guitar, a typical Adorno line would curl back on itself, obscuring its original intention: 'Life has become the ideology of its own absence' was a classic example. Others were just as good: 'Art is magic delivered from the lie of being truth,' or 'The splinter in your eye is the best magnifying glass.' At times it was simply brilliant verbal white noise: 'Intelligence is a moral category.' 'All reification is a kind of forgetting.' 'The joke of our time is the suicide of intention.' 'The fully enlightened earth radiates disaster triumphant.' Above all, there was Adorno's most famous line: 'After Auschwitz, there can be no more poetry.' Why exactly the great philosopher thought there could be no more poetry we did not know, but his words were powerful for being enigmatic, and quoted endlessly in the corner at the back of the schoolyard where the cool kids in battered army parkas would meet for roll-ups and black coffee. France will always have Sartre, Germany will always have Adorno.

Theodor Adorno was also a household name in another sense. When we eventually got around to unpacking the removal boxes that were stacking up in our living room, I discovered that Adorno's *Dialectic of Enlightenment* must have been part of our household furniture for some time. For here, at the bottom of one of my mother's boxes, was an old, faded paperback copy of the book in a Fischer edition, with simple sky-blue typography on a navy background. Why would my parents bother to transport a three-hundred-page tome of deeply enigmatic continental philosophy across the Channel? Had they ever read it? The spine looked suspiciously uncreased.

One way of learning to understand the Germans is to accept that they have a peculiar attitude to matters of the mind in general, and to printed matter of the mind in particular. According to the sociologist Benedict Anderson, nations begin to perceive themselves as communities only once printed books or scripts written in a common vernacular language circulate around a country, allowing different scattered communities to join in shared discourses. In this respect, Germany has always been a relatively early developer, if not a pioneer, with Gutenberg's invention of movable type in 1450 and Luther's translation of the Bible into vernacular German in 1521/22. Even by the time of Germany's supposed 'philosophical revolution' of the late eighteenth century, literacy rates were already unusually high. Reading societies were springing up across the country by the hundreds, and there was talk of a widespread *Lesesucht* or 'reading addiction'. Elementary schools and laws that made their attendance compulsory had been established in the eighteenth century, something the British didn't get around to until the 1880s. In the early nineteenth century, literacy rates in Prussia and Saxony were unmatched anywhere in the world except New England – by the end of the century illiteracy was as low as 0.5 per cent, half the rate of Britain and one-eighth of the sophisticated French. Germany might have been slow on the uptake when it came to parliamentary politics and industrialisation, but in thinking and writing it has often led the way.

The nation-building poets and thinkers of the late eighteenth and early nineteenth centuries added intellectual grist to the publishing industry's mill. The key concept to emerge from this period is *Bildung*, which is often translated as either 'culture' or 'education', but means so much more in the original. *Etwas bilden* also means 'to put something into shape': *Bildung* is not merely the extension or training of one's intellectual capacities, but the formation of the very essence of a human being. With Kant, the father of the German Enlightenment, *Bildung* became more important than religion, an idea later spelt out by the poet Friedrich Schlegel: 'Religion is merely a supplement to or a surrogate for education . . . the more educated we are, the less religion we need.' The fiery poets of the *Sturm und Drang* movement which followed in his footsteps conceived of a *Bildungsstaat*: a state whose overriding purpose was the perfection of our mental lives. Goethe invented a new kind of novel in which that same development would stand at the centre of the action: the *Bildungsroman*. Goethe's close friend Schiller proposed that the very best kind of *Bildung* would not take place in a classroom, but in an art gallery: only by undergoing an 'aesthetic education' could the mind be truly liberated. Goethe and Schiller enjoy such an elevated status in the German canon not just for their writing, but also because they came closer than anyone else ever did to realising a *Bildungsstaat*, when the two writers worked under the patronage of the court of Weimar in the 1790s.

With the Romantic movement of the nineteenth century, *Bildung* itself was elevated into a kind of art, which is to say that it became less of a constant activity than something which could be concentrated into individual pieces or projects. In particular at the university of Göttingen a more formalised framework began to grow around research and seminars. Even though it is commonly accepted that the first ever PhD was awarded at the university of Bologna in 1219, there is little dispute that it was at Germany's self-governed universities that the idea of the doctoral thesis was elevated into a type of cult. Academic qualifications matter to

Germans outside academia in a way they don't to English people. Courses last longer, for a start, with the equivalent of a bachelor's degree often taking four or five years. Even the equivalent of a master's degree – usually a year's full-time work at a British university – can in Germany take the shape of a major research project. I remember a friend of a friend who had his mind set on becoming a sports teacher at a primary school but ended up completing a several-hundred-page dissertation on the evolution of dunking techniques in basketball. Those that do complete a thesis rarely do so before their thirties. Pride in academic rank, once attained, is immense. Flick through any respectable German newspaper and you will find rows of doctors and professors among the contributors; skim the biographies of the German parliament and you will get an overwhelming impression of lengthy stints in university libraries (in March 2011, one fifth of the Bundestag, the lower house, held PhDs, including chancellor Dr Angela Merkel – compared to three per cent of the American Congress). In Germany many people insist on being referred to as 'Herr Doktor' or 'Frau Professor' even if they're no longer employed in academia. In England, on the other hand, when people saw the Prof. Dr.-Ing. on my father's business card, they often assumed that he was either a practising medic or simply a fraud.

The number of higher degrees a country produces doesn't tell you everything, of course. A 2001 survey revealed that as many as 58.5 per cent of chief executives at German businesses had PhDs, compared to 1.3 per cent in the US. Yet the overall percentages of people embarking on a doctorate were fairly similar (1.3 per cent of the population in Germany, 1.5 in the US). If anything, this indicates a modern trend whereby tertiary degrees in Germany are mainly regarded as career boosters, rather than genuine research intended to further knowledge. In 2009, an exposé about professors at German universities handing out PhDs in exchange for financial donations seemed to confirm the trend, as did the controversial doctoral thesis that led to the resignation of the high-flying German defence minister Karl-Theodor zu Guttenberg (or Googleberg, as he came to be known) in March 2011: a postmodern patchwork of a thesis, in which several long passages had been hastily copied from other sources.

But *Bildung* is not just about titles in front of surnames. The best way to describe its significance these days is as a kind of secular belief system. The modern-day embodiment of the educational ideals of the eighteenth and nineteenth centuries are the so-called *Bildungsbürger*: middle-class citizens who define themselves not through their financial income or their political leanings but their cultural choices. Classic indicators of *Bildungsbürger*-dom include a subscription to a weekly magazine or newspaper such as *Der Spiegel* or *Die Zeit*, a professed enthusiasm for French cinema or Italian cooking, or even just a loyal relationship with *Tagesschau*, the 8 p.m. news programme in which, more than half a century after the invention of the teleprompter, presenters continue to read the news from a sheet of paper.

Traditionally, *Bildungsbürger* were teachers, architects, pastors, lawyers, doctors or engineers, but in a country as prosperous as late twentieth-century Germany, it was a broad church. It could easily be stretched to include someone like my mother: a woman who had for the most part of her life been a full-time mother and part-time social worker. From an early age, she had installed in me the belief that money spent on a book was a sound investment, whatever the cost. Books had their own value, a value that could not be measured in terms of financial gain or loss. Our first step towards furnishing our new London home – weeks before we had properly begun to unpack – had been to erect a majestic bookshelf in my bedroom, claiming our ground like the US soldiers who drove their country's flag into the ground at Iwo Jima.

All this goes some way to explaining the discovery of Theodor Adorno's *Dialectic of Enlightenment* in our removal box. From the box, the book was eventually moved to my new bookshelf, where the navy-blue spine took pride of place amidst a row of bright orange Penguin classics. For the next few weeks, it stared at me like an evil eye. One rainy Friday evening I eventually gave in and tried to get my head around what Theodor Adorno was really about.

As it turned out, even though Theodor Adorno had to me always been synonymous with that forcefield of *Bildung*, he was actually fairly critical of the German cult of education. *Dialectic of Enlightenment* was a detailed dissection of the eighteenth-century belief that humankind could be enlightened and 'made whole' through culture. In a particularly memorable passage, Adorno likens the traditional model of *Bildung* to the myth of Odysseus' encounter with the Sirens. Knowing that he has to pass his boat through a narrow strait occupied by creatures whose song will turn his head and lead to his death, Homer's cunning hero devises a clever plan: having advised the crew of his ship to tie him to the ship's main mast and seal their ears with wax, Odysseus can hear the Sirens' song, but not act on their call. Adorno likens Odysseus to the typical bourgeois *Bildungsbürger*, whose enjoyment of art is only made possible by the enslavement of those who beat the oars of his ship. This, he resumes, is the sinister truth behind the enlightenment ideal of education: *Bildung* always goes hand in hand with barbarity. The German obsession with *Hamlet*, to Adorno, was further proof of the link between the idealism of German high culture and an inherent negativity. Hamlet symbolised that very German taste for self-reflection followed by self-destruction, 'the first wholly self-aware and despondently self-reflecting individual'.

To Adorno and Horkheimer, then, the 'good' Germany of enlightened *Dichter und Denker* and the 'bad' Germany of the Third Reich were not polar opposites, but mutually dependent: the existence of one presumed the existence of the other. And this wasn't mere theoretical nit-picking, but a fact that was powerfully backed up by historical reality. Only seven kilometres from Goethe's 'Enlightened Republic' in Weimar, the Nazis had been able to build Buchenwald concentration camp. *Bildung* was of little use to the estimated 56,000 prisoners who died there between 1937 and 1945. The presence of a 'Goethe Oak' on the site of the camp makes a mockery of the German cult of high culture, just as the fact that Germany enjoyed some of the highest literacy rates in the world when *Mein Kampf* was published raises a question about the German valuation of learnedness. In Germany, culture and non-culture had always gone hand in hand. That famous declaration (less sweeping than I had remembered it) that 'to write a poem after Auschwitz is barbaric' only really makes sense in a specifically German context, in which poetry and culture are traditionally conceived of as the cure to all social evil. 'What is German?' Adorno once asked himself. 'The absolute underwent reversal into absolute horror.'

I say that I got all this from reading *Dialectic of Enlightenment*, when strictly speaking it isn't true. The first time I tried to read the book I understood absolutely nothing at all. The aforementioned fondness for sentences that curl in on themselves was perfect for producing enigmatic one-liners, but it made for frustrating reading when whole paragraphs were written in that style. Adorno was a master of the German *Schachtelsatz*, the Russian-doll sentences that snaked across the pages, awkwardly held in precarious balance by a 'yet', a 'therefore', a 'however'. Again and again, I found myself coming to the end of a page and realising that I had been staring at the white paper without deciphering the black marks on it.

It was only much later, after I had taken seminars on Adorno at university, that I realised that this cryptic style of writing, the 'Adorno sound', was part of the point the author was trying to make. Adorno once described *Dialectic of Enlightenment* as a 'message in a bottle', which is to say that its true meaning wasn't meant to be apparent to its readership on publication in 1944, but only to a later generation. The main reason for this was that Adorno believed that in his own lifetime culture and barbarity had so far converged as to be practically inseparable: culture was no longer culture but a 'culture industry' whose methods resembled the industrialised processes of political fascism, in which human beings were treated like machines. It was obvious, then, that any philosopher who wanted to speak truthfully could no longer express himself through the mainstream, but had to relay messages in a more covert way.

The alternative voice that Adorno envisioned was the voice of modernist art. He wanted to do to philosophy what Samuel Beckett had done to drama, Arnold Schoenberg had done to music or Franz Kafka had done to storytelling: to make its medium reflect the complicated nature of the message it was trying to convey. In particular, Beckett's play *Endgame* appealed to Adorno, for here was a more cryptic and cynical assessment of the state of the world: Hamlet had been suitably cut down and dismembered to become Hamm, one of Beckett's characters. This is what Adorno meant when he said 'The splinter in your eye is the best magnifying glass': in order to tell us something about the brokenness of the world, language had to be broken too. And yet, even though Adorno thought the German cult of culture was the source of all its problems, culture also held the solution to those problems. In that respect, as in his infatuation with stationery, he was still as typical of the German *Bildungsbürger* as could be.

*

If reading Adorno was a difficult task in its own right, it was even more difficult to read Adorno in England. The problem wasn't that England was uncultured – on the contrary. In the nineteenth century, German travellers had been able to mock England as 'the land without music', but in the late 1990s that insult would have rung hollow. The economic upturn had injected the country's culture industry with cash and confidence. Even suburban Middlesex, which at first had left me with an overwhelming impression of monotony and boredom, turned out upon closer inspection to be a hive of cultural activity. Every stretch of high street seemed to have a record store or second-hand bookshop tucked away down a side alley. Classmates who at first sight had struck me as grey and faceless bores turned out to be avid collectors of 1960s New York underground cartoons or fanatical art-rock enthusiasts.

That first summer in England a band from Wigan called the Verve released a hit single which played on heavy rotation on all the radio stations and music channels. The video for 'Bittersweet Symphony' featured singer Richard Ashcroft loafing down a London high street in a wrinkled leather jacket. Ashcroft was oblivious to what was going on around him, stepping out in front of cars, knocking into people but never once breaking his stride: a perfect symbol of Britain's extreme confidence in its cultural powers. This was a *Kulturnation* with a swagger.

The problem, then, was not that England didn't *do* culture, but that it did it differently. In particular the distinction between high art and low art, between *Kultur* and entertainment – so crucial to Adorno – was much harder to locate here than it had been in Germany. In our household, the boundaries had always been clearly defined: books were good, television was bad. '*Was guckst Du da für einen Schund?*' – 'What's that trash you're watching?' – my parents would say if they walked in on me watching a soap opera, an action film, or even just the news on one of Germany's down-market private channels. Here in England, however, even the more highbrow broadsheets carried lengthy essays on the merits of particular TV programmes. Shakespeare, on the other hand, the favourite Englishman of Germany's educated classes, enjoyed an elevated status in his homeland precisely because his plays effortlessly negotiated the boundaries of art and entertainment. When Mr P took us on a trip to Stratford to watch *Hamlet* in performance, I was struck by the diversity of the audience, and by the way the play was able to cater to all kinds of taste: from the philosophical sophistication of Hamlet's soliloquies to the knockabout humour and naff double entendres of the sung interludes.

It would have been interesting to see what Adorno would have made of the 1995 'Battle of Britpop': an endlessly hyped rivalry between one band that was supposedly more working-class and macho, and another that was seemingly middle-class and effete. You'd expect Adorno would have described this distinction as a 'false choice', since the culture industry cared very little about which band's albums you bought as long as you parted with your hard-earned cash. But Adorno's theories only really made light of the situation until you listened to the music itself. In 1997, Blur released their self-titled follow-up album to *The Great Escape*, the record that had put them at the centre of the Britpop scene. One particular song stood out: 'Essex Dogs', a nine-minute track at the end of the *Blur* album, which started with what sounded like a malfunctioning lawnmower fed through a distortion pedal, only to segue into a mumbled monologue about suburban wastelands and post-clubbing ennui. I thought 'Essex Dogs' was pure genius: not only because I recognised the British landscape that Damon Albarn described in his lyrics, but because the music itself painted a picture of broken, industrial suburbia – a kind of Adorno sound, if you will. Blur blurred that fine line between painful modernism and pure pop with ease.

If the English out-swaggered the Germans in cultural matters, they would pussyfoot around when straying into more abstract terrain. The other boys in my English set oozed self-belief when it came to wit and wordplay: it was obvious that they could spot an ambiguity or double meaning in Wordsworth's poems faster than I could, that they had more precise words at their disposal to describe the exact nature of Hamlet's predicament than I had. But when it came to explaining big, abstract ideas the same boys suddenly went all shy and quiet. Occasionally, someone would tentatively try to venture forth on some grand theory about Hamlet's 'psychological interiority' or 'existential condition', but they would promptly be shot down, like soldiers who had poked their heads too far over their trenches. Anyone who dared to utter the word 'philosophy' would instantly be declared a 'pretentious twat' or simply labelled 'the professor'.

Being 'pretentious' was the worst of crimes in many of my schoolmates' books: a word that was used so rarely in German that I had to look it up in the dictionary. 'Pretentious' meant 'claiming or demanding a position of distinction or merit, especially when unjustified', or 'making or marked by an extravagant outward show'. The latter aspect appeared to be crucial: while it was perfectly fine to be clever, the prevailing social code decreed that it was definitely not fine to make an outward show of one's own cleverness. Some boys had affected a confusing verbal tic that Mr P later taught me to call a 'rhetorical fallacy': at the start of a conversation they would do their utmost to emphasise their own ignorance, only to disprove that very ignorance over the course of the ensuing debate. It took me months to figure out that 'I haven't revised at all for the exam tomorrow' really meant 'I am so confident about doing well in tomorrow's exam that I've taken a day off.' 'I don't know anything about the Victorians' really meant 'I know everything about Victorian history, including the names of Queen Victoria's cousins once removed.' 'I wish I spoke German' meant 'I am practically fluent in German, though there is room for improvement in my use of the Plusquamperfekt tense.' The perfect embodiment of the obsessive English penchant for understatement was the 'essay' form, which we learnt to write in our first term. An essay was nothing but a grandiloquent advertisement for one's own genius, a long, subjective opinion piece, yet the word – coming from 'assay', to test or attempt – implied that it was nothing but a humble experiment.

My initial ignorance of the English fear of appearing overtly intellectual worked to my advantage in more ways than one. I was still as good as mute in the classroom, but when it came to the first mock exams at the end of term, I saw little reason to restrain myself from holding forth. When the exam papers were returned to us on the last day before half term, I had one of the top marks in my class. 'And he's a bloody German as well,' murmured one of the boys on the row of desks behind me. After class, Mr P asked whether he could speak to me for a minute. Had I considered doing an A level in philosophy? There was a small class of four students who had been studying philosophy since the start of the year. I would have to play catch-up for the first few weeks, but he didn't think that would be a problem.

I had heard about the philosophy set. To the rest of the school, they were invariably known by their nicknames. There was Supernanny, a boy with the body of a man and the face of a toddler, who wore the kind of beige three-piece linen suits you would expect to see on a nineteenth-century explorer. Toryboy, who already looked like one of the cartoon depictions of front-bench politicians which he had glued to the inside of his folders, with a cowlick haircut, a steely hawkishness in his eyes and dreadful acne. Winegum, who was into medieval roleplay and Goth rock and claimed he was a nihilist. And finally, Jonesy, a Church of England Christian with a permanent look of terror and bewilderment on his face, like a prize poodle who had just received an electric shock. At the start of the second term, I found myself in a room with this select cast of distinguished eccentrics: Supernanny, Toryboy, Winegum, Jonesy and Phil-the-German. Our teacher was Mr C: a small, owlish man with Pinocchio cheekbones, who wore woolly short-sleeved cardigans and closed his eyes when you talked to him. In our first lesson, Mr C entered the room and handed us a stapled pile of photocopies. 'Today we will have a look at A. J. Ayer and the problem of metaphysical language.'

I had never heard of A. J. Ayer before, but Mr C filled us in. Ayer was part of a philosophical movement known as logical positivism, which had been heavily influenced by a group of Austrian philosophers known as the Vienna Circle. In spite of the continental bend to his thinking, Ayer was one of the most important and influential English philosophers in the country's history. The photocopied pages were from *Language, Truth and Logic*, a book that Ayer had started in 1934 and finished two years later, aged only twenty-five. The book was written in short, sharp sentences, linked together by a clear, rational argument. So easy was Ayer's writing style that I was almost shocked at how simple it was to follow the author's reasoning. Ayer's writing was like 1960s bubblegum pop to Adorno's grunge guitar.

Like Adorno, Ayer wanted to break with traditional philosophy. But whereas Adorno had taken specific issue with the Enlightenment cult of *Bildung*, Ayer's starting point was more elementary. According to Ayer, there were only two types of meaningful statements we could make about the world. The first type were empirical statements, which could be verified by means of sense investigation. 'I have broken my arm' is a meaningful statement because a doctor can check my limbs to determine if I have snapped a bone or merely got a fracture. The second type were statements which could be proved true or false by means of logical deduction. 'Triangles have three sides' is a meaningful statement because the definition of a triangle is that it has three sides.

Any statement which didn't fit into either of these two categories, Ayer argued, had to be 'consigned to the flames': they weren't meaningful statements but 'pseudo-statements'. There is a *Beyond the Fringe* sketch called 'Oxford philosophers', which parodies all the talk of 'language games' and 'pseudo-statements' that came from the logical positivists. 'Pseudo-statements', Alan Bennett says in the sketch, were like saying 'There's too much Tuesday in my beetroot salad.' This actually comes very close to the heart of Ayer's philosophy. The only difference was that for Ayer, it wasn't just obviously nonsensical statements such as 'There is too much Tuesday in my beetroot salad' that were nonsensical, but even statements that sounded utterly serious, such as 'There is a God.' Since neither of them could be verified by any empirical or logical means, they were in effect meaningless. As Mr C explained, what made Ayer a true radical was that he didn't apply his verification principle just to religion and beetroot, but to all of language. Even weighty moral statements such as 'Killing is wrong' weren't spared. As there was no empirical way of proving that killing was bad, the statement made sense only, said Ayer, as an expression of the speaker's emotion: 'Killing is wrong' really meant 'I really feel strongly that killing is wrong.' In short, Ayer was challenging philosophy to rebuild itself from scratch.

Initially, I wasn't much impressed by all this. Ayer struck me as a very English sort of philosopher. By concentrating purely on language, he seemed to give philosophy very little scope for rebuilding itself into anything particularly impressive. Philosophy of the Ayer school was essentially a kind of bullshit detector: a way of correcting what people said when they were being vague and fanciful. The really exciting work, however – the verification business, the truth-finding missions – was left for science, while philosophy was only playing second fiddle. In *Language, Truth and Logic*, Ayer mocks the overambitious scope of metaphysical philosophy when he writes: 'In order to determine whether it will rain tomorrow, I need not take into account the present state of mind of the Emperor of Manchukuo.' But at least a scientist could give you some idea of whether there would be rain or sunshine, while Ayer could only really comment on the way we talked about the weather – another feature that marked him out as a quintessential Englishman.

The bell rang. Mr C packed his wad of paperwork into his leather satchel, said his goodbyes and left the room. I too had packed my bag and was about to get up when I realised that the other boys had stayed in their seats. 'Do you really think there is no way of proving that killing someone is wrong?' Jonesy said, evidently disturbed. 'Some Satanists feel very strongly that killing people is a good thing,' Winegum said, sharpening an imaginary pair of knives. 'Killing people *is* wrong,' Toryboy said, flicking back a lock of hair. 'Behold the word of the Lord!' Supernanny shouted, jumping up from his seat and pacing up and down the classroom while clutching the lapels of his linen suit in a gesture of mock-seriousness, 'he who telleth us that sticking knives into people's backs be a bad, bad thing to do.' There were hisses, tuts and boos, and howls of approving laughter. The whole scene reminded me of the scenes from Prime Minister's Questions I had seen on television, or a Monty Python sketch: it was theatrical and absurd, for sure, but also pretty clever. Eventually, Toryboy turned around and fixed his hawkish gaze on me. 'What does the new member of the class have to say on this?' I coughed to clear my throat, but before I had got to the end of my sentence I knew that my argument would fail to pass the verification principle: 'Well, you know what Adorno said: "To write a poem after Auschwitz is barbaric."'

*

You hear people talk about 'the German genius'. Even English people who are sceptical about the European Union and distrustful of continental politics tend to show a flicker of admiration for Germany's history of producing great thinkers and inventors. Germans, on the other hand, rarely speak about 'the English genius' these days.

And yet, the more time I spent in England, the more I was convinced that such a thing did exist beneath the seemingly bland facade of duffel coats and Sunday roasts. The schoolboy parliamentarians in my philosophy class were all formidable logical positivists, in the best possible sense. They were rhetoricians, who realised that ideas could not exist outside language. At the same time they were instinctively sceptical about mere phrasemaking. If an argument didn't match up, it was criticised and dropped. Above all, they seemed to *enjoy* debating with each other: philosophy, in their hands, was a living, breathing thing, rather than something that belonged in libraries. I have heard many English people tell me that Germans would discuss philosophy in their local pubs, while the English merely gossip about football and reality TV. And yet, in my own experience, the English pub is a veritable hub of the Anglo-Saxon passion for debate and learning. What is the traditional pub quiz but *Bildung* under the guise of non-intellectual sportsmanship?

A. J. Ayer might not have been a particularly ambitious philosopher by German standards, but he realised that in order for philosophy to remain relevant after the shock of the First World War, it had to be rooted in experience. His biography brings this out as much as his philosophical writing. While a student at Oxford, Ayer used to be a regular visitor to a basement club called The Nest on Kingly Street, off Regent Street, where he would dance, drink and listen to black jazz musicians visiting from the States. In the late 1930s, he and an eighteen-year-old Lauren Bacall made a record in which she sang 'Chattanooga Choo-Choo' while he recited Andrew Marvell's ode to empiricism of the sensual kind, 'To His Coy Mistress'. In the late 1940s, he became a season-ticket holder at Tottenham Hotspur, where he was simply known as 'The Prof' among the regular crowd. In 1987, Ayer confronted Mike Tyson at a party where the boxer had been paying unwanted attention to a young Naomi Campbell. Tyson allegedly replied, 'Do you know who the fuck I am? I'm the heavyweight champion of the world.' Ayer's reported response was: 'And I am the former Wykeham Professor of Logic. We are both pre-eminent in our field. We should talk about this like rational men.' It's hard to imagine Adorno coming up with a similarly quick-witted response, though it's also hard to imagine Adorno at a party.

Adorno's and Ayer's time at Oxford overlapped by three years, in which they were even taught by the same supervisor, the philosopher Gilbert Ryle. I've tried to imagine them meeting on the streets of that dreamy city. Did they share a bottle of port at high table? Did they wave as they passed each other on their bicycles outside the King's Arms? Did they stand in the same queue shopping for groceries in the Covered Market? But I struggle to picture any of these scenarios. It's more likely that they observed each other from a distance, and didn't much like what they saw when they moved closer. In his memoir *Part of My Life*, Ayer remembers Adorno's 'dandified manner and appearance, and his anxiety to discover whether other refugees had been accorded the privilege, which he had not so far obtained, of dining at High Table'. The content of the 'leetle cards' Adorno sent from his room at Merton don't do much to dispel that impression. Did he know, he wrote to the Austrian composer Ernst Krenek, that Merton was 'the oldest and one of the most exclusive colleges in Oxford'? (which is a white lie: Merton shared that with Balliol and University College). Explaining the 'true basics of my philosophy' to an Englishman, he wrote in the same letter, was 'practically an impossibility'. In order to talk to anyone, he had to scale back his work to a 'child's level'. Sharing his meals with the undergraduates in Merton's oak-floored thirteenth-century dining hall was 'like going back to school, in short: an extension of the Third Reich'. The city of dreaming spires was 'a fear-filled nightmare'.

The one piece of writing that Adorno managed to complete in Oxford was an essay called 'On Jazz', published in the journal *Zeitschrift für Sozialforschung* in 1937, under the pseudonym Hektor Rottweiler. It is, in essence, an unrelenting attack on the musical fashion of the day. Jazz, Adorno claimed, was a 'pseudo-democratic' form of music, which glossed over class difference and belied its own promise of individualistic liberation. The improvised nature of the genre was only a facade: in actual fact, jazz was closer in spirit to military marching music than real art – a thesis that Adorno found supported by the dominance of the saxophone, a staple of the marching band, and the dance style that went with it, the jazz 'step'. The Nazis had denounced jazz as 'negroid music', but Adorno was nonetheless convinced that jazz was the natural soundtrack of totalitarian regimes: it was 'ideal for fascistic usage'.

Adorno elaborated his jazz theory in a series of Merton-crested letters he sent to his friend Max Horkheimer in 1937. Could the prevalence of syncopated notes in jazz be the musical expression of a premature orgasm? At the same time, and unaware of the apparent paradox, he thought jazz symbolised a profound fear of castration, an anxiety which was expressed not only in the razor-like appearance of the double z in 'jazz', but also in the propped-up piano lid which formed the centre of any jazz orchestra – an accident waiting to happen. 'It is plausible', wrote Adorno, that the English word 'jazz' derives from the German word *Hatz*, the chase, 'intimating the idea of a slow creature being hunted down by a pack of bloodhounds'. And didn't the word 'ragtime' suggest an image of that same creature being torn to shreds? The eminently jazz-like Debussy record 'Général Lavine, eccentric' evoked in Adorno's mind the German word for avalanche, *Lawine*, designating 'that which erupts, bursts forth without rhyme or reason, and terrifies', 'a destructive social force'. The mute trumpet struck him as 'a parody of a scream in fear'. In particular, he singled out 'Tiger Rag', a jazz tune originally recorded by the Original Dixieland Jass Band in 1917 which, according to *Melody Maker*, had been covered more than fifty-two times by 1934, by artists including Louis Armstrong, Duke Ellington, Glenn Miller and Art Tatum. 'Tiger Rag' reminded Adorno of 'a tiger's mating call, as well as the fear of being eaten or castrated by the animal'. Worst of all, in Adorno's book, was the term 'jitterbug', used to describe various types of swing dance: 'It refers to an insect who has the jitters, who is attracted passively by some given stimulus, such as light. The comparison of men with insects betokens the recognition that they have been deprived of autonomous will.'

In Adorno's defence, it's worth remembering that he

wrote these words long before Charlie Parker, Charles Mingus or Miles Davies turned jazz into complex, difficult, Adorno-esque music. And yet one can't help feeling that this is a case of a man spectacularly missing the point. Reading those letters now, one is led to assume that in 1937 the world was coming to an end in Oxford, England, and not in the Third Reich. The man who would make his name criticising the educated German's failure to stop the rise of Hitler evidently spent a large chunk of the years from 1934 to 1937 attacking not the rise of fascism but the popularity of an innocuous musical style. Reading Adorno and Ayer in parallel, it's hard to shake off the impression that the years between the wars had had a very different effect on the respective national characters. If the 1930s in England had reawakened a healthy cynicism, the decade saw Germany develop an all-pervasive, nihilistic pessimism.

4

Kurt Schwitters Reinvents Dada by Grasmere Lake

On the morning of 22 August 1944, two hours after a German V-1 flying bomb fell on one of the neighbouring Georgian townhouses, a group of English artists and intellectuals gathered at the Institut Français in South Kensington. The doors and windows of the building, patched up after previous raids, were blown out, but the structure as a whole looked stable enough for the event to go ahead as planned. Many of the visitors might have even thought the smell of burnt brick-dust appropriate. After all, this particular symposium, organised by the London branch of International PEN, the association of poets, playwrights, editors, essayists and novelists, was also promising to be an explosive affair. Organised to commemorate the tercentenary of Milton's *Areopagitica* (1644), it inevitably invited the question whether, in the middle of a national crisis, English artists were any freer to speak their minds than they had been when this radical polemic against book censorship was published three hundred years previously. During the war years, the Ministry of Information exercised almost complete control over what was written in the newspapers and what was said on the radio. Was the mind of a creative person working in Britain still 'free to grow, free to express itself, free to blunder, to make mistakes, and try again', as poet Herman Ould put it in a paper from that day?

E. M. Forster delivered the opening speech. This appeared fitting. Few other English writers had devoted themselves to the 'novel of ideas' in the way this London-born cosmopolitan and humanist had. A trademark of a Forster novel is that fairly early on it will feature a public event at which people from opposing walks of life meet: there's the concert at which the middle-class Schlegel sisters meet working-class Leonard Bast in *Howards End*, the dinner at which uptight Lucy Honeychurch meets free spirit George Emerson in *A Room with a View*, and the garden party at which Brit abroad Adela Quested meets Indian Dr Aziz in *A Passage to India*. Anyone who has read these novels knows such meetings are good things, because they make people question their own principles and prejudices – in the long run. In the short run, they are comical affairs, full of social awkwardness and mixed-up items of apparel, in which heated discussion and fiery debate would be unlikely features. So it was in South Kensington that day: tempers were kept, and manners stayed mild. Many of the talks were only of tangential relevance. One professor concluded that the real issue of the day wasn't freedom of expression, but 'the relation between Mind and Spirit'. Even Forster's keynote speech had only a half-hearted crack at the Ministry of Information and the British Council, recalling an amusing anecdote from the previous war, in which the government had prosecuted the London Library for stocking banned German books only to find itself having to borrow the same books in order to write propaganda literature: a good-natured nudge rather than a passionate attack.

In a review of the symposium, a noticeably frustrated George Orwell asked: 'Considering the age we live in and the kind of things that have been happening to writers and journalists during the past fifteen years, wouldn't you expect such a gathering of people to be a bit more vehement and a bit more precise in their accusations?'

Nonetheless, one aspect of the morning's proceedings made it into the diaries of several of the literati in attendance. In particular, their attention was commanded by the activity of a tall, balding man in the front row. Clad in the 'grey, worn-out suit of a German refugee', as one Polish visitor put it, the man wore shoes but apparently no socks. In his hands was a two-foot-long piece of convulsed iron wire, which he had evidently picked up from the smouldering bombsite next door. Unaffected by Forster's speech, the man was instead concentrating on bending the material into a complex shape. Who was he? An undercover officer sent by the MOI? A madman? Some visitors concluded that he must be a plumber who had strayed there by mistake. At the end of Forster's speech, he left the building on his own.

*

Kurt Schwitters never looked his part. There is a photograph of him in his mid-thirties: seated upright with his hands folded in his lap, a white shirt with a starched collar and a tweed tie, an insurance-broker moustache and slicked-back hair, he looks like a scouring-pad salesman from the provinces, rather than a bohemian *homme du monde*. The look was in keeping with a lifestyle. An avid writer of letters, Schwitters kept up correspondence with artists in Holland, Russia, Paris, New York, Berlin and Hamburg, but he always lived and worked in Hanover, the medium-sized Lower Saxon city in which he was born in 1887. And yet a number of art history books will insist that Kurt Schwitters was one of the most radical artists of the twentieth century, and one of the leading figures in the radical art movement known as Dada. What was Dada? In spite of the catchy name, this is notoriously hard to get down on paper. At its peak in the early 1920s, several of Dada's leading practitioners published manifestos, but they are full of red herrings and contain only a few statements of genuine intent: 'Dada is affirmative,' 'Dada is negative,' 'Dada is a virgin microbe,' 'Dada is a dog or a compass,' 'Dada is idiotic,' 'Dada is dead'. In fact, Schwitters never used the word Dada, and, at any rate, looking at his artwork will tell you more about the man's desires, fears and aspirations than manifestos or photographs ever could.

Kurt Schwitters made art from scraps. A typical collage would feature a playing card, a torn bus ticket, a cutting from a newspaper and a rusty nail, scattered across a canvas in carefully considered chaos, belying a deep interest in the rules of artistic composition. To call such an approach 'radical' is not much of an exaggeration, especially in 1920. In an era still shell-shocked by the experience of the First

World War, the aesthetic of a Schwitters collage was that of a bombsite. An aesthetic of cut-ups and broken shards, where even an old bit of metal twisted by the impact of a V-1 was considered worthy of gallery space. 'Only connect . . .' an optimistic Forster had written as the epigraph of *Howards End* in 1910, '. . . Live in fragments no longer.' After the war, Schwitters's motto was much blunter: 'Everything had broken down in any case and new things had to be made out of fragments.' Schwitters called his own distinct brand of Dada Merz, which is in itself a cut-off from a longer word (Commerzbank) chosen at random.

In Schwitters's mind, Merz was not so much an artistic technique as a general philosophy that could be applied to poetry, children's stories, theatre, sculpture, journalism, advertising, carpentry and even architecture. His own house in Hanover became the apotheosis of this worldview, an ultimate work of art: a walk-in collage which he christened the Merzbau, the Merz building. Merz rhymes with *Scherz*, joke, but also with *Herz*, heart, and *Schmerz*, pain, which was too much of a paradox for some. From about 1933 onwards, the Nazi party had run numerous smear campaigns against modern artists. Schwitters's collage *Das Merzbild* from early 1919 was included in the 1937 exhibition of 'degenerate art', annotated with a sign that read: 'Even this kind of thing was once taken seriously and cost a lot of money!' Schwitters had effectively been blacklisted from paid artistic activity in the Third Reich. Luckily the artist had already been out of the country for six months: in January 1937 he left his Hanover home for Norway, and when the Nazis invaded Norway in 1940, he moved on to Britain, which once more looked like the final bastion of free speech.

Schwitters had a miserable time trying to explain Merz to the English. Dada was an international movement, with autonomous centres in Berlin, Paris, Zurich, New York and Tokyo, but Britain proved stubbornly resistant to the lure of the avant-garde. In 1940, there was no Dada London HQ. Gallery owners were shunning Schwitters's offer to show them his work. A friendship with Barbara Hepworth and Ben Nicholson, promising lucrative links to fellow artists and gallery owners, was called off after Nicholson dismissed Schwitters as 'an ass and a bore'. Schwitters was left drawing penny portraits of pedestrians in order to earn a basic income, and doing what he had always been good at: writing letters to friends around the world. 'The English people are conservative and don't understand art at all,' he wrote to one. 'We Germans appreciate Shakespeare more than the English do,' he wrote to another (it was as if he had read *Howards End*: 'Frieda, you despise English music. You know you do. And English art. And English literature, except Shakespeare, and he's a German').

It's hard to grasp the irony of Schwitters's situation unless you look at a collage from this period. There's a cheekily doctored portrait of King Edward's eldest son, Prince Albert Victor: half of his mustachioed face has been blacked out, and a razor blade has been glued across his chest in a reference to the (discredited) claims that the prince was Jack the Ripper. It doesn't just look shockingly ahead of its time, but also unmistakably English: a piece of pop art not unlike the cover of the Beatles' *Sgt. Pepper's Lonely Hearts Club Band* LP or the Sex Pistols' 'God Save the Queen', only with a razor blade in place of the safety pin. A scrawl explains that this used to be a portrait of His Royal Highness, adding: 'Now it is a Merz picture. Sorry!'

If that collage tells the story of what could have been, another artwork makes for a more realistic mood picture. There's a wire sculpture dated to 1944, possibly the same piece of metal he toyed with while being lectured at by Forster at the Institut Français. The wire grows upwards out of a clump of plaster and then snakes back on itself, like a dead tree on a craggy rock. It makes you wonder if one reason Kurt Schwitters might have found it hard to relate to Forster's lecture was that the issue of censorship didn't really apply to him. His problem was that people didn't want to listen to him in the first place. 'You always talk very quietly in England, at least the middle classes do,' he wrote in another letter. 'If you talk loudly you count as "common", not a gentleman . . . Talking loudly is just as bad here as being unshaven or having dirty fingernails. It's not done. But what results is a typical English attitude. The English don't defend their ideas, because then they'd have to talk loudly. They know what's right, and that's enough.'

To make things worse, the bombs that spared Forster hit their target when it was Schwitters: in February 1945, he found out that RAF raids over Hanover had destroyed the Merzbau. Having suffered a minor stroke in April 1944, he eventually decided to leave London in mid-1945, moving to a small town in the English Lake District called Ambleside.

By rights, Kurt Schwitters's English journey should have come to an end there.

There's one more picture from the archives worth closer inspection, though. At first, it looks like a filing mix-up: a picture by a different artist, put away under 'Schwitters' by mistake. It's a painted portrait of a man, with some rough brushwork in places but, overall, very realistic. The man is sat in a chair by the side of a barn or shed, hands folded in his lap, an indifferent, slightly bored look on his face. Nothing much of interest here, I thought when I first saw the picture, until I showed it to a photographer friend of mine. He pointed out something unusual about the picture: there was a shadow on the man's face. This was either an extremely basic mistake or a deliberate decision, my friend explained: any serious portraitist would position his subject facing the sun in order to catch the glint in their eyes. Looking at it again, you realise that it's quite an odd picture: less a portrait of a man than of a man's surroundings. To the left of the man you can glimpse a garden in full bloom. There's a triangle of blue sky, and the sun seems to be beating down: the plants and bushes are shining bright, like a chest of gold in a fairytale castle.

The picture is both authentic Schwitters and an accurate portrait of the sitter: Harry Pierce, a retired landscape gardener who had trained under Thomas Mawson, author of the seminal *The Art and Craft of Garden Making* (1900). In 1942 Pierce had bought a small estate in a tiny village called Elterwater – nestled in the Lake District hillside, less than an hour's cross-hill hike from Grasmere and

Wordsworth's garden at Dove Cottage – with the intention of turning it into a garden full of flowers, trees and shrubs: not a manicured park of the French variety, or a traditional wild English garden, but 'a combination of man's imagination and Nature's lavish profusion'. Schwitters and Pierce had been introduced by a mutual friend, and in the summer of 1947 Schwitters took a bus from Ambleside to Elterwater to paint Pierce's portrait.

It's unclear what exactly had changed by the time Schwitters finished the last stroke of the portrait. What's certain is that some kind of connection between the artist and the gardener must have taken place, because by the time the paint had dried, Pierce had agreed to rent out the shed in the picture to the German artist. Built on the site of a former gunpowder factory, the barn was now a makeshift storage space for hay. It had rough stones for a wall and bare earth for a floor. Over the next five months, Schwitters and Pierce moved a tiny oil stove into the building, fixed the roof and began to assemble ingredients for a new collage sculpture: stones, pieces of glass, oddments of metal, broken picture frames, a china egg, a child's ball and some of Pierce's gardening tools. In October 1947, Schwitters wrote a letter to a friend. 'I am working three hours a day, that's all I can do. But I'll need three years.'

The 'Merzbarn' was never finished: in the middle of winter, Kurt Schwitters fell ill with pneumonia and was taken to the hospital in Kendal. He died on 8 January 1948. Shortly beforehand, he had written to another friend: 'Thanks to England, we live in an idyll, and that suits me just fine. England in particular is idyllic, romantic, more so than any other country.'

*

I had thought of England primarily as an urban place before I moved here: a nationwide Greater London, with places like Manchester and Leeds as larger suburbs on the edge of an enormous great cityscape. Every German schoolchild knows about Big Ben and Tower Bridge, about red double-decker buses and black cabs. But the Lake District, the Cotswolds, the New Forest, Mount Snowdon – Albion's lauded beauty spots simply don't have the same alluring ring in Schleswig-Holstein and Mecklenburg-Vorpommern. The main reason for this is undoubtedly the climate: we don't make the same fuss about northern European natural wonders that we make about the Spanish coastline, the Italian mountains and the French countryside, because we know that drizzle, fog and cloudy weather can ruin the most glorious view. Architectural features aside, there is relatively little that sets the Yorkshire Dales apart from the Rhineland. Another reason – and this may sound controversial – is that the English themselves aren't all that proud of their countryside. Mutual suspicion governs relations between city-dwellers and rustics, as Evelyn Waugh once put it: 'There was something un-English and not quite right about "the country",' he wrote in his 1938 novel *Scoop*: 'the kind of place where you never know from one minute to the next that you may not be tossed by a bull or pitchforked by a yokel or rolled over and broken up by a pack of hounds.'

The German attitude to the countryside is radically different – you just have to look closely at the way we talk about it. The translation of 'we are going to the country for the weekend' would be *wir gehen übers Wochenende aufs Land*. But I know few Germans who ever go *aufs Land*. In the south of Germany, near the Alps, some people go *auf die Alm*, but this is usually more than a weekend stint in the countryside: a quasi-monastic retreat high up in the mountainside, with little electricity, no human contact and only the company of goats. Most often, Germans would say they go *in die Natur* or *ins Grüne*, 'into nature' or 'into the green', which is not just a square of lawn, but more of an abstract idea of going back to the basics of nature. When Germans talk about the countryside, they aren't talking about country estates or villages, but about nature as such. While English families will go on a day trip to visit a country house, German families will often embark on lengthy car journeys with the sole aim of visiting a lake, a mountain or a forest. Once arrived, they will abandon their cars and engage in that quintessentially Germanic activity, the *Wanderung*, for in Germany everybody goes walking: children, teenagers, pensioners and even politicians. When the German president Karl Carstens retired in 1984, the first thing he did was go on a long walking tour from the Baltic sea via the East–West border all the way down to the Alps. Writers including Goethe, Heine and Fontane have all written entire books about extended rambles across German land, and the filmmaker Werner Herzog once walked all the way from his apartment in Munich to the Paris home of the silent-era filmmaker Lotte Eisner when he had heard that she had fallen ill.

In my family's case, this return to nature took the form of a strict ritual: an annual trip to the Harz mountains, the northernmost of the German mountain ranges north of the Alps. On the last day of every year, the whole family would squeeze into our metallic blue Volvo and drive from Hamburg to Hanover, where we would have *Kaffee und Kuchen* at the house of my parents' old student friends. From there, we went on to the Harz forest, where we had booked several tables in a rustic inn decorated with stags' antlers and stuffed birds. Sometime after midnight, when the inn's owners were too drunk to care, Onkel Christian, whose moustache was even bushier than my dad's, would pick up one of the antlers and hold them up to his head, chasing us around the table like a medieval wildman from the woods. The next morning, we would march out into the virgin snow – it was always snowing in the Harz. The grown-ups tried to walk off their hangovers, and we kids threw snowballs at our suffering parents. The walks would last hours. I have abiding memories of the twinge of pain when cold mountain air hit my lungs, the ache in my legs and feet after hours of trekking through the snow, and the rush of blood to my cheeks when we finally returned to the inn. The German countryside, those trips taught me, wasn't there to be looked at or admired, but to be conquered on foot.

Geography, in spite of our shared climate, goes some way towards explaining these different attitudes. Britain's defining feature isn't its landscape but the mass of water at its edge. When Britons tell stories about themselves, they look to the sea and to their rivers. The Thames in London has had its praises sung in William Wordsworth's 'Upon Westminster Bridge' ('Never did sun more beautifully steep/In his first splendour valley, rock, or hill'), Charles Dickens's *Our Mutual Friend*, T. S. Eliot's 'The Waste Land' and the Kinks' 'Waterloo Sunset'. No paintings are more universally adored in Britain than J. M. W. Turner's riverscapes. Jerome K. Jerome's *Three Men in a Boat*, George Eliot's *The Mill on the Floss*, Kenneth Grahame's *The Wind in the Willows* and Richard Adams's *Watership Down* pay tribute to the constant flow of traffic through the country's rivers and canals. 'The seaside' is the place in the English imagination where the nation goes to fight its enemies and to recharge its batteries.

Germany's defining features, on the other hand, are its mountains and forests, which dwarf anything found in England. For example, the highest peak in the Harz mountains, the Brocken, might not be particularly high by German standards (the Zugspitze rises 2,962 metres above sea level), but at 1,142 metres, it is still fifty-seven metres higher than the highest British peak south of the Scottish Highlands, Mount Snowdon. The contrast is even more extreme if you compare English and German forests. Natural historians reckon that at one point, England might have contained a relatively large area of woodland: the Anglo-Saxons' Andredsweald has been estimated to have been 120 miles long and thirty miles wide, stretching from the marshes of Kent to the New Forest in Hampshire. According to the Domesday Book, 15 per cent of Britain was covered in trees in 1086. But a growing population, large-scale farming and a moist climate that turned fertile forest floors into boggy marshes meant that the woodland areas of Britain shrank by the century. Few people saw any intrinsic value in woodland other than that it might be used as a giant tree-growing factory. Even then, native wood was considered to be of inferior quality and in the days of empire it was cheap to import timber from abroad. The idea that forests were ecosystems which might need professional care to be kept in balance was an alien concept until Queen Victoria hired three German forestry experts, Sir Dietrich Brandis, Berthold Ribbentrop and Sir William Schlich. The latter set up the first British Forestry Institute at the University of Cambridge and published a multi-volume work called *Forestry in Britain*, in which he passionately pleaded for the island's woodland to be nurtured. Yet all this was too little, too late. By the end of the nineteenth century, only 4 or 5 per cent of British land could be counted as forest.

In contrast, the size of the German forests has been relatively stable at 30 per cent through the centuries. There is an oft-repeated story that a German squirrel can travel from the north to the south end of the country without ever having to touch the ground. This is an exaggeration, but it is true that several of the German forests link up to form one vast woodland patchwork. Even on their own, most of them are bigger than any single forest in Britain. England's largest, the New Forest, is 571 square kilometres. Germany's largest woodland, the Black Forest, covers an area of twelve thousand square kilometres. Even the Harz, one of Germany's smaller forest areas, is almost four times the size of the New Forest: there are parts of Germany in which getting lost in the wild is a concrete possibility. No one has evoked the nightmarish quality of a vast forest more powerfully than the brothers Jacob and Wilhelm Grimm, who used to collect folk wisdom on German customs, laws and language in a journal called *Altdeutsche Wälder*. To English children, their tale of Hansel and Gretel must have sounded like a wild fantasy, far removed from everyday concerns – to German kids, the bit about dropping breadcrumbs to help you find your way home came across as practical advice.

But there's more to the German relationship with nature than just geography. Travelling around a bombed-out Germany straight after the end of the Second World War, Stephen Spender felt that the landscape told you more about the people who lived there than about the land itself. 'Germany has not the cultivated look of Italy or France, but rather a *carved* or *hewn* look; as though the curve of the hill in Westphalia, even the vineyards on the shores of the Rhine were carved and hewn, out of wood or stone, out of the landscape, instead of having grown there with the years.' Germany's landscape, concluded Spender, had not been civilised, but 'thought of and thought into', its rugged edges a product of violent fantasies and vivid daydreams. Poets, artists and philosophers of the Romantic school spent an inordinate amount of time engaging with their natural habitat. Werner

Herzog points out that walking in Germany is never just a means of transport, but a spiritual activity:

> When I am walking I fall deep into dreams, I float through fantasies and find myself inside unbelievable stories. I literally walk through whole novels and films and football matches. I do not even look at where I am stepping, but I never lose my direction. When I come out of a big story I find myself twenty-five or thirty kilometres further on. How I got there I don't know.

Forests, in particular, trigger something in the German imagination, having produced a seemingly endless stream of poems, songs, essays and aphorisms. 'People who suffer like to visit forests,' the Swiss novelist Robert Walser wrote in his essay 'The Forests'. 'To them it seems as if the forest suffers with them in silence, as if it understands how to suffer and be quiet and proud in its suffering.' 'Trees are sacrosanct,' wrote Herman Hesse, 'those who know how to speak and listen to them will find the truth.' The nineteenth-century writer Ludwig Tieck even invented a new term, *Waldeinsamkeit*, in order to describe the sensation of loneliness when entering a forest. In art, no painter did more to evoke the German affinity with woodland than Caspar David Friedrich. Friedrich is best known for *Der Watzmann*, a panorama of the Bavarian Alps which proved such an inspiration for Hitler that he built his summer home at Berchtesgaden in order to recreate the vista, and *The Wanderer above the Sea of Clouds*, an enigmatic, almost hypnotic image of a man high on a mountaintop, which has been endlessly reproduced and parodied. But his most interesting picture is *Der Chasseur im Walde* from 1814, the time of the Napoleonic wars: a painting of a French Grande Armée soldier in a forest clearing, separated from his division and dwarfed by the enormous conifers that surround him. There's a raven perched on a tree stump, patient in the knowledge of his imminent *petit déjeuner* – a comical touch in a serious picture. Serious, because it reminds us how difficult it is in Germany's case to separate romanticism from nationalism, art from politics.

The Nazis, for one, were great tree enthusiasts. The idea of woodland ethnicity played a key part in shaping the National Socialists' idea of *Lebensraum*, 'living space', after Hitler came to power in 1933. Göring, Himmler and Rosenberg, the chief ideologues of the Nazi party, thought forests should inspire the structure of their new political programme: unchanging, mystical, with a clearly defined internal hierarchy. In their view, German society was a *Waldgemeinschaft*, a woodland community – markedly different from the Jewish 'desert people'. In 1933, so-called 'Adolf-Hitler-oaks' were planted across German towns and cities, and Nazi marching songs turned the tree into a symbol of national strength and endurance: 'On Adolf Hitler Square there is a young oak that reaches for the sun, let her be an example in bravery and resilience to everyone'. There is a collage by Kurt Schwitters's Dada colleague Helmut Herzfelde, more widely known under his English moniker John Heartfield, in which Hitler is shown trying to construct a swastika out of a Christmas tree: the ultimate joke about the absurd German fixation with the forest, were it not for the fact that the Nazis were even better at satirising their own obsession. In the Uckermark area in Brandenburg a group of Nazis planted interlocking rows of larches in a pine forest: a woodland swastika visible only to the gods above and the Luftwaffe's angels of death.

It's possible to imagine that without German forest romanticism, there might not have been an invasion of Poland, no bombs over London. And it is hardly surprising that many German émigrés arrived in England with what might be described as a woodland trauma. Schwitters, who kept a diary of his dreams during his time in England, wrote down the following sketch in 1947:

Whenever you are standing on a high mountain you feel free and happy. You see around you bigger and smaller mountains, you feel the music they play together, nothing irritates you, nothing seems to trouble your sight. You feel happy.

I often felt happy, and could not think that this happiness would not last forever. I was healthy, had all I wanted, could look around and see a happy future.

Then suddenly clouds came between me and the horizon, they came nearer, they were already covering the nearest mountains, and finally I could not see at all any more.

After a while the clouds disappeared again, and I could see. But I was no longer on a high mountain. I was in a narrow valley with plenty of trees which made frightening shapes. The clouds walked like ghosts between the trees, it was dull and dreary, no hope, no light, no horizon. I did not even know the way back to the high mountain I had lost. I was really sad and unhappy. All I tried was wrong, there was no hope at all.

His fellow London exile Elias Canetti, a Bulgarian who wrote novels in German, might have been able to offer a useful key to the symbolism in Schwitters's dreams. 'The Germans' mass symbol was the army,' Canetti wrote in *Crowds and Power* in 1960, 'but the army was more than just an army: it was a marching forest.'

The German émigré's fear of the forest might also explain why Schwitters was able to get on better with English gardeners than with English artists. Shortly after the outbreak of the Second World War, the Austrian writer Stefan Zweig had tried to encapsulate the English attitude to nature in his essay 'Gardens in Wartime'. Zweig, who lived in England from 1934 to 1940, had been puzzled by the calm and collected manner in which the English received news of war in 1939. In 1914 in Vienna, people had rushed out onto the streets; there had been spontaneous chanting and flag-waving, and wannabe generals flooded the cafes to debate the lie of the land until the early hours. England, by contrast, went on with its daily business as usual. Zweig was convinced that the secret behind this intriguing aspect of the English national character was a regular but restrained interaction with the natural world. 'For a long time, I thought like everyone else, that the love and affection of the

English belongs to their homes. But, in reality, it belongs to their gardens.'

Curiously, Germany's forest myth didn't stop with the end of the Second World War. It just changed party membership. No sooner had the Nazis' 'German Oak' been cut down to size in 1945 than the forest was reclaimed by the German left: in 1947, an alliance was established to protect the German forest from citizens desperate for firewood. The *Schutzgemeinschaft Deutscher Wald* still exists today, though it's only a minor organisation in comparison to the group that sees itself as the main protector of woodland in Germany: the Green Party. Originally conceived as an opposition movement, in 1983 *Die Grünen* became the first European Green party to move into a national parliament. Their theatrical entrance onto the political stage came with familiar props: on 29 March a group of Green MPs pushed a papier-mâché globe through the streets of Bonn all the way to the Bundestag; at the front of the group walked Petra Kelly – one of the party's founding members – carrying over her shoulder a conifer tree that had been severely damaged by acid rain.

The rise of the Green Party in the 1980s coincides neatly with a particularly German anxiety about the effect of industrial emissions of sulphur dioxide and nitrogen oxides on the health of the native woodland: the so-called *Waldsterben* phenomenon. In 1984, the weekly news magazine *Der Stern* had claimed that no conifer forests would be left in Germany by 1990, that beech forests would disappear soon after, and that by 2002, there would be 'hardly any forest left' whatsoever. Some politicians talked about an 'ecological Hiroshima'. The fear of dying forests contributed significantly to the rise of the German Greens: led by Fischer, they formed a successful ruling government coalition with Gerhard Schröder's Social Democrats in the mid-1990s and continue to be a considerable force in national politics to this day.

The word *Waldsterben*, however, is nowadays more likely to cause awkwardness than pride in the party ranks, because by the early 1990s, most of the country's conifer forests were still in place. In 1995 forestry experts published a study which showed not only that the German forest was healthy, but that it was growing faster than ever. Spurred on by visions of a forestless Germany, the number of new trees planted was actually outstripping the number of trees dying by nine to one. Depressingly, this seems to hint at the continued existence of all those unpleasant traits Margaret Thatcher had thought essential to the German character: angst, egotism, an inferiority complex and an overriding sentimentality. The end of the war in 1945 was meant to be a *Stunde Null*: a complete reboot of the system, a clean slate. *Waldsterben* suggests that this was mere talk and self-deception, and that the deeper flaws in the national psyche had survived. It made Germany seem like a country which behaved in the manner of a rational intellectual but deep down still thought like a romantic teenager.

The meeting between Kurt Schwitters and Harry Pierce suggests that national identities aren't always as easily pinned down as that. Schwitters was a romantic modernist:

someone who could appreciate abstract art as well as the traditional pleasures of a landscape garden. The German Green Party likewise inherited not just the traditional German woodland myth, but also a good dose of the spirit of Merz. Not only did they originally conceive of themselves as an anti-party party in the same way that Dada was an anti-art art movement, they could also count an artist among their founding members. Joseph Beuys – a tall, hollow-eyed man who always wore old-fashioned clothes and a Borsalino hat – created installation art out of found objects including strips of felt, tins of fat and bags of sugar. In 1982 he spent a grant from the city of Kassel on planting seven thousand oak trees around the city – making him by far the closest Germany got in the second half of the twentieth century to anything resembling a Merz artist. These days, the core of the Greens' values has little to do with the myth of Germany as a woodland nation and much to do with Merz philosophy. One of their greatest achievements is Germany's fantastic rate of waste recycling, which is as high as 70 per cent in some regions and averages around 54 per cent. What is this but an enactment of Schwitters's principle that even rubbish can be salvaged and turned into something beautiful?

*

In the winter of 1997–8, my parents and I went to stay with their friends in Hanover for New Year's Eve, and on the first day of the new year we went for our annual walk in the Harz mountains. More than any other part of Germany, the woodland of the Harz has a symbolic value. Between

1940 and 1990, the East–West German border used to run straight through the forest. The Brocken was a designated *Sperrzone*, a no-go area surrounded by a three-metre wall, because the East German secret police, the Stasi, had built a radio tower there to listen in on phone calls as far away as the Channel. On 3 December 1989, groups of protesters scaled the peak from the eastern and western side of the mountain and forced the Soviet guards to reopen the top to the public. Some of them carried placards that read 'Free Brocken = Free Citizens'.

A *Brocken* in German is a lump or a chunk, which seemed an appropriate name, for as we walked up the steep forest path to the top of the mountain, we found ourselves having to stop every few metres because dead trees or large boulders were blocking our path. The path snakes around the mountain in tightening concentric circles, but since I worried that I would break my neck if I took my eyes off the ground, I walked for almost two hours without really taking in the views around me. I noticed that I had reached the top of the mountain only when a gust of wind hit me, full force, and I realised that I wasn't sheltered by trees any more.

'The Brocken is a German,' wrote Heinrich Heine, who climbed it in 1824. 'With German efficiency he presents us with an enormous panorama.' But what struck me about the view from the Brocken was not how orderly everything was, but how messy Germany looked from above: not a neatly squared-up set of lots, but a series of oddly shaped, intertwining jigsaw pieces. It looked a mess, but a happy mess. Germany from here reminded you less of the unified vision of Caspar David Friedrich's Romantic imagination, and more of a Merz collage, with all its imperfections and idiosyncrasies. (Years later, I was pleased to find out that even the master of German romanticism had been a Merz artist at heart: Friedrich's Bavarian idyll *Der Watzmann* was in fact a collage of several mountain sketches from across Germany, with the unassuming Brocken next to the triumphant Alpine peaks.)

When I returned to school at the start of the new term, I asked several of my schoolmates where they usually went on holidays with their parents. I realised that contrary to my previous impression, the English did care about the countryside after all. They just happened to have a very specific idea of what 'the country' is, what it looks like, and what they like about it. This much I learnt: 'the country' wasn't within the M25, or in fact anywhere within an hour's drive of London, but then it couldn't be that far away either, because many of the kids at my school would go there for half term or a bank-holiday weekend. When I asked what 'the country' looked like, I found out that the country could contain haystacks, cows and Waugh's pack of barking dogs, but that these elements were negotiable. The bit that was never missing from 'the country' was 'the village pub', and next to it 'the village green': a perfectly manicured, not too dry and not too muddy square of lawn, populated by men in cricket whites who would occasionally disappear into the village pub for refreshments. Years later I went on my first trip to the Lake District and realised that one of the reasons this part of England enjoyed such a status in the national imagination was that it conformed closer to the English ideal of the country than any other place on this island: a landscape which was rugged and wild, but at the same time habitable and cosy, dotted with small villages that made you feel like you hadn't strayed too far from the civilised world. The English countryside was never just green, but green and pleasant (one of the reasons opponents of wind turbines and high-speed rail lines continue to wield more power in England than in Germany is that such installations would crush such ideals of pleasantness, while they are perfectly in keeping with the vision of nature as awe-inspiring and intimidating).

In Ambleside there is a small museum, half of which is dedicated to the memory of Schwitters's time in the area. The other half contains drawings and sketches by Beatrix Potter, which are the perfect embodiment of the English attitude to the countryside: a vision of nature not red in tooth and claw but clad in knickerbockers and mob caps. If the Germans went to the countryside to discover their inner wilderness, the English found only reminders of Nature's inherent civility.

5

The Beetle Overtakes the Mini

The day we moved into our new English home, my father had walked up to the living-room window and very slowly pushed up the lower frame. '*Ein* sash window – *hast du so was schon mal gesehen?*' Had I ever seen anything like that? He had let go of the brass handle. The ledge had stayed in position, drawing an involuntary whistle from my father, followed by a grunt and a nod of the head. This acoustic code was well known in the family, a tell-tale sign that my father was admiring the robustness of a piece of furniture or machinery. The hung sash window, my father had explained, was a masterpiece of British craftsmanship: a complex pulley system of weights and counterweights elegantly hidden in the window frame, centuries old and yet still state-of-the-art.

To him, the oblique charm of the sash window typified the appeal of the new English home. It might have been small – smaller than the house my parents had been able to afford in Germany – but it made ingenious use of the little space it had, creating a *Through the Looking-Glass* effect whereby the internal space was disproportionately larger than you expected from outside. When the architect Hermann Muthesius took up a post as cultural attaché of the German embassy in London in 1896, he was bowled over by the cleverness of domestic architecture on the island. Homes were 'homes' in the truest sense of the word, which is to say that they felt like houses even when they were the size of flats. Unlike the multi-storey urban houses of Vienna or Berlin, with their wide central stairways and high ceilings, Victorian architects had pioneered a cluttered look with bay windows and 'cosy corners', creating an instant impression of friendliness and emotional comfort. England might once have been 'the country without art', Muthesius wrote in *Das englische Haus*, but in terms of domestic architecture it was 'pointing the way to the world and the world was following'. To Germans, it is extraordinary to find that most Londoners still live in the same buildings that Muthesius described nearly a hundred years before. And like Muthesius, we were charmed by our new English home, its nooks and crannies, its eccentric use of stairs and its damp bathroom carpets – for my parents, it felt like the final step of their Anglo-German metamorphosis.

The road to Englishness wasn't always smooth, however. We soon discovered that the sash window had an irritating habit of rattling in the frame each time an aeroplane passed overhead (which was frequent: we lived under the Heathrow flight path). One or two of the windows didn't rattle – they had been painted shut, which was just as irritating. Cleaning a sash window proved to be difficult, if not impossible, because you couldn't reach the area where the two sheets of glass overlapped. Within weeks, a neat rectangle of filth crystallised in the middle of the window. When winter came, we had to move the sofas away from the windows to avoid the draught that sneaked through the gaps in the window frames.

Other features we had originally admired began to grate. My mother's key snapped off in the lock of our front door; several days were spent wondering why no one had thought of equipping the door with a handle, thus taking the pressure off the key when opening. There was an awkward encounter with a plumber who spent a week trying to fix a burst pipe before breaking down in tears and admitting that he didn't have a clue what he was doing.

My parents also expressed annoyance at the roadworks outside our house: a patchwork of tarmac and cement which was ever-changing but never completed. '*Eine Arbeitsbeschaffungsmassnahme*,' my father said in a mouthful of compounds, a measure to keep people in work. No wonder England's unemployment figures were so low.

My parents still loved England, though now with an increasingly desperate edge. One evening my father returned from work brandishing a fold-up push scooter and declared to my mother's bewilderment that he would from now on make the journey to his office on two wheels. That was what English people did – they were eccentric! But something wouldn't click into place. Our home, with which we should have been familiar by now, remained stubbornly strange. Nowhere was this as true as in our bathroom.

Using an English bathroom if you are used to German bathrooms was, I imagine, how it would feel to have been struck down by a severe nervous disease: the most basic things suddenly felt unfamiliar. There were never any light switches in English bathrooms, for example – even if these existed in the rest of the house. Instead, a piece of string dangled from the ceiling, occasionally with some wooden or ceramic ball attached, but often ending in a useless little knot. There were no power sockets, or if there were, they were made for strangely shaped plugs. English bathrooms, like English pubs, were also frequently carpeted – 'to keep your feet warm', a girlfriend later explained to me. A rectangular square was cut out from around the toilet.

German toilets, the American novelist Erica Jong explains in *Fear of Flying*, are 'a fixture unlike any other in the world'. Uniquely, they are equipped with 'a little porcelain platform for the shit to fall on so you can inspect it before it whirls off into the watery abyss'. The key difference from the French toilet model is that there is no water in the toilet bowl until you flush it – in fact, French toilets are built to make the faeces disappear from view and into the underwater world as swiftly and discreetly as possible. What set the classic English toilet apart from the French model, I discovered, was its flushing mechanism. It usually worked, though when coaxing it into action you needed the dedication and instinctive sense of rhythm usually required for starting the engine of a classic car. German flushes, in contrast, consisted of two buttons – one for big, one for small ('water saver') – and sprang to life with the mighty roar of a rocket launcher.

Either way, the toilet wasn't the real centrepiece of the English bathroom; that was the sink. There were two taps: one for hot water and one for cold. The cold water was freezing, the hot water was boiling. Right here was a Puritan

manifesto against the luxuries of modern living: the invention of the mixer tap had been stubbornly shunned. It took
me years to internalise the hand-washing routine that I can
now perform in my sleep – criss-crossing my soapy hands
between the two jets of water while regulating the water
pressure with my wrist. In my vocabulary notebooks,
between the words 'acquiescence' and 'bugle', there is a hastily scribbled entry which reads: 'bog standard: average quality, verging on poor'. I remember how much sense that word
made to me at the time, for the standard of English bogs
really was below par.

One crystal-clear January morning something finally
cracked, physically and metaphorically. I walked into our living room to find that the overnight frost had left an enormous fissure across the lower part of the previously revered
sash window. Enough was enough, my father announced.
We needed new windows: not any old bog-standard window, but 'tilt-and-turn', German standard. At that point I
had a brainwave. I suggested to my father that we should
contact a local window-fitting company owned by the father
of one of the boys at my new school: Sam W, who wore
dark skater shoes to school and smoked cigarettes behind
the sports hall. Workmen turned up at our house, fitted new
windows and left, but instead of becoming my new best
friend, Sam started to ignore me at the bus stop. It was another two years before I found out the reason. After sash had
given way to tilt-and-turn, my father had written a letter to
Sam's dad. 'Thank you for repairing our windows. However,

it has to be said: in Germany everything is much more efficient.'

In hindsight, this story sounds like the punchline to some stupid joke. Like the one about the German child who never says a word until one day its mother forgets to change the bedding ('Mother, my bedclothes are messy.' 'You can speak! But why did you never say anything until now?' 'Because until now, Mother, everything has been satisfactory'). A few weeks at an English school had taught me pretty quickly that this was what Germans were meant to be like: humourless, efficient, robotic. Apparently we also shouted '*Ja?*' at the end of every sentence, like a burst of static electricity. What exactly was German efficiency? Was it being organised? I wasn't very good at being organised. Was it punctuality? I overslept on the day of my first AS exam. Or was it good workmanship: tilt-and-turn, Siemens, Miele, *Vorsprung durch Technik*? My father was undeniably German in that way. As a small boy, he had spent hours on the dyke outside his house studying the large container ships that travelled up and down the river Elbe: no ship could enter Hamburg's port without being meticulously logged by Gerd Oltermann in a game of real-life Top Trumps. For his PhD in engineering, he had spent six years examining the viscosity of water as it approaches boiling point under high pressure. This was important, he once explained. As water turned into steam it expanded, and as steam turned into water it condensed – nature was left playing catch-up. *Horror vacui*, nature's abhorrence of empty space, was key to understanding why matter could be animated. I usually glazed over at this point:

nothing bored me more than engines. But my father was a genius at building and repairing things. We had a cellar in our old German home – *ein Bastelkeller* – from which he would emerge triumphantly every now and then, brandishing a newly repaired chair or a fixed toaster. I, on the other hand, was an utter failure when it came to DIY. One afternoon my father and I went down to the *Bastelkeller* so that I could learn how to fix a puncture on my bike. We emerged several hours later: the tyre still flat, my father's head hanging with despair, my own in shame.

*

Machines mattered to my father's generation. Born two years before the end of the Second World War, he had grown up in the decade of the so-called *Wirtschaftswunder*, when Marshall Plan money, the introduction of the Deutschmark and Ludwig Erhard's liberal market reforms enabled Germany to pass from postwar gloom to economic boom with miraculous speed. Nothing symbolised that rapid uplift in living standards more powerfully than the automobile: between 1951 and 1961, the number of passenger cars in the country multiplied sevenfold. Industrially, Germany didn't just catch up with its competitors, it moved into the fast lane: in 1953 it overtook Britain as Europe's leading car manufacturer.

My father's first car was a Volkswagen Beetle, the most German of German machines. Like everything else in this country, it had an uncomfortable past: ripped off from a model by the Czech manufacturer Tatra, it had been embraced by the

Nazis, who decided to overlook its Slavic ancestry. Hitler had sponsored the Volkswagen prototype and christened it the 'Strength-through-Joy' car: it was the car that promised to motorise the *Volk*. Yet its physical appearance was almost comically harmless. Roland Barthes once described the Citroën DS as 'the Gothic cathedral of modern times', but the little Beetle was neither awe-inspiring nor opulent. If American cars with their rocket-shaped headlights and their flamboyant wing mirrors seemed to imitate B-movie spaceships, the Beetle was comparable to twentieth-century office stationery: less concerned with marking its space than making use of as little room as possible. Could a car with headlights that looked like frog's eyes hurt anyone?

My parents bought their first Beetle for roughly double their joint monthly wages, 2,300 Deutschmarks. This was 1967, when my father was still an engineering student and shortly before my mother fell pregnant with my older brother. There is a photograph of baby Ralf peering through the passenger-seat window on their first family holiday. It was taken in 1969, when my parents should really have been out on the streets protesting, or at least smoking weed in student communes. Instead, their life resembled one of those Volkswagen adverts of the time, in which young families zoomed into the sunburst 1960s with big grins on their faces, using their new car as a sort of motorised picnic hamper. 'The big day . . . finally a Volkswagen owner', was the kind of slogan these adverts usually carried. The saving grace of the car in the photo is the fact that it has exactly the same eggshell colour of the Beetle you can see on the cover of the

Beatles' *Abbey Road* album of the same year, strategically placed between a denim-clad George Harrison and a bare-foot Paul McCartney, a slightly obvious but forgivable visual gag: the fifth Beatle.

*

The British had their own equivalent of the 'people's car'. The Mini had a boxier shape than the Volkswagen, and its wheels were tiny; it looked as if an invisible hand was trying to pin it to the ground. Even more so than the Beetle, the Mini was a lifestyle symbol, inextricably tied up with music, art and fashion. Initial sales of the car were poor – at £350 it was pricey for flat-cap workers. Things only changed once the newly married Princess Margaret and her husband Antony Armstrong-Jones were spotted in a Mini which the car's inventor, Alec Issigonis, had given them personally as a wedding present: the little car captured the imagination of an upwardly mobile nation. Sales rocketed as Marianne Faithfull was spotted driving a Mini to pick up Mick Jagger from rehab. Peter Sellers presented Britt Ekland with a Radford Mini de Ville GT for her birthday. Steve McQueen owned a Mini with chromed wheels and a sunroof. Twiggy advertised a Mini wearing a mini.

In 1969, the same year that the Beetle was featured on the cover of *Abbey Road*, Michael Caine drove a Mini Cooper down the steps of Turin's Gran Madre di Dio church in *The Italian Job*, a film which perfectly encapsulates the Mini's very British mix of understatement and arrogance. Watching that movie now, you are struck by how the film's cool cocktail of music, fashion and slapstick comedy is interspersed with several nasty little digs at Britain's continental neighbours, and continental cars in particular. Most of the jokes are at the expense of the Italians: there is a deliciously prolonged shot of a red Lamborghini Miura crashing down a mountainside within the first ten minutes of the film. In another scene the Minis race the Italian police on the roof of the Fiat factory. But a certain German car also gets a brief cameo. Seconds before the end of the famous opening sequence, and thus easily missed, there is a glimpse of a Beetle, stranded on the side of a mountain road.

In fact, the Beetle was a common object of ridicule in 1960s Britain. In August 1959 a BBC news report on the Mini not only praised the cars' ability to 'corner at amazing speed', but also pointed out that 'they look like showing the Volkswagen and similar invaders just where they get off'. A year later, Issigonis published a brochure called 'A New Concept in Light Car Design', in which he outlined the faults of 'that German motor'. The weight distribution was all wrong, he explained. The vehicle was too heavy at the back, and it was plagued by what motoring critics call 'oversteer': a tendency to start swerving when the car takes corners at high speed. In addition, the gearbox was at the back of the car, so changing gears was unnecessarily elaborate. There were two small luggage compartments – one big one, Issigonis thought, would have been more practical. The petrol tank was at the front, which increased the risk of a fire in a crash. Extra material was required for heating or ventilating the engine: depending on the weather it was either boiling hot or freezing inside the car. In the Mini, on the other hand, the engine was fitted transversely at the front, sharing a space with the gearbox. The ten-inch tyres hardly protruded into the passenger cabin. Only 20 per cent of the car's inner space was taken up by machinery, making 80 per cent of the Mini inhabitable. Issigonis felt strongly that he, not the Germans, had built the first truly efficient people's car.

*

After the episode with the cracked window, I sat down at my dad's computer and learnt that the bog standard had nothing to do with toilets at all. In fact, it was an acronym: 'British Or German standard', a term which, linguists claimed, originated from the car industry during the 1960s and 1970s and denoted a particularly high standard in engineering. I liked this: it hinted at an era of shared values and respectful appreciation, rather than the mutual mockery which I'd seen dominate Anglo-German relations in the 1990s.

A few weeks later, I went to watch a Godard film at the National Film Theatre. *British Sounds*, made in 1969, starts with a ten-minute tracking shot of men working on an assembly line inside a car factory, slowly cutting, welding and screwing an automobile into existence. In what might seem now almost a parody of agitprop cinema, the footage is overlaid with a male voice reading from the *Communist Manifesto*: 'Masses of labourers loaded into factories and offices are organised like soldiers.' As it happens, Godard filmed this sequence in the BMC factory in Cowley, Oxfordshire, which was producing the Mini. The Cowley plant, as I later found out, was notorious for its disastrous working conditions. In 1969 alone there were six hundred strikes. Health and safety standards were practically non-existent: the lighting inside the factory was poor, the floor filthy with oil, the air heavy with lead dust. There was a glass roof which was occasionally removed in hot summer months. When the sun shone, you could see the lead glittering in the air. On their walk home, workers spat black phlegm onto the pavement.

One year the Cowley workers were invited on a tour of Volkswagen's main factory in Wolfsburg, Lower Saxony. During the war, the plant had been bombed heavily by the Allies: when the British occupying forces arrived here in 1945, they found 60 per cent of the buildings and equipment damaged or destroyed, and nearly shut down the site altogether. In the end British pragmatism prevailed: officer-in-charge Ivan Hirst ordered the repair of the building, re-commissioned machine parts and starting exporting the first Beetles to Holland in 1947, thus laying the foundation for the success of the car. But when British workers from the Cowley plant arrived in Wolfsburg twenty years later, they were shocked to find how different the standards in the German factory were. The main hall was bright and clean; there was an open space in the centre of the factory, where the entire workforce would assemble for general meetings. A third of the machinery used to build the German car was regularly taken out for overnight maintenance, substantially lowering the chances of faults and accidents. In Cowley, it took between fifteen and twenty men to equip the Mini with a door. In Wolfsburg, the Beetle was placed on a mechanical crucifix and turned on its side: the door-fitting process required one operator. David Buckle, one of the Cowley workers, remembers going home from that trip with the realisation that 'technologically, Germany was ten years ahead of us Brits'. The Germans had become very good at putting together their poorly thought-out car, while the British had become very poor at putting their ingenious design into action.

You could describe what had happened as a kind of sash-window syndrome: outdated methods and machines kept in use out of habit and sheer sentimentality. Some people referred to this as 'the English disease' – a term later more commonly used for football hooliganism. From a German perspective, Britain in the Swinging Sixties looked like a country full of people who were not very good at working hard, but were very good at importing expensive goods from abroad. As early as 1966, the *Guardian*'s finance editor, William Davis, was lectured by German economists who told him that they felt 'sorry for British people'. 'Before you know it', they said, 'people will start to laugh at you.' Viewed with a sense of historical dimension, the tale of Britain's industrial decline really did have the shape of a joke. At the end of the nineteenth century the inventors of the steam engine and the electric light had expressed concerns about imports of inferior manufactured goods from the continent. The Merchandise Marks Act of August 1887 required that every product had to carry a stamp or insignia indicating its country of origin, a rule that was tightened during the First World War to facilitate the boycott of enemy goods. It was thus the British who provided Germany with the slogan that would later boost its worldwide reputation as a high-quality manufacturer just as Britain's own stock began to plunge dramatically: 'Made in Germany'.

Another oft-repeated story has it that at some point in the early 1960s, Alec Issigonis went on a skiing holiday in Switzerland and got stuck at the bottom of a mountain, with no way of getting back up other than being dragged by a Volkswagen Beetle. Issigonis complied eventually, but not without screaming abuse at 'that German motor' all the way to the top. It's an anecdote tragically emblematic of the wider economic shift in the middle of the twentieth century, with Germany steadily trucking on to new heights while Britain is left at the bottom of the valley.

Over the course of the next thirty years, the 'BOG standard' lost all meaning. Under the Conservative governments of the late 1970s and 1980s, the decline of British manufacturing was not halted but sped up. Under Margaret Thatcher, industry had been neglected at the expense of competition policy. It was, as J. B. Priestley had written in an article in the *New Statesman* in 1970, as if 'the idea of serving machines did some injury to the English psyche'. The middle classes, ill at ease with the prospect of a career in industry, pushed into the City, which had the plush offices and social cachet that the factories of the North lacked. The City of London rose to become the most powerful financial centre in Europe and the British economy boomed. Factories, meanwhile, shut down all over the country.

The return of a Labour government in the late 1990s did little to stop this trend. In fact, by the time we moved to England the manufacturing sector had shrunk further and British manufacturers had been sold off to global conglomerates. Even the Mini wasn't owned by a British company any more. In 1994 Rover Group, which owned the Mini, was bought up by BMW, the large Munich-based car maker. The takeover was headed by BMW chairman Bernd Pischetsrieder, a cousin once removed of Alec Issigonis. Pischetsrieder once said that his single abiding memory of Issigonis as a child was that his British cousin wouldn't let him play with his train set, which makes the business of buying and selling car marques seem like child's play. In actual fact things were more serious than that: the day BMW bought Rover marked the first time in over ninety years that Great Britain did not have a native mass-manufacturer of cars. The Romantic aphorist Jean Paul had once mocked the English predilection for machines by saying that 'one day the English will invent a machine that invents machines; that way they'll be finished and useless'. Little did he know that he would one day be proved right: the only machine the English government seemed to care about in the 1990s was the one that would calculate their profits.

If the marriage of BMW and Rover didn't last long, this was at least in part because the Labour government didn't seem to see much value in the business of building cars. The German company was also to blame, not least for failing to implement the famed high standards of German engineering. With a strong pound, English cars sold poorly abroad and Rover's factories continued to lose money – in Germany, the company came to be known as *der englische Patient*. In 1998, BMW pressed the panic button and Bernd Pischetsrieder approached the TV producer-turned-politician Peter Mandelson, now Labour's secretary of state for trade and industry, to get government support for the struggling manufacturing sector. In Germany, state subsidies like these were common. And yet Mandelson rebuffed Pischetsrieder's approach. The love affair between BMW and Rover was essentially over there and then; 'If they didn't care, why should we?' Pieschetsrieder said in an interview. Rover was sold off two years later, even though the Mini was kept and later relaunched as a safe but unexciting German car inside British wrapping.

It was also around this time that I found out the BOG standard might never have existed in the first place. Flicking through the TV channels one evening, I chanced upon a panel quiz show in which the host elaborated that 'bog standard' was really a bastardisation of the term 'box standard': a labelling format that was common among mass-produced toys such as the Meccano train set. In fact, continued the host, Meccano could be credited with not just one, but two popular phrases. For discerning parents with disposable income, there was the train set in the 'box deluxe' edition: a phrase that later entered common parlance by Spoonerist inversion as 'dox beluxe', or 'dog's bollocks'.

I wasn't all that surprised. Whether or not the explanation was actually correct didn't matter – it certainly rang true. For the boys in my English sixth form, cars had long lost the utopian glow they had had for their parents. That is not to say that automobiles weren't popular: I learnt that one of the most talked-about TV shows among my peers was a programme called *Top Gear*, in which cars fell either into the 'box standard' or 'dox beluxe' category, being either toys or outlets for pent-up testosterone. The business of making cars was rarely dealt with on *Top Gear*, however: it must have struck the producers as too repetitive, too grimy and dirty, too much at odds with the shiny world of New Labour's Britain.

*

In Germany, meanwhile, the manufacturing sector became indispensable. The country that had once looked with existential anguish at Britain's smoking factories went through a period of industrial expansions that was much more than a teenage growth spurt. In stature, at least, the German Hamlet is now a giant. In 2011, Germany was the world's second largest exporter of goods, having only been pushed off the spot by China in February 2010. Even being overtaken by China didn't cause much of a panic, however, since 2010 also saw the biggest growth of the German economy since reunification in 1989.

There are various theories to explain the rise and rise of Germany's industry. Many point to the famed Protestant work ethic, according to which hard labour could lead to personal salvation: after the Second World War, Germans sought atonement not at the altar but in their factories. Others point to the federal system, which avoids England's gravitational pull to the south-east and allows medium-sized family-run businesses to flourish across the regions, engineering anything from solar panels to rollercoaster parts and prosthetic limbs. Others, again, attribute it to the strong tradition of apprenticeships and guild-based crafts that underpins any kind of manufacturing work done in the country. Unlike in Britain, it is still fairly common even for people who finished secondary school to end up in a crafts-based job. There's also the fact that Germany has done fairly well out of a struggling common currency, which has guaranteed that quality German goods have remained not just in demand but also affordable in other EU countries. For now, however, there is no way around German cars. Car-making accounts for almost half of all national exports, with approximately 4.8 million vehicles rolling off the assembly line every year and every seventh job being somehow tied to the industry.

The car is still the ultimate symbol of German self-belief, summed up perfectly by a record from 1974. On the cover of Kraftwerk's album *Autobahn*, we see a practically empty section of German motorway. A black Mercedes is about to exit the picture in the foreground, upstaged by a little Beetle driving into a glorious sunrise in the opposite direction. The Beetle isn't just the star model on the cover, it's also a guest musician on the record itself: the first track starts with the characteristic tin rattle of a starting Volkswagen engine. The car gives a cheery beep of its harmonium horn before a vocoder dawn chorus kicks in, humming '*Autobahn, Auto-bahn, Autobahn*'. The sound of the engine gives way to a drum machine, first clip-clopping hesitatingly, then galloping at full pelt. One minute and eighteen seconds into the track, we hear a barely syncopated sequence of high synthesiser notes: rays of sunshine reflecting in the windscreen. At 1.55, a deeper synth sound, moving from right to left: cars passing in the opposite direction. Then the chorus: '*Wir fahr'n, fahr'n, fahr'n auf der Autobahn*'.

'Autobahn' is, in part, a very clever parody of the Beach Boys song 'Fun, Fun, Fun', itself a hymn to automobiles and their promise of redeeming us from the everyday ('And she'll have fun fun fun 'til her daddy takes the T-Bird away'). But with its proto-techno beat, it's also a satire of the German love of machines. More specifically, Kraftwerk managed to pinpoint a strange psychological side effect of the rise of German industry: my parents' generation didn't just adore machines, they also wanted to become more machine-like. Germany in the miracle years was hard-working, but also increasingly dour, humourless and downright boring. Between 1949 and 1969, the conservative CDU was re-elected no fewer than five times in a row. The sleepy-looking chancellor Konrad Adenauer – a man who campaigned with the utterly uninspiring slogan 'No Experiments' – became the face that defined the nation.

In Germany's haste to mature into a fully industrialised nation, more sensitive issues fell by the wayside – or were simply ignored. It's a conveniently forgotten fact that in 1953 – just as the economic boom was at its height – an astonishing 10,936 people died on German roads in a single year. Over the next two decades, as Germany churned out more and more cars, that figure more than doubled. By 1973, all major motoring countries in Europe had introduced upper speed limits – only West Germany didn't play by the rules. Even today you can zoom down the autobahn at full throttle: a tribute to a very German blind faith in the perfectibility of machines. It's as if Germans don't want to accept that even cars can sometimes let you down. When my father was a small boy, he was sitting on his grandfather's lap when their overladen Opel collided with an ambulance on a country road. He crashed through the windscreen but survived unscathed; his grandfather died. Years later my father's brother was fatally injured when he lost control of his Ford in a tight corner. Another brother had died in a similarly tragic industrial accident. We didn't talk about this much in our family, and I grew up knowing very little about the two uncles I had never met. Only two unfamiliar faces next to my father's portrait on my grandmother's living-room cabinet hinted at a vacuum in the family. Rapid expansion followed by rapid extraction equals animation of matter: *horror vacui* theory didn't explain just the physics of the steam engine, but also a change in the German mentality after 1945. Once we're moving, the feeling seemed to be, why stop and look back?

In 1978 Kraftwerk would release another album, which was called *The Man-Machine*, but it would be wrong to conclude that Germans really are as cold, calculating and machine-like as they pretend to be. Heinrich Heine made that mistake when he came to industrial England in 1827 and saw only 'colossal uniformity and machine-like movement'. Behind the German obsession with the automobile lies a human heart that beats to a sentimental tune. The Hamburg suburbs where I grew up are dotted with car recycling centres – automobile graveyards crammed with rusting write-offs – which are haunted by men and women in their fifties, ambling down the aisles in a philosophical trance. If you ask them what they are doing, they will mumble something about 'spare windscreen wipers' or 'those rubber bonnet stay rods that Audi stopped doing years ago', but deep down they know that they are really there to breathe the smell of petrol and dream of a safer, less vulnerable and more car-like life.

*

Back in England, meanwhile, our English house started to feel a little bit more like a German home. Our new double-glazed tilt-and-turn windows kept us warm and cosy, I was starting to get my head around English washbasins, and my mother discovered the joys of our tiny back garden. In *Das englische Haus*, Muthesius singles out the lack of thresholds as a defining feature of English domestic architecture: 'There is not even a suggestion of a threshold, the floor-boards simply run through,' he writes. The drawbacks of this are more apparent than the advantages, because it means that English houses always have a small gap underneath the doors, making rooms vulnerable to draughts. But there were unexpected positive effects too. Much more than our house in Germany, our English home felt like a single interconnected unit, rather than a series of closed-off cabins. You could slam the door to your bedroom shut, but you couldn't really seal yourself off from the outside world.

The thought of spending so much time in close proximity to my parents had initially terrified me, but in practice the whole thing wasn't so bad. In Germany, I had always been the baby in the family: the child that couldn't tie his own shoelaces or walk to school without his sisters. In England, I was not just an only child, I was more like an equal. Because I was more directly plugged into the hidden conventions of English than my parents, there were things they couldn't do without me. When my mother needed to call British Gas, she would wait until I was home from school so I could do the talking. When my father needed to write an important email to his golf club, I got to translate. We were a team. I didn't even feel awkward about going to restaurants with them any more.

The German word *Schwellenangst* doesn't translate easily into English. In common usage, it is used to refer to the anxiety that comes with change of any form, with transitional phases, with moving from one place to the next. It also literally means 'fear of thresholds'. After living in England for a year, it struck me as quite appropriate that there was no straightforward translation for *Schwellenangst* in English, because we had surprised ourselves to find that being in between was quite a comfortable place to be.

6
Freddie Frinton Teaches the Germans to Laugh

It could have gone like this: a late afternoon, August 1962. Summer in Blackpool, and the rain was beating down on the promenade like badly timed drum rolls. Peter Frankenfeld and Heinz Dunkhase were running down the seafront, ineffectively trying to cover their heads with rain-sodden newspapers. They took a sharp right turn onto Victoria Street and sprinted the last hundred metres to the entrance of the Winter Gardens theatre. Inside the foyer they peeled themselves out of their soaking overcoats. '*Scheussliches Nest*,' said Dunkhase, the shorter of the two men. Frankenfeld tugged at his trademark chequered suit and stroked his greying sideburns.

Both men worked for NDR, northern Germany's regional television channel. Dunkhase was a producer, Frankenfeld a comedian, talkshow host and all-round TV luminary of considerable fame. When a large number of young people were interviewed about German celebrities for a survey in the late 1950s, 100 per cent of them said they would recognise Frankenfeld on the spot. Only Konrad Adenauer, the German chancellor at the time, could match his record – a mere 9 per cent had heard of Karl Marx. Born in 1913 in Berlin's Kreuzberg district, and a late recruit for the Wehrmacht in 1940, Frankenfeld had started his comedy career in the army, as an entertainer for the American troops in Marienbad. He became the first German to emulate the style of American late-night entertainment pioneered by Art Linkletter and Arthur Godfrey – between 1948 and his death in 1975, Frankenfeld hosted and performed in more than twenty regular slots on TV and radio. '*Toi toi toi*' – the Berlin slang expression for 'Good luck' he used to say to his contestants before sending them on wacky errands – became a national catchphrase. By the summer of 1962, Frankenfeld started to feel that his current show, *Guten Abend, Peter Frankenfeld*, had run out of steam, and he and his producer went abroad in search of new acts.

Blackpool was not such an odd choice as it might seem: throughout the first half of the twentieth century, the town's reputation for excellent music-hall entertainment was enormous. Thousands would flock to the seaside resort every summer – in some months it was as if entire cities across England would shut down and emigrate to Blackpool for a week. Many Germans also made the trip: Sigmund Freud went beachcombing here in 1908 and loved it; Marlene Dietrich visited Blackpool in 1943 and had a picture taken of herself in front of the Pleasure Beach's new wooden rollercoaster, the Big Dipper. On the warm nights of the summer season, the hard-earned cash of months of labour was spent willingly. The shows in Blackpool's main music halls – the Winter Gardens, the Grand and Palace theatres –

were accordingly lavish and spectacular. There would be two shows on each stage every night, the first starting at ten past six, the second at twenty to nine. The line-up for an ordinary evening would include jugglers, magicians, bell-ringers, Tiller Girls dancing, an eighteen-piece pit orchestra, large fountains of water being pumped across the stage, and often a depiction of a 'spectacular scene' such as a train crash.

Yet the fortunes of the Blackpool music halls had already taken a downward turn. When ITV started up in 1955, the promise of a career in television drew many acts south. Theatres across the country were struggling to find plays and acts to fill their evenings. In Blackpool, this led to a temporary closure of the Grand Theatre in the autumn, and a permanent closure of the Palace Theatre at the end of the year. Variety, people from Blackpool say nowadays, died in the winter of 1955.

When Peter Frankenfeld and Heinz Dunkhase entered the auditorium of the Winter Gardens, they couldn't see the stage in front of them. On rainy days, shows at the theatre were delayed because the evaporation rising from the heads and clothes of the damp audience would make the stage invisible. Once the mist cleared, however, there was little that would have truly excited the two Germans. There was no water spectacle and no train crash, only five Tiller Girls and a big band that didn't deserve the name. Dunkhase rolled his eyes and started to shift in his seat. Twenty minutes before the end of the show, there was a sudden blackout for a scene change. When the lights came up again, the audience was faced with a bare stage, with only a long table at the centre and a tiger skin to the right. An elegant elderly lady entered on the left, followed by a butler in tails. Twenty minutes later Dunkhase and Frankenfeld were backstage, frantically knocking on the door of the dressing room.

*

The sketch the two Germans saw is called 'Dinner for One', and it is easily described. The curtain opens on butler James laying a lavish dinner table. The lady of the house, Miss Sophie, wearing an elegant evening dress, descends a flight of stairs stage left, and sits down at the head of the table. We soon realise that it is her birthday (for those who don't, there is the hint in the subtitle, 'The ninetieth birthday'), and we also realise that something is not quite right. 'Is everybody here?' Miss Sophie asks. 'They're all here waiting, Miss Sophie, yes,' James says, gesticulating towards the empty seats around the table. 'Sir Toby?' Sophie asks. 'Sir Toby is sitting here,' James says, patting the back of the chair on Miss Sophie's right, and continues to assign seats to the imaginary guests named by his mistress: 'Admiral von Schneider', 'Mr Pommeroy' and 'my very dear friend, Mr Winterbottom'.

The evening continues to unfold in this vein. James serves four courses: mulligatawny soup, haddock, chicken and fruit. With each, Miss Sophie requests a different type of drink: first sherry, then white wine, then champagne, then port. In the absence of any actual people around the table, James impersonates the different guests and toasts the host of the party on their behalf: a growling 'Cheerio!' from Sir Toby, a Nordic 'Skôl!' from Admiral von Schneider, an effete 'Happy new year, Miss Sophie' from Mr Pommeroy and from Mr Winterbottom a familial 'Well here we are again, me old luvvie', in the broad vowels of a Yorkshire pub land-lord. With each course, James's walk becomes less stable, his tour around the dining room more haphazard.

Like so many good comedies, 'Dinner for One' works by the law of repetition: it sets up its own rules and patterns, and then creates moments of surprise when it breaks them. Every time James passes around the table, he nearly stumbles over the head of the tiger skin to the right of the stage – so that the one time he *doesn't* stumble, he takes himself by surprise and stops in confusion. Much of the comedy in 'Dinner for One' is slapstick, knockabout stuff too: James spills wine, drops food, crashes into furniture and downs the water in the flower vases instead of what's in the port glasses. But the most memorable comic moment in the sketch is verbal. Before each change of wine, James stops short: 'By the way, the same procedure as last year, Miss Sophie?' The mistress of the house looks accusingly at her servant: 'The same procedure as *every* year, James.' At the end of the sketch, Miss Sophie decides to retire to her bedroom. James, now completely drunk, offers his arm. For a final time, there is the catchphrase of the sketch – but this time, the effect is different:

'Same procedure as last year, Miss Sophie?'

'Same procedure as *every* year, James.'

'Well, I'll do my very best.'

As he is dragged offstage, James winks at the audience, baring his gappy teeth for a Cheshire-cat grin.

*

Who are the two performers in the dressing room? The man who played the butler, James, is called Freddie Frinton. Born in Grimsby in 1911, Frinton left school at fourteen to work in a fish-processing factory, but was sacked for distracting his co-workers: his boss walked in on him putting his head through the belly of a plaice and pulling faces. After the Second World War, he began touring the theatres in holiday resorts up and down the country. Like most actors on the music-hall scene, Frinton soon found himself a specialist stage act: the drunk. 'I have played the drunk for as long as I can remember,' he said in an interview a few years before his death from a heart attack in 1968. He played a heavy drinker in his first film role, Peter Sellers's debut *Penny Points to Paradise*, and in most of the revues and variety shows in which he appeared. The pockets of his stage jackets were stuffed with his trademark prop, a cigarette snapped in half. When he walked down the Blackpool promenade in the daytime, people would shout at him: 'Having another drink, Fred?' In real life Frinton was neither very funny nor very drunk. Offstage, he didn't smile much and wore sensible shoes. A committed father of four and family man, he would often rush to Blackpool station after his last show on a Saturday night in order to catch the last train back to London. When he arrived home in the morning, he would start frying pancakes for the entire family. He rarely touched a drop of alcohol, neither after shows nor at family weddings.

Frinton made his Blackpool debut in October 1949, but 'Dinner for One' wasn't part of his repertoire then. The sketch was not even his own: originally part of a double bill with a sketch called 'The Lavatory Attendant', it was performed throughout the 1920s by the duo Binny Hale and Bobby Howes, and scripted by the variety playwright Lauri Wylie. Frinton watched it for the first time in 1954 and fell in love with it: it became like a fifth child of his, the Frinton family says. In the summer season of 1954, he first performed the sketch with the young actress Stella Moray, later a sidekick of the music-hall legend George Formby. By the time Dunkhase and Frankenfeld saw 'Dinner for One' at the Winter Gardens, Frinton had tried out a number of different actresses in the supporting role.

After the 1954 season, Frinton fired Stella Moray and hired another young actress in her twenties for a run of the show at the opera house in Jersey. Audrey Maye had just given birth to her third child, but she was keen on joining her husband Len – another music-hall actor specialising in drunk comedy – on his trip to Jersey. Again, 'Dinner for One' was a success with audiences, and requests from playhouses across the country continued to pour into the office of Frinton's agent. Audrey Maye had already been booked for a musical in the following season, so when Frinton asked her to take their act to Shrewsbury and Brighton with him, she had to decline. Frinton begged her, but Maye stood firm. Why didn't he ask her mother, Maye suggested. Frinton laughed. He should meet her mother, Maye said, then he wouldn't be laughing. When Heinz Dunkhase and Peter

Frankenfeld hammered on the door of the Winter Gardens' dressing room in 1962, the two people inside were the fifty-two-year-old Frinton and Audrey Maye's mother, May Warden, a seventy-two-year-old veteran actress.

Frinton opened the door. What did the two men in the loud chequered suits want, he tried to ask, but before he could get a word in Frankenfeld had started to talk. He loved the sketch, he said, it was the funniest thing he had ever seen the timing was so spot-on where on earth did they get that tiger skin from and did they want to come to Hamburg to perform the sketch on his show on primetime German TV. All the time, Frankenfeld was shaking Frinton's hand. Frinton looked at Frankenfeld's hand, then at Frankenfeld, then at May Warden, then back at the hand. After the show, Frinton's mentor, the comic Jimmy Edwards, had told him, you had to eat your sandwiches and be quiet. But he liked Frankenfeld's enthusiasm. Like Frankenfeld, Frinton had performed his early shows in front of soldiers: first as a solo entertainer for the Royal Engineers stationed in Wales, and later as part of the 'Stars in Battledress' company that also included Bill Pertwee and Arthur Haynes. He had never had to fire a gun, and he held no personal grudges against the Germans – his family had even had a German au pair. It had always been a dream of his to perform 'Dinner for One' for television. Frinton nodded and shook Frankenfeld's hand.

On 8 March 1963, Frinton and Warden flew to Hamburg and performed their sketch live on Frankenfeld's *Guten Abend* show. In July they were back in the city, this time to do a proper recording of 'Dinner for One', at the old Theater am Besenbinderhof. Frinton received DM4,150 for the performance, the equivalent of £3,100. The 'Dinner for One' reel was soon ferried between Germany's different regional stations. On New Year's Eve 1972, NDR screened the sketch at 6 p.m., and something clicked. In fact, something amazing happened: Germany fell utterly in love with the sketch. People put down their plates of potato salad and left their frankfurters to cool on their plates; entire parties huddled around the television set to watch Frinton and Warden perform their strange ritual. The following year each of the regional channels showed 'Dinner for One' at 6 p.m., and a few showed a repeat four hours later. Since 1963, the sketch has been screened 231 times to German audiences (nineteen times in 2003 alone), making it the most repeated show on German television, and – according to the *Guinness Book of World Records* of 1988 – the most popular show in TV history. In 2004, 15.6 million Germans watched as the two British actors performed their act on TV.

As the popularity of 'Dinner for One' in Germany rose, music hall's decline in Britain continued. Between 1950 and 1960, the number of TVs in British homes rose from around five hundred thousand to more than ten million. Those who didn't fancy staying indoors all summer flocked to the beaches of France and Spain, not to the Pleasure Beach in Blackpool. Frinton and Warden too turned their backs on music hall in favour of a career in television. Within a few years, they both reached national fame. May Warden was offered the role of the grandmother in *Billy Liar*, where she was meant to be killed off after just five episodes, but remained in the show until her actual death in 1978. Frinton too had found a national audience: millions watched as he did his turn as Thora Hird's husband Freddie Blacklock in the TV comedy *Meet the Wife* – a show later immortalised in the Beatles' song 'Good Morning, Good Morning' ('It's time for tea and *Meet the Wife*'). Frinton would never see for himself the fame that butler James found on the continent: he died of a heart attack in 1968, two years before the sketch started to go on heavy rotation on German television. In Britain few people under fifty remember his name. To this day, there have been no documented screenings of 'Dinner for One' on British television.

*

I know 'Dinner for One' practically off by heart. The first time I watched it I was five – it must have been either the first New Year's Eve that I was allowed to stay up late or the first time I actually had the stamina to. German New Year, *Silvester*, is a different affair from what goes on in England. There is plenty of drinking, dancing and hugging, but the whole event is wrapped up in an air of mystery and ritual. Fireworks play a large part in it. The reason behind Guy Fawkes Night in Britain is arguably quite mundane: after all, the exploding fireworks and bonfires enact an event that never happened in the first place. In comparison, the symbolism of German fireworks is almost ridiculously esoteric: fireworks, we kids were told, were meant to frighten off the demons and ghosts that fly around the skies on the first night of the new year. Pyrotechnics are traditionally less popular than explosives, what we used to call *Böller* or 'bangers'. Germany in the week before New Year's Eve can be a terrifying and dangerous place. One boy from my primary school used to put fireworks into sandwiches and throw them into postboxes, for reasons that still escape me. Another girl I knew lost two fingers because she held on to a firecracker for too long. Dinner-table entertainment too is less like a straightforward party than a shamanistic ceremony. *Bleigiessen* is popular: small lead figures are held over a candle on a spoon until melted, and then quickly thrown into a bowl of cold water. The results are expressionistic miniature Giacomettis, which are fished out of the water and interpreted according to a little booklet. Horseshoes bring good luck, hearts mean you will fall in love, bees herald an impending marriage. In my experience the lead never resembles anything but nondescript species of fish – which means that people are talking about you.

All this emphasis on ritual only intensified the sense of mystery I experienced when I stumbled into my parents' bedroom on 31 December 1986. 'What are you doing here?' I asked my siblings and cousins, who had gathered around the television set. 'Come back into the lounge and play with m—'

'Shhhhh!' my sister interrupted, 'It's time for "Dinner for One".'

It was like I had walked in on a bunch of schoolfriends drinking beer or sharing a packet of cigarettes. For the next twenty minutes, I scrutinised the events on the screen and tried to pick up clues. When James stumbled over the tiger's head for the first time, they chuckled. I chuckled. When James stumbled over the head for the fifth time, and the plate of chicken in his hand went flying out of frame, they howled with laughter – and I howled with laughter. When James downed a vase full of water (mumbling 'I'll kill that cat!') they shrieked hysterically, and I shrieked hysterically too.

Through my teens, the sketch stayed with me and continued to reveal new layers of interest: I felt smug when, aged eleven and just out of my first year in secondary school, I first noticed the grammatical mistake made by the German presenter Heinz Piper, who introduces the sketch: he says 'Same procedure *than* every year' rather than 'Same procedure *as* every year'. When puberty stirred, the double entendre of the line mystified me more than anything. 'I'll do my very best.' Best what? He didn't mean *that*, did he? They're so . . . *old*. And if so, where? And how? And for how long? The ambiguity drove me insane. Perhaps the fact that 'Dinner for One' dealt in such universal taboo subjects as sex between the elderly and getting drunk in public accounted for some of its cult status. But then why was the sketch so popular only in Germany?

One reason might be that there is so little talking in the film. By wooing the audience for laughs with physical gestures rather than words, Frinton's sketch managed to tap right into the German traditions of silent cinema, cabaret and *Sprachkrise*. Even today, most comedy in Germany is generally more physical and knockabout than in Britain.

This is not to say that it is all as crude and basic as a Benny Hill sketch. Growing up in Germany, I was reared on a wide range of comic acts. At one end of the spectrum was Otto Waalkes: a modern version of the circus clown, with oversized dungarees, a bald pate, a trademark bunny-hop walk and goofy laughter. At the other end was the late Vicco von Bülow, better known as 'Loriot': a more subtle act, whose sketches were usually set in the socially awkward realm of the upper middle class, a world of fine dining, book clubs and boardroom meetings. And yet the core of Loriot's acts was essentially physical. One of the most popular Loriot sketches is reminiscent of 'Dinner for One': a couple are sitting at a table in a restaurant, eating a bowl of soup; the man noticeably nervous. As he wipes his mouth with his napkin, a noodle gets stuck on his chin. The woman tries to point this out, but the man interrupts her. For the rest of the sketch, the rogue noodle travels from his chin to his finger to his forehead to his earlobe. The comic effect is heightened by the fact that the man is trying to have a serious conversation about their relationship, but the popularity of the sketch is essentially all down to the noodle. It is perhaps no coincidence that the only Loriot sketch which relies almost completely on words is about the English language, or more specifically about the German trouble with the English language: in '*Die englische Ansage*' the actress Evelyn Hamann plays a TV presenter who introduces a new episode of the classic English serial *The Two Cousins*, but gets hopelessly entangled in names like 'North Cothelston Hall', 'Nether Addlesthorpe' and 'Gwyneth Molesworth'.

German humour's reliance on the physical is not just apparent on television, but also in the way Germans act on a day-to-day basis. The clue is all in the body language. After or before they have made a joke, many Germans will make a physical gesture to signpost their intention: sometimes just an expressively raised eyebrow, sometimes something more emphatic than that. Not for nothing are jokes also known as *Schenkelklopfer*, 'thigh-slappers'.

The decorum of English joking couldn't be more different. When the boys at my school made jokes, there was nothing in their body language to demonstrate it – no funny voice, no grimacing, no slapping of thighs. Particularly in my first year, I was caught out innumerable times by this. There was the vocabulary test that my classmates had warned me about that never happened, the boy who said his father was the prime minister who wasn't, the teacher who said he had been drafted into the Oxford and Cambridge boat race at the last minute who hadn't. They had all told blatant lies without raising an eyebrow. The 'deadpan face' strategy of joke-telling seemed to come from the same mentality as the art of understatement: the point was that you would by all means avoid making an outward show of what was going on inside your head.

In Germany, the signposting of puns and punchlines is particularly common in the gigantic beer tents of the Munich Oktoberfest and the cities of Mainz and Cologne, where people dress up in clown costumes every November (on the 11th, incidentally, at 11 a.m. – the same time as Armistice Day) to celebrate Karneval. *Büttenreden* are a staple of the German carnival tradition. They used to involve a comedian standing on an upturned tub (a *Bütt*) telling a jokey story in rhyming iambic pentameter. Nowadays *Büttenreden* are conducted on stage in vast festival tents or concert halls, and the speeches are often televised – but the way they are delivered hasn't changed for centuries. Their secret lies in the regular rhyming structure, which makes these 'jokes' terribly predictable and mannered. It gives the audience a clear signal when they should laugh – particularly useful since the speeches are often extremely unfunny. Here is an example:

> *Ihre Gesichtszüge sind ihr total entglitten,*
> *Sie dachte wohl jetzt an ihre Titten.*

Without the rhyme on the last syllable, it translates as: 'She had lost control of her facial features/ She was probably thinking of her tits.' In case someone in the audience should have missed their cue, a trumpet will sound after each punchline: da-doo da-doo da-doo. They might as well hold up signs reading '*Bitte lachen sie jetzt!*', 'Please laugh now!'

Cologne might give another clue to the enduring appeal of 'Dinner for One'. Carnivals turn social hierarchies on their head: at the Cologne *Karneval*, grown-up men behave like children, while children are symbolically elevated to public office: the highlight of the annual carnival is the crowning of a young 'carnival prince' and his wife, the *Funkenmarie*. Yet the very fact that carnival happens only once a year, and that the citizens of Cologne will return to their regular jobs once the season is over, undermines and contains the anarchic element in the festivities. You might say that just in the same way that slapping your thighs after you've made a joke helps to clarify whether you are being serious or funny, an annual carnival helps to make a distinction between 'work time' and 'leisure time'. Like *Karneval*, butler James and Miss Sophie enter the German imagination at a fixed date every year – thus striking a chord not just with the *fin de siècle* tradition of *Sprachkrise*, but also with the recently reaffirmed work ethic. The overriding impression one gets from visiting the Cologne carnival – in spite of its emphatic silliness – is, in fact, one of supremely efficient organisation. Apart from the crowning of the carnival prince, highlights include the parade of the *Blaue Funken*, the 'blue sparks', a military unit whose comedy powdered wigs and period dress are somewhat undermined by the military precision in which they are organised. There is nothing spontaneous, nothing unpredictable about *Karneval*; even joining the elite ranks of the *Blaue Funken* requires a two-year probation period.

In the evening, Cologne citizens tend to go to glorified *Büttenreden* events in large halls known as *Sitzungen*, in which the audience will link arms and sway in unison as a local band plays a jolly song. Many of these songs are so familiar that people know them by heart: in fact, many of the songs are about the fact that people gather at carnival every year to sing them – a mirrored hall of self-affirming platitudes. People I know from Cologne like to think of their city as a place apart – an island of jolliness in a sea of seriousness. Like Bavarians, they like to refer to people from outside their region as 'Prussians'. Personally, Cologne's *Karneval* strikes me as the most Prussian institution in the whole of Germany. Then again, I come from north Germany, where they say '*zum Lachen gehen wir in den Keller*': if we want to have a good laugh, we go down into the cellar so that nobody sees us. But even as a dour northerner, I understand and recognise the spirit that jokes and laughter are associated with in Germany: we call it *Gemütlichkeit*, cosiness. Not the eccentric cosiness of an English home, but a uniform, mainstream sort of cosiness.

*

This takes us to the final, perhaps decisive factor behind the success of 'Dinner for One': the German idea of 'British humour'. I did not really register that this idea existed until my parents and I went back to Germany for a weekend break in February 1998. The occasion for the visit was my mother's annual family reunion, a north German tradition called *Grünkohlessen* where you are served green cabbage alongside fatty slices of pork, sausages and generous glasses of schnapps. At the end of the meal, one of my uncles – known only as 'Knuddi' in family circles – came up to me. 'So,' he asked, 'how are the English treating you?'

'It's good,' I said, 'I'm enjoying it.'

'*Und der britische Humor*? Do you understand it yet?'

That meeting was the first time it became clear to me that Germans treat 'the British sense of humour' with a remarkable degree of curiosity and fascination. It will always carry a sense of being a different language, a code that Germans are able to decipher only in exceptional circumstances. To *understand* British humour – that, in my uncle's mind, would have been quite an achievement. That a German could *practise* British humour, or make an Englishman laugh, on the other hand, was quite inconceivable.

The stereotype of the humourless German isn't new, but it isn't exactly timeless either. In the eighteenth and nineteenth centuries, German literature could count some of the world's finest satirists in its ranks: Jean Paul, Georg Christoph Lichtenberg, Friedrich and August Wilhelm Schlegel, Friedrich Nietzsche. Many of them, like Heine, were Jewish. Even in the first two decades of the twentieth century, there was still a vibrant tradition of satirical cabaret, often coupled with the anarchic spirit of Dada nonsense: a comedy culture which was all about reacting against *Gemütlichkeit*. The picture that sums up that tradition perfectly is another John Heartfield collage. It portrays a respectable middle-aged gentleman wearing a top hat over a Prussian *Pickelhaube*, a dinner jacket draped over a military uniform and a proud moustache. His mouth is agape, and from it escape the words of the first line of the first verse of the old German national anthem: '*Deutschland, Deutschland über alles*'. The sense of national unity, however, is undermined by the ragdoll appearance of the man: Heartfield's collage is a satire on National Socialism. The picture is used on the cover of a book by the satirist Kurt Tucholsky, who once coined the immortal line 'Germans, buy more German lemons!'

By the 1940s, however, Germans' confidence in their own funniness had collapsed. The Austro-Hungarian playwright

George Tabori recalls how, as an émigré playwright in Hollywood in the 1940s, he once attended a party with Thomas Mann, Charlie Chaplin and Greta Garbo. Mann, whose novels have often been praised for their understated irony, had been told on his arrival in the US that the only way any English-speaking person would start a speech was by making a joke. When Charlie Chaplin started to play practical jokes with confetti bombs on the guests around the dinner table, Mann thought his time had come. He got up and announced that he wanted to share a little joke. His thousand-page novel *The Magic Mountain* had never been intended to be read as a serious book at all, Mann said, but as a parody of his novella *Death in Venice*. There are no reports of Chaplin's reaction, though it is unlikely that this would have left him on the floor in stitches. The fact that the anecdote is set abroad seems key: with leading Jewish playwrights and songwriters fleeing the country, the Nazi era drained Germany of its natural comic resources.

The idea of 'British humour', however, was always about a bit more than just a general comedic inferiority complex. The generation of Germans who grew up in the 1950s and 1960s have a very specific idea about what it is and what it does. In 1957, a critic for the *Berliner Stimme* newspaper described his shock at seeing an English comedy performed on the German stage: 'It wiped the laughter off our faces. We had to learn how to stomach this "black comedy" first.' Peter Frankenfeld, too, was intrigued by *der britische Humor*. In particular, he was fascinated by the way it made Germans laugh about things they shouldn't really laugh about.

'Americans laugh about black humour of Anglo-Saxon origin. Black humour deals in the grotesque and the macabre; ~~death and murder~~, ~~scabies~~, lumbago and consumption are all normalised through nonsense, punchlines can give you shivers.' Nothing illustrates the idea of 'British humour' better than an anecdote from the life of Frinton's co-star, May Warden. In October 1978, Warden was lying on her deathbed, suffering from painful convulsions and drifting in and out of consciousness. A doctor and a nurse stood at her bedside. In the hope of easing the convulsions, the doctor suggested that the nurse should give Warden some brandy. 'Shall I give it to her with milk or with water?' the nurse asked. Suddenly May Warden's eyes opened. 'Neat,' she said. It was the last word she spoke. She died in the early hours of the morning.

Few people spent more time thinking about what Germans should and shouldn't laugh about than Theodor Adorno. In 1958, Adorno wrote an essay in which he tried to come to terms with a play he had just seen. 'The laughter that it encourages', he wrote, 'should really suffocate all other laughter. Because that is what humour has turned into since it has become antiquated as an aesthetic medium, without any consensus about what one can laugh about and what one can't; without a place of reconciliation from where we can laugh; without a harmless place between heaven and earth which we could possibly laugh about.' Adorno was a lot more radical in his approach to humour than my uncle Knuddi. He didn't just think that he wasn't very good at it – he thought there was something fundamentally wrong with things that make you laugh. It is not well known that Adorno refined his most famous soundbite, 'To write a poem after Auschwitz is barbaric,' in another essay in 1967. 'After Auschwitz', he wrote in 'Ist die Kunst heiter?', 'humorous art is unimaginable.' The idea of a comedy about the Holocaust, for Adorno, was impossible: 'Comedies about fascism turn themselves into accomplices of the stupid idea that it has already been defeated.' For Adorno, it was as if every joke was a little Bergen-Belsen, every pun a Mauser to the head.

The play that made Adorno first put his thoughts on comedy to paper was not 'Dinner for One', of course – it was Beckett's *Endgame*. They are two very different plays: the former is lowbrow, popular entertainment, the latter a sophisticated piece of absurdist theatre, but in a way, they are also very similar. *Endgame* was written in 1957, five years before Frankenfeld and Dunkhase discovered 'Dinner for One', and like the music-hall sketch, it was received with great enthusiasm across Germany. Both *Endgame* and 'Dinner for One' are plays about the relationship between a master and servant, and they involve the servant being sent on meaningless errands by his master, scuttling across the stage in repetitive circles. Both plays are set in a hermetically sealed world, where time appears to have stopped: they are melancholy, in that they show us old people who are unable to let go of the past and so opt for illusion instead of reality. And they are slightly disturbing. They hint at war, death and destruction: what, after all, has happened to the British and German gentlemen who are no longer with James and Miss

Sophie? Above all, however, they are funny plays, and they are funny in spite of the bleak subject matter. The secret of their success in Germany was that they allowed the Germans to chuckle about a very sinister thought: that history was only ever repeating itself in meaningless loops, that nothing was ever changing. And in a roundabout way, to break the greatest taboo of them all: to laugh about the war.

*

We are left with the question of why 'Dinner for One' has never found a home in the country it came from. In March 1998, I brought a VHS tape of 'Dinner for One' along to an after-school film club. Many of my schoolmates chuckled, some of them thought the sketch was genuinely funny, but none of them were as overwhelmed as Dunkhase and Frankenfeld had been back in 1962. Unlike tragedy, which appeals to the universals of right and wrong, comedy, where the devil is in the detail, ages badly. Slapstick, once the height of comic inventiveness, is now considered passé, the stuff of dusty Benny Hill collections, not primetime TV. The visual spectacles of the variety shows – water fountains, train crashes, live animals – are a thing of the past. Everyone in my sixth form loved stand-up comedy and quoted their favourite lines endlessly. Stand-up was a descendant of the music-hall tradition, of course, but it was a slimmed-down version, which relied almost exclusively on the verbal.

With the slippery, bendable qualities of the English tongue, the evolution of comedy from physical to verbal was a much smoother transition in England than in Germany.

German, with its suspension-bridge structure and modal particles, is poorly equipped to create moments of surprise. 'A German comedy is like a German sentence,' George Eliot once remarked. 'You see no reason in its structure why it should ever come to an end.' English, on the other hand, with its malleable sounds and one-syllable words, feels custom-made for comedy. An English sentence can be flipped upside down like a pancake, its meaning completely changed by the mere variation of a syllable. The pay-off at the end of 'Dinner for One' – 'Same procedure as *every* year, James' – gives a hint of what the English language can do, but the Eddie Izzards, Jo Brands or Bill Baileys of the 1990s were so much faster, so much slicker than that. I remember watching an episode of *Have I Got News for You* in which Paul Merton said: 'There are various ways to give up smoking – nicotine patches, nicotine gum ... my auntie used to pour a gallon of petrol over herself every morning.' This was so much darker, so much more daringly surreal than what Freddie Frinton could have got away with; it makes the ending of 'Dinner for One' look very safe and toothless.

In Germany there has been much speculation about why the nation's favourite sketch has been ignored in its country of origin. On the occasion of the sketch's fortieth anniversary in 2003, *Der Spiegel* published an article called 'Why the BBC is still shunning "Dinner for One"', in which author Sebastian Knauer suggested that social anxiety might have played a part, since the sketch subversively poked fun at the English class system. The portrayal of heavily intoxicated aristocrats such as Sir Toby and dangerously seductive aristocratic figures such as Miss Sophie, suggested the article, made the sketch an 'anti-monarchical tract', which would never be allowed on the traditionalist BBC. At best, such arguments are badly researched. Class has always played a central part in British comedy, not least in the music hall: the toff decked out in a top hat, the 'Champagne Charlie', was as much a stock character of the holiday-resort theatre scene as the drunk or the 'old dear'. Subversive or not, class relations – and particularly master–servant relations – are often at the heart of English comic masterpieces, from Hogarth's *A Rake's Progress* through P. G. Wodehouse's Jeeves and Wooster novels to Roy Clarke's 1990s BBC sitcom *Keeping Up Appearances.* Class even plays a central part in the show that made Frinton's name in the UK: Thora Hird's character, who pronounces 'yes' 'yay-es' and 'Fred' 'Fray-ed', doggedly aspiring to an upper-middle-class lifestyle, truly paved the way for Hyacinth Bucket, or as she would have it, 'Bou-quet'.

Even if we were to ignore the history of class-based comedy in Britain, the logic here is surely flawed. In *The Interpretation of Dreams*, Freud defined comedy as 'surplus of energy which has to be discharged in laughter'. It's a deliciously complicated way of pointing out that the appeal of comedy lies in its safety-valve function: when we laugh, we let off the steam that has built up inside. It allows us to break taboos and act out our fantasies – jokes, as Freud put it later, are really just the superego speaking kind words of comfort to the intimidated ego. Which is why so many jokes and comedies address anxieties about wealth and status – it is no coincidence that the example Freud gives in his book *Jokes and Their Relation to the Unconscious* is about someone who claims to be quite 'familionairely' with Baron Rothschild. To suggest then that 'Dinner for One' could have been unsuccessful *because* it dabbled in subject matter that was too close to the bone is surely absurd. If anything, the social dynamic between Frinton and Warden should have propelled it to broadcasting success.

Perhaps the main reason why 'Dinner for One' never found a following in Britain is not that it deals with awkwardness about class relations, but that TV sketch shows were no longer the only places where that awkwardness could be dealt with. Before the war, music halls in seaside resorts used to be the British equivalent of the Cologne carnival – a safety valve for national surplus pressure, or as George Orwell described it in a famous essay on dirty seaside postcards, 'a sort of saturnalia, a harmless rebellion against virtue'. But is it still? Local historian of Blackpool Barry Band remembers seeing the sketch at the Winter Gardens in 1954, when he was in his teens. 'The bit we laughed at the most was Freddie: it was hilarious to think that someone could drink so much as to become befuddled and trip over his own shoes. Very few people in the audience would have been that drunk in their lives ever.' Today more people come to Blackpool not to laugh, but to drink. The only clientèle the city council can rely on is the never-ending stream of hen and stag parties. People becoming 'befuddled' and 'tripping over their own shoes' are not so much a rare occurrence as a regular feature of a Friday night.

Comedy in twenty-first-century England is no longer an exception to the norm; it is the norm. The public figures my classmates adored most were neither politicians nor writers, neither pop stars nor Hollywood actors, but comedians. All the brightest boys in my year were eager to get into Oxbridge, not because the teaching was so good there, but because that was where their comedy idols had started their careers. In England, comedians write newspaper columns, they host political discussion shows and campaign for reform of the voting system. In Germany, comedy still patrols the closely guarded border between seriousness and silliness, between work and leisure – in post-industrial England, however, those borders were increasingly being broken down. To the rising population of investment bankers, property developers and media creatives, it was hard to tell where working started and playing stopped. Comedians ruled supreme and comedy became the English gut reaction to anything big, clever or vaguely intimidating.

By the time I moved to England, there was a commonly expressed view in the German press that England was a country tragically stuck in the past, obsessed with its glorious role in the Second World War, unable to shake a German's hand without making some daft joke about the Nazis – all true, to an extent, just not the whole truth. In many ways one British comedy had already come up with a much more convincing explanation for this. John Cleese's Basil Fawlty desperately tries to be serious when he meets his German guests at Fawlty Towers, yet he cannot stop himself from reverting to the English instinct of black-humoured wordplay: 'That's two egg mayonnaise, a prawn Goebbels, a Herman Göring and four Colditz salads.' Basil Fawlty reminds us that postwar Anglo-German relations weren't just complicated by changing economic fortunes and a rapidly unfolding European project, but also by increasingly divergent ideas of what humour could and should do.

7

Kevin Keegan Runs past Berti Vogts

On the match ticket, there are two angry cockerels with colourful plumage, pictured mid-fight. The one on the left sports greens and blues; the one on the right pink and red. The writing on the ticket reads: *Union Européenne de Football Association. Roma. Stadio Olimpico. Coppa Finale Del Campioni*, the final of the European Cup. *FC Liverpool vs Borussia Mönchengladbach*. On the evening of 25 May 1977, there are about twenty-five thousand football fans with these tickets in their pockets outside the stadium in Rome. Roughly three quarters of the fans have made their way from Merseyside, the rest are German, or Italian locals. It's a hot summer evening.

On German and English television, the cameras switch to a view inside the stadium. The two teams are gathering on the pitch. 'That's Kevin Keegan with the number seven shirt, you'll recognise him, ladies and gentlemen,' says the commentator Rolf Kramer on German WDR. 'There is no doubt that the German defenders are concerned about Kevin Keegan,' Barry Davies confirms on the BBC and uses the opportunity to remind viewers that Keegan scored twice when the two teams met in the UEFA cup final four years before. Liverpool won 3:0. Keegan is only five feet eight inches tall, but he is the biggest star in English football.

'I wonder if Mönchengladbach will decide to man-mark Keegan,' says Davies. 'And if so, who they can trust to do the job.' The camera eyes up the players gathered around the centre circle. Liverpool are wearing red shirts, red shorts and red socks. Gladbach are wearing a white kit, with a black-and-green streak running down their sleeves and the sides of their shorts. The searching lens comes to a halt on a blond German player in the white number 2 shirt. 'And there is Berti Vogts,' says Kramer on the WDR. Hans-Hubert Vogts, whom the commentators call Berti, is two inches shorter than Keegan. He plays left-back in the German national team, and tonight he is wearing the captain's armband for Mönchengladbach. Vogts and Keegan are standing by the centre circle, on either side of the white line. Just before the referee blows his whistle at 7.45, Vogts tugs at the seam of his shorts and winks in Keegan's direction.

'And off we go!' Gladbach kick off. Bonhof to Heynckes, who loses the ball to Hughes. A long ball into the German half. 'Here's Keegan. Vogts at his back.' Keegan jumps. Vogts jumps higher. Vogts tumbles over, but Klinkhammer gets a foot on the ball and hoofs it out of the danger area. 'The two smallest players on the pitch playing against each other,' Kramer says. 'We'll be seeing more of that in this match.' Twenty-seven minutes into the match, Keegan receives the ball on the left in the German half. Vogts tries to tackle, slips, Keegan turns and sprints, pretends to shoot. Vogts is back on his feet, misses Keegan – '*Kee*gan,' Davies says –

who drags the ball back with his left, another sprint past Vogts, *shoots*. Goal kick. 'This is going to be a difficult task for Berti Vogts,' says Kramer. Two minutes later. Liverpool on the attack again. Heighway cuts into the centre from the right. Clips a pass through to McDermott. Where is Vogts? 'Goal, goal!' '1:0 for Liverpool!' In the fifty-second minute Gladbach equalise through Simonsen. Eight minutes later Keegan runs into the penalty area. Vogts tackles. Both players go down. 'No penalty, no penalty,' begs Kramer. 'The referee says no,' Davies says. Vogts gets up, tries to jump over his opponent's body, Keegan trips him up, he's on the floor again. Is Keegan going to lose his temper, as he did when he punched Leeds's Billy Bremner in the Charity Shield game in 1974? The two players stare at each other furiously as the camera follows the ball into the other half.

In the sixty-fourth minute it's a corner for Liverpool. The red number 4 jumps higher than all the German defenders. 'It's a goal!' 'Oh *yes*,' Davies says. 'It's 2:1 for Liverpool.' A Liverpool fan is escorted off the pitch by four men in army gear. The commentators go quiet. The Liverpool fans in the northern block are celebrating. They unroll a banner that says *Joey Ate the Frogs Legs, Made the Swiss Roll, Now He's Munching Gladbach*. German fans are biting their nails. On the running tracks by the sidelines, photographers sit huddled together in groups, like penguins waiting for the end of a storm.

In the eighty-first minute, several things happen very quickly. Keegan has the ball. Forty yards out, right of the centre circle. 'Keegan,' Kramer says. Vogts between him and the goal, legs wide apart, eyes on the ball. Keegan tries to take the ball past Vogts on his left, both players running, tussling, elbowing, shoving – '*KEEGAN*' – clinging, shirt-pulling, 'IT'S A FOUL.' '*BUT HE'S GOING ON!*' Vogts leaps feet first for a last-ditch sliding tackle – Davies is screaming incoherently. Keegan falls. '*AND IT'S A PENALTY!*' Kramer's voice is a hoarse croak: '*UP AND er . . . QUICK, er . . . BITTER SECONDS FOR BERTI VOGTS AND BORUSSIA MÖNCHENGLADBACH!*' Photographers in flared trousers run over from the sides to position themselves behind the goal. Liverpool's Phil Neal gently cushions the ball as he places it on the penalty spot, like a prehistoric egg. He takes a deep breath, runs, no, jogs – and scores. After the final whistle Keegan punches his fists into the hot air. Vogts walks off the pitch with shoulders hanging.

*

The late South African anthropologist Clifford Geertz's celebrated essay 'Deep Play: Notes on the Balinese Cockfight' analyses what happens to a society when it develops an abnormal interest in sport. Balinese men, he observed while living on the island with his wife, were 'cock crazy': they were so obsessed with cockfighting that they would spend hours ruffling the birds' feathers, cropping their combs, bathing them in ceremonial ointments of tepid water and medicinal herbs, and habitually betting more money on the highly illegal fights than they could afford. Geertz described their relation to sport as 'deep play'. Cockfighting was not mere leisure, not just a distraction from the pressures of daily life, but a symbol of everything Balinese society held most dear.

'Deep play' is also a good term to describe the English and German relationship with football. Football is played everywhere on the globe, but there are few places where it has carved out such a central and immovable role at the heart of public life as in Germany and England. Arriving in England keen to shake off memories of the Euro '96 final, I found football everywhere: on television, on massive bill-boards, on magazine racks, even on sweet wrappers. 'What's your team?' was the question that started my first conversations with my new schoolmates, and 'Did you see Arsenal/Spurs/ManU last night?' the social glue that held together every working environment I've passed through since. Such was football's all-importance that politicians could attribute electoral defeats to football matches without anyone batting an eyelid, as Harold Wilson did in 1970, or that heads of state visit not just World Cup finals but comparatively insignificant qualifying games and demand to be photographed afterwards shaking the hands of the goalscorers in the dressing room, as Angela Merkel did after a 3:0 win over Turkey in 2010.

In Europe, at least, Germany and England are without match in this respect: Italy, France, Spain and Holland all have had memorable football triumphs and traumas but, historically speaking, their interest in the sport is still fresh. English public schools engineered the modern rules of the game in the nineteenth century, while Germany has been taking football seriously since the 1920s and chalked up its first World Cup win in 1954. Mythological moments such as the *Wembleytor*, the 'Hand of God', the 'Miracle of Bern' or the 5:1 in Munich are so deeply embedded in our national memory, they cannot be shifted. Among French Left Bank intellectuals or Basque separatists, it might still be possible to ignore the scoreline of the latest international – in Germany and England, in this post-*Fever Pitch* era, it would be socially unacceptable. *König Fussball*, as they say in Germany, reigns supreme.

Geertz also made the observation that 'deep play' got even deeper when it was played among respectable and well-off members of the community. The more expensive and well-groomed the cockerels, the higher the pile of money on the table. In other words, when the opponents were better matched, there was more for the winner to win and more for the loser to lose. International football matches between England and Germany – be they the national sides or club teams – are never just a simple matter of twenty-two men chasing a football around a green lawn, but serious diplomatic affairs in which nothing less than national honour and respectability are in play. The stakes are far too big to hide.

Another reason why Germany vs England always matters in football is that we cannot help but read these games as verdicts on the way we do things differently in the two countries. It doesn't just matter who wins, but also how. The European Cup final of 1977 did not just pit two of the leading European club teams against one other, but also the perfect ambassadors of two perfectly clashing football philosophies. Kevin Keegan's qualities, perhaps more than those of any other footballer of his generation, were perfectly suited to the style of football known as 'kick and rush'. Technically gifted, though perhaps not exceptionally so, his greatest asset was speed. Keegan was quick not only in the sense that he was a fast sprinter, but in that he was a quick thinker when he had the ball. A typical Keegan goal would start with a long, high ball from the sidelines or near the centre circle, knocked down by the head of a taller strike partner – usually Liverpool's six-foot forward John Toshack – which the curly-haired son of Doncaster would then volley, flick, head or simply bundle into the net before a defending player could put his body in the way. When other players controlled the ball and passed it sideways, Keegan tried an ambitious nutmeg, a volley or an overhead kick. Often the trick failed, but frequently little Kevin managed to produce a piece of sheer magic. Keegan's ability to improvise goals out of the unlikeliest situations and to think on his feet – displayed beautifully in that mazy catch-me-if-you-can with Berti Vogts – made him the first truly international star of English football. Out of 225 career goals, my favourite is his first in the other, 1973, UEFA Cup final against Gladbach: a flying header which meets the ball at such an odd angle that it catches the German goalie completely by surprise. It's the kind of thing that wouldn't have worked if he had thought about it for a second: a product of pure instinct.

Unpredictable gut reactions also remained Keegan's trademark off the pitch. When he decided to record a pop song in 1979, he gave it the suitable title 'Head over Heels in Love'. Could Kevin Keegan fall in love in any other way? A short career as England coach came to an end when he decided on the spur of the moment – sat on the toilet one half time – that he 'simply wasn't up to the job'. The fact that the match was a home friendly against Germany which his team lost 1:0 did little to garner sympathy. When I tried to get Keegan to agree to be interviewed for this book, he had quit professional football altogether and was managing a a football-themed amusement park in Glasgow, the Soccer Circus. After calls to various press offices at his old clubs had failed to get me anywhere, I typed the name into Google and simply dialled the first number that came up. A man answered.

'Could I speak to the press officer?' I asked.

'She's not here, what's it about?'

'I wanted to find out how I could best contact Kevin Keegan.'

'You're talking to him right now. What do you want?'

Recovering my composure, I asked politely if he would let me interview him.

'Sounds like hassle, and I don't need hassle while I am concentrating on my business. Let's talk in December.' And he hung up.

All this was pure Keegan: an unorthodox, refreshing directness, paired with a frustrating tendency for short-term thinking. By December, of course, Kevin Keegan was no longer 'concentrating on his business' and had dropped the Soccer Circus for a second, inevitably short-lived stint as coach of Newcastle United.

Berti Vogts, by contrast, was not a man known for head-over-heels decisions. Over the years, most footballers usually acquire a nickname which sticks in the public imagination because it pinpoints something about them as a player. Keegan became 'Mighty Mouse' because of his short stature and his incredible speed over short distances. The similarly speedy Argentine Alfredo di Stefano became known as *Saeta Rubia*, 'the Golden Arrow'. Rotund striker Gerd Müller's devastating impact in the opposition's half helped him acquire the nickname *Der Bomber*. Germany's legendary skipper Franz Beckenbauer became the Kaiser, because of his statesmanlike gait. Berti Vogts, however, was always *Der Terrier*. He made his name not by a masterly dribble, a visionary pass or a dramatic goal, but a career-long dedication to single-minded ankle-biting. This is not to underestimate his value to his team, but Vogts didn't so much add anything to the side he was playing for as sap the energy of the team he was playing against. In his greatest match, the World Cup final against Holland in 1974, he had niggled and hassled the mercurial Dutch forward Johan Cruyff into utter despair this way.

Footballers like Keegan, Cruyff and Beckenbauer are often called 'natural' footballers because they make difficult things look easy. Berti Vogts, on the other hand, could make very easy things look incredibly difficult. His shoulders always looked hunched, his head always thrust forward, as if he was pushing a plough through muddy soil. Every run, every tackle appeared like an act of willpower rather than instinct. 'If I played football like Berti Vogts,' the Frankfurt striker Klaus Toppmöller, another 'natural', once said, 'I would burn my boots.' After his retirement, Vogts worked hard to improve his image. In 1999, he accepted a guest role in the popular German crime series *Tatort*; the idea was that he would portray a friendly neighbour who returns an escaped bunny rabbit to the lead character's home and notices a gas leak in the kitchen, thus saving the lives of a young family. Watch it on YouTube. When Vogts smells gas in the air, the look on his face is the disgust of a club captain who has just seen his back four fail to work the offside trap. For a second, you worry he's going to snap and boot the rabbit into touch. Berti acting was like someone trying to play the piano with a pair of oven gloves.

The two players' individual qualities didn't just hint at ineradicable national characteristics, but also at the strategies and tactics employed by their teams. Keegan's speed and adventure won against Vogts's work ethic not least because Mönchengladbach had taken the 'playing-as-working' approach to an extreme. Lining up against a team of terriers, you had to concentrate on making creative use of the holes in the German system. In an interview with Brian Glanville, the English striker explained that 'in England games are won or lost in the midfield. In Germany, they surrender the midfield. They keep a spare man at the back, the libero, but everyone else waits and marks man to man. It means that if you beat a man you can have a fifty-metre run in empty space before you reach the next man.'

English football, on the other hand, had developed a tactic which made maximum use of the empty spaces on the pitch. 'Kick and rush', or 'the long-ball game', was first pioneered by the retired RAF commander and amateur statistician Charles Reep in the 1950s. Taking detailed notes on thousands of professional matches, Reep had noticed that a high percentage of goals scored, 80 per cent, had involved only three passes or fewer in the build-up to the shot on goal. Skill was overrated, Reep thought: what use was a player's ability to control the ball with the sole of his foot if he was nowhere near the opposition's goal? Chance, on the other hand, was vastly underrated. Playing a long ball could be a risky business and the chances of gifting the ball to the opposition were greater than they were in a short pass. But by playing a long ball directly near the opponent's penalty box, you were shifting the game of percentages into the part of the pitch where it really mattered. Any team should therefore concentrate on maximising its chances of scoring by getting the ball into the other half as quickly and directly as possible. In many ways, Reep's long-ball theory was another example of English no-nonsense empiricism at its best.

It was increasingly popular among managers too. From the late 1970s onwards, more and more English teams took his philosophy to heart. Recently the term 'kick and rush' has fallen out of fashion; it is only really used as a term of abuse for teams lacking in skill. But the core of Reep's idea has never gone away. You don't need to go into the lower leagues of English club football to hear people talk of 'playing the percentage game', 'throwing the ball into the mixer' or simply shouting at each other to 'hoof it!' Just go to a pub to watch England the next time they are playing a big match. If they are losing with ten minutes to go, there'll inevitably be someone shouting for the gaffer to 'start lumping it to the big fella in the box'. The long-ball game is still irredeemably part of English football's DNA.

Chance, of course, is always part of any football match. But Commander Reep's emphatic pioneering of kick and rush heralds a wider change in the psychology of English sport. The Argentinian writer Jorge Luis Borges's short story 'The Lottery in Babylon' helps to illustrate this development. Initially, the lottery is played as we'd expect it today: a draw is held in the middle of the day, the lucky winners receive silver-minted coins. Over the years, however, the rules of the lottery are changed. Winners can 'win' a punishment as well as a prize. Later the measure of the punishment – a mere fine, the red-hot poker or public execution – is also determined by means of a lottery. A lottery is then created to determine the identity of the executioner. Soon there are lotteries for everything of utmost importance and utter insignificance, from state decisions to whether 'a grain of sand be withdrawn (or added) from the innumerable grains on a beach'. What Borges describes in the story is essentially the next step on from Geertz's 'deep play': the seeping of play into every aspect of a society. 'The lottery', Borges writes, 'is an interpolation of chance into the order of the world, and to accept errors is not to contradict fate, but to merely corroborate it.'

By pinning one's hopes for a football match on something which is essentially decided by chance, Reep sent English football down a precarious path. One striking feature about English sports is the enormous gambling industry that is attached to its various forms. This industry exists in Germany, too, but it isn't as public: there used to be a bewildering number of shops on route to my English school which were displaying fantastical football scores in their windows such as 'Wales 4–Brazil 1'. In German cities, you can find betting shops, if you're looking, in the seedier parts of town, by the train station or in the red-light district. In England, on the other hand, they had been plonked onto the high street. 'Going to the bookies' appeared to be a perfectly acceptable thing to do for all classes. Years after finishing university, I bumped into someone I had known through the student magazine, an immeasurably posh young man in tweed overcoats who used to write articles comparing Philip Roth to Virgil. When I asked him what he was doing now, he simply said: 'Oh, professional gambling, mainly.' I laughed, because I had assumed he was joking, but he wasn't.

As in Borges' Babylonian lottery, the percentages game of gambling seems to have rubbed off on the game itself. It's evident in the vast amounts of money English clubs are willing to splash out in the transfer market, but also in the style of football itself. Only in English football can you hear people talk of a so-called 'fifty–fifty' tackle: a flying challenge in which the attacking player's chances of catching the ball or the shins of his opponent were exactly in the balance. In many English commentators' view, a 'fifty–fifty' was generally a good thing: a sign of passion and commitment. But surely if there was a 50 per cent chance of breaking your opponent's legs, any responsible footballer shouldn't be making that challenge in the first place? Calling it 'fifty–fifty' seemed merely a way of shedding all responsibility and shrouding the game in yet another layer of pure chance.

The part of football where the 'pot-luck' mentality has manifested itself most obviously is the penalty shoot-out. It hardly bears repeating that England have exited five of the last nine tournaments they've played in on penalties; with a 17 per cent success rate, they have the worst record in penalty shoot-outs of all the major football nations. Germany hasn't lost on penalties since 1974 and has a success rate from the spot of 71 per cent. You don't need to be a statistician to detect a pattern here. And yet English journalists cling to the well-trodden line that penalties are 'a cross between Russian roulette and the OK Corral', as a leader in *The Times* put it after losing to Germany in 1996. After a shoot-out defeat in 1990, the same paper wrote that England had 'innocently lost not a football match but a lottery'. Penalties, it reasoned, 'have always been a bizarre form of punishment, since the distance from goal is so short as to make scoring much more a matter of luck than of skill.' Too short? When it came to penalties English logic suddenly went all wonky. So a free kick scored from the halfway line was a piece of skill, but a penalty kick pure luck? Applying that same logic to golf would mean that a ball putted from within the green was a bit of good luck, while a birdie struck from the tee must be the result of clever calculation. Sports minister Tony Banks even suggested that games ending in a draw should be decided by tossing a coin instead: a real lottery, so to speak, as opposed to a virtual one.

This change in England's football psyche neatly mirrors similar developments in the British economy. It's certainly true that as the country fell out of love with making things, it became increasingly comfortable with the idea of gambling for a living. Margaret Thatcher had still been fairly critical of the gambling industry – because she felt that it undermined the notion of hard labour leading to just reward – yet her policies had paved the way for a world in which everyone was playing their own kind of lottery for a living: stockbrokers were playing with hedge funds, homeowners were playing the housing market and parents were playing the postcode lottery. John Major said he was 'morally neutral' on the issue of gambling, while Peter Mandelson proclaimed that the Labour government was not just comfortable with the idea of people making huge gains on the stock markets, but 'intensely relaxed about people getting filthy rich'. While France and America tried to outlaw online gambling in the new millennium, the British government seemed to encourage it, with minister Tessa Jowell actively propagating plans for a 'super-casino' and Richard Caborn, the then Minister for Sport, writing in a leaked note to the managing director of the online betting company Betfair that 'it is government-wide policy, and that includes HMT [Her Majesty's Treasury], that Britain should become a world leader in the field of online gambling, in order to provide our citizens with the opportunity to gambling [sic] in a safe, well-regulated environment'. In 2006, Britain spent

£80 billion on gambling. The lottery had become the ultimate symbol not just of the English approach to penalties,
but of the way the country was run as a whole.

Incidentally, I have never heard anyone in Germany say
that penalties are 'just luck'. Of course they wouldn't have
used the word 'luck' anyway, but *Zufall* or *Glück*, which
can translate as both 'good luck' and 'happiness'. 'When
you are learning a new word', Christopher Isherwood once
said about the German language, 'you must never say to
yourself *it means*. A table doesn't *mean* "ein Tisch". The
two things are essentially different, because they've been
thought about differently by two nations with different
cultures.' Unlike English, German also has the word *Pech*,
meaning 'bad luck', which hints at the fact that Germans
are instinctively sceptical about matters of chance. The
word for penalty is *Elfmeter* or 'eleven metres', which makes
it sound less like a pending punishment than something
which is still part of the game: easy, achievable, a routine
exercise, only eleven metres. Penalties are considered a skill
that can be honed and perfected, but something which still
requires some strength of character; more than at any other
point in the game, the penalty shoot-out puts the player's
ability as an athlete under the spotlight.

Penalties are also the part of a football match which is
most in line with the traditional German approach to sport.
The nineteenth-century nationalists' recreation of choice
was not football but gymnastics. *Turnen*, the flamboyantly
patriotic gymnast Friedrich Ludwig Jahn claimed, had absolutely nothing to do with the English word 'to turn', but

was based on the old German *Torna* or *Turna*, indicating an ancient Germanic predilection for fighting and combat. Gymnastics were opposed to the English idea of sport in every other way too: there were no competitions or tournaments, but only 'continuous examination'. At Jahn's gymnastic events there was always a *Kontrollbuch* in which the progress of the athletes would be monitored: no aspect of the exercise was considered out of bounds. When football first became popular in Germany, it was widely condemned as an 'un-German' pastime: 'an English disease' which caused injuries and a 'monkey-like' posture, as the gymnast Karl Planck warned in a 1898 book called *Fusslümmelei* ('Foot-hooliganism'). Even though neither Jahn nor Planck could stop the spreading of the English disease, *Fussball* became Germanicised as it gained popularity in the country, not just in name but in spirit too: it became a sport which was more about continuous control and willpower than about speed and chance.

By and large, it has to be said, that approach has worked pretty well for Germany. Until the late 1960s, England dominated the Anglo-German football rivalry in the same way it dominated world football. Germany vs England used to be such a one-sided affair that in the run-up to the 1966 World Cup final, a cocky reporter in the *Sun* could afford to write that England 'never lost to Germany – at soccer neither'. But not long after the Volkswagen Beetle overtook Alec Issigonis's Mini, the Germans went from catching up with the English to leading the field. Berti's 'working-as-playing' philosophy played a key role in this: in 1968, a year after the

Terrier had debuted for the national side, Germany eked out a 1:0 win against a lacklustre FA side in what looked like a meaningless friendly at the time. It effectively turned the tide. Since then, Germany has won thirteen times against England and lost only five games – a record so bruising that it led ex-striker Gary Lineker to declare defeat to 'the Hun' a universal law: 'Football is a simple game: twenty-two men chase a ball for ninety minutes and at the end, the Germans win.'

When a retired Berti Vogts was put in charge of the national team in 1991, many of the gymnasts' values came to the fore once more. At their best, Berti's Germany were not a loose ensemble of individuals, but a genuine team in which everyone worked for and with each other. '*Die Mannschaft ist der Star*,' Berti said, leaving at home divas like Lothar Matthäus and Stefan Effenberg, relying instead on selfless collectivists like the humourless East Frisian Dieter Eilts or Marco Bode (of whom Nelson Mandela had once said that he looked 'exactly like Steffi Graf'). Berti's Germany would always be in complete control of a match, even if that meant passing the ball from the striker back to the midfielder, from the midfielder back to the defender, and from the defender back to the goalie – with the inside of the foot, to make sure the ball wouldn't bobble. They also usually won: under Vogts's guidance, Germany raised three trophies: he was assistant coach for the World Cup in 1990, and in charge during the European Cup in 1996, as well as a (relatively unimportant) US Cup in 1993. His record of sixty-seven wins in 102 games is second only to that of his old mentor Helmut Schön; his points-per-match average of 2,196 (both under the old two-point rule and the new three-point rule) is better than that of any German coach apart from the current holder Jogi Löw.

The great irony is that even though German football became incredibly successful by becoming incredibly German, the German public was anything but impressed – on the contrary. At its worst, Berti's Germany could be both uninspired and uninspiring, like a live version of the popular board game which goes under the name Ludo ('I play') in England, but the more appropriate name *Mensch ärgere dich nicht* ('Don't get angry, man') in German: a game in which the objective is not to win, but to stop everyone else from doing so. Watching Germany in the 1990s involved a complex emotional double-bind. We cheered when the ball went into the net, but we were taken aback when we saw the celebrations. Was this the ugly Germany they talked about abroad?

It's worth returning to Clifford Geertz to explain this phenomenon. A national cult around a sport, Geertz notes, does not mean that everyone in the country identifies with the sport. Balinese men obsessed with cockfighting in spite of a wider social taboo around animal-like behaviour. Balinese babies, for example, were taught not to crawl on the floor in public, and in the eyes of the law bestiality was seen as a much more horrific crime than incest. Cockfighting, in fact, is outlawed by the national government. In identifying with his cock, the Balinese man was not identifying with his ideal self, or even his penis, but also with what he most despised. In Germany's case, the compound that best summed up these ambivalent feelings was *Siegesscham:* shame in victory. Berti Vogts, in particular, as the journalist Roger Willemsen put it, 'had become the perfect surface onto which the Germans projected everything they hated about themselves'.

Perhaps this was the reason I never really got into football as a child in Germany: a suspicion that it might only be a thinly disguised displacement activity for something else. Italians, Winston Churchill allegedly once said, lose wars as if they were football matches, and football matches as if they were wars. Didn't Germans play football matches like they were wars? Sepp Herberger, father of Germany's World Cup victory in 1954 and former Nazi party member, once wrote that 'a good footballer is also a good soldier'. What if all those articles in the British press about 'Blitzkrieg counter-attacks' and 'Panzer defenders' had a point?

*

Rome, Stadio Olimpico, 25 May 1977. Two hours after the final whistle. Ed van Opzeeland, a Dutch journalist, walks into the lobby of Rome's Hotel Raphael and notices teetotal Berti Vogts propping up the bar, nursing a glass of whisky.

'Why are you drinking, Berti?' the journalist asks.

'Keegan,' Vogts says.

An hour later the German captain is seen entering the Travel Inn where the Liverpool squad are celebrating their victory. Vogts walks past a row of puzzled Englishmen. Stops in front of Kevin Keegan. Outside the hotel, English and German fans are gathering in the bars around Piazza

Navona in the city centre. 'We were shit-scared of the Eng-lish,' remembers Mönchengladbach fan Klaus Christ, then twenty years old. 'We thought things would kick off any minute.'

But they didn't. Vogts shook Keegan's hand and congrat-ulated him; Liverpool and Mönchengladbach fans bought each other rounds of drinks; and Klaus Christ ran back to his hotel room to share his stash of Kölsch beer. Twelve years later, when ninety-six Liverpool fans died in the disaster at Hillsborough stadium, Mönchengladbach fans donated more than £8,000, and even today there is an annual 'Friend-ship Trip', where fans from the two teams visit each other for home games and sing Liverpool's club anthem, 'You'll Never Walk Alone', together before kick-off. Throughout the 1980s, fan violence and the crowd disasters at Hillsbor-ough and Heysel gained club football an increasingly bad reputation, but it's often forgotten that the English game's 'dark years' came on the back of a period of flamboyant pan-Europeanism, where sport's ability to build ties was more evident than its tendency to sever them. With Liverpool regularly making it to the last rounds of international tour-naments, their fans felt at ease with continental ways, their cosmopolitan side expressing itself in the Italian-inspired dress of 'casual' fashion and the daring avant-garde modern-ism of the bubble perm. From the dark days of the 1990s, it looked like a blissful lost decade of intercultural understand-ing and benign tolerance.

No footballer embodied this open-minded attitude more than Kevin Keegan, whose curly mop had matured into a magnificent mane when he quit Liverpool the day of the 1977 final and became the first English footballer in history to move to a German club. At Hamburg SV, Keegan became Bundesliga champion, was twice crowned European foot-baller of the year, reached the top ten in the German charts with 'Head over Heels in Love' and inspired an entire gener-ation to name their children Kevin. With an annual salary of £15,000 and a fee of 2.3 million Deutschmarks – a record-breaking sum of money at the time – it would be naïve to cast his transfer as an act of selfless idealism: Keegan crossed borders because he was a good businessman. But it's worth remembering that in the 1970s playing for a foreign club was considered such an unpatriotic thing to do that players from abroad were often banned from their national side. During the 1978 World Cup, Nottingham Forest's acerbic manager Brian Clough turned on Keegan during a live panel show: 'Well, young man, who have you bet your Deutschmarks on?' Keegan, quick on his feet as always, replied: 'That ter-rific suntan of yours, you didn't get that by being patriotic, did you?'

Like a distorting mirror, football has a habit of throwing back some of the less flattering aspects of our national char-acter. But this has little to do with the game itself, and all to do with the extent of its reach and appeal. In fact, it's easy to forget that at its heart, football is a moral and virtuous game, which teaches you to act within the law and respect your enemies. In spite of the chants, the fouls, the cocky celebra-tions, it is a supreme model of socialisation, which doesn't drive people from different countries apart but brings them together.

*

Towards the end of the spring term at my new English school, my parents sat me down on our living-room sofa for a chat. Our agreed 'trial period' was coming to an end, and the time had come for me to decide whether I wanted to stay in England and finish my A levels or return to Germany. They had noticed that I wasn't going out much, but my grades had improved and at the last parents' evening one of the teachers had even suggested that we should 'give it some thought' as to whether I wanted to apply to 'Oxbridge'.

I said I wasn't sure, which was true. In German, we have a word for the nagging feeling that you might be missing out on a better life: *Torschlusspanik* describes women racing against their biological clock, men in the throes of midlife crisis and teenagers anxious not to be the last in their circle of friends to have sex. It literally means 'gate-closing panic' and comes from the time when cities used to have a gate which closed at nightfall, though a common mistake is to spell the word *Torschusspanik*, 'goal-shooting panic', not just because the two compounds sound alike, but because being 'put on the spot' in football evokes a similarly pressurised situation, and one that is much more easily visualised in our football-saturated culture. Sitting on that sofa flanked by my parents, I could definitely hear the gate closing, even if I wasn't sure which side I should be on. Would I be better off back in cosy, safe Germany, where I could impress girls at my old school with my English accent and my knowledge of obscure Britpop records? Or was it more fulfilling out here in London, where being a bit of an outsider was the norm and where young men didn't just listen to bands but played in them? The other problem with *Torschschlusspanik* was that the more you thought about it, the more panicky you became, and the more difficult it was to make a decision. My parents and I agreed that I would have another month to make up my mind.

The next day, I did something strange. One month before my eighteenth birthday, I bought my first football: a blue-and-white number from the bargain bin outside JJ Sports, with the Liverpool crest on one of its panels. For the rest of the holiday I would start each day by packing my new football, a sandwich and my notebook into a bag and walking to the nearby park. I would side-foot the ball against a wall or tree stump, wait for it to bounce back to me, flick it up, volley it back against the wall. Ten times. Fifty times. Hundreds of times, until the sun came down and I couldn't see if I had hit the wall or not. At the start of the summer term, I joined my first ever football team. After several trial runs, I had been rejected for the first eleven, and the second eleven, and the third eleven, but there was a casual sixth-form team called the Reggae Boyz, run by a bunch of lads in my year who said they could do with a big man up front for the annual grudge match against the teachers' team.

The weather on the day of the match was perfect: a wet and windy afternoon after weeks of prolonged rainfall. We wore yellow shirts and black socks, the teachers wore black shirts and blue shorts. The pitch was deep and slippery, and for the first half the Reggae Boyz struggled to get a grip on the match. After ten minutes we fell behind due to a controversial penalty. Shortly before half time, we managed to equalise, though my personal involvement in the effort was limited. I was struggling to keep up with the relentless pace of what I had falsely believed to be an irrelevant friendly. At one point I thought that I had finally managed to outpace the player marking me – a maths teacher who was the spitting image of Mr Bean – when I was tackled with a robust fifty–fifty challenge that left me face down in the mud, snot running down my chin. 'This isn't the Premier League, you know,' said the Business Studies teacher who had dished out the tackle, offering me a hand. I was unsure whether this was meant to be a backhanded compliment or straightforward abuse.

In the second half, I started to feel more on top of things. I was beginning to learn that English football was at least as much about words as it was about moving your body: whenever you had the ball, there would be at least five people shouting at you from all directions. 'Long ball!' 'One-two!' 'Send it!' 'Back door, mate, back door!' At first, this could be incredibly intimidating, but the flip of the coin was that your teammates would keep on talking to you even when you lost the ball. 'Never mind, mate,' 'Good effort!' 'Tackle!' Having since played in a number of amateur games for English teams against international opposition, I am convinced that emphatic verbal communication is a uniquely Anglo-Saxon trait. It can look and sound embarrassing from outside – particularly when you realise that a team's voices normally rise as they lose control of the match – but when you're on the field yourself, it provides immense comfort.

We were deep into extra time when several things happened very quickly. Sam G, a gold-chain-wearing troublemaker with a shaven head who would be expelled from the school a few weeks later, managed to dispossess the head of the Spanish department near the centre circle and punted a long ball into the opposition's half, which cut through their defence like a hot knife through butter. The ball was skidding very fast on the wet surface. Towards me. In books, this is the point in the story at which 'time seemed to slow'. Time slowing down in dramatic moments is convenient for writers because they can sit back and think of powerful yet poetic ways of describing the moment on which their story centres: the rain on the wet leather ball sparkling like hunger in the eyes of a puma, stuff like that. But that would imply that footballers have as much time to ruminate over decisions as writers. And that's just not true.

What really happened was this: the ball was in the net. In the side netting, to be specific, still spinning. I looked up, with a vague feeling that I might have played a part in this state of affairs, a feeling that was confirmed by every single one of my teammates running screaming towards me, with an overjoyed Sam G leading the pack. Weeks later, stories would still circulate around the common room about how I had celebrated by pulling off my shirt and belly-diving onto the wet grass, but this too is only a hazy memory. My legs had learnt to do some decision-making that afternoon, and luckily they couldn't talk. What I do know is that I continued to play for the Reggae Boyz for the rest of the season, and that, on the weekend after the match, I told my parents over breakfast that I wanted to stay in England.

8

Astrid Proll Wishes She Wasn't on Joe Strummer's T-shirt

Victoria Park, also known as 'Vicky Park', is an eighty-six-hectare municipal green space in east London, bordering Hackney to the west and Bow to the east. In the nineteenth century, Victoria Park enjoyed a reputation as 'the people's park', mainly because it had several 'speakers' corners' at which people would gather to debate matters of political and religious importance. William Morris was a regular presence on top of the soapboxes of Victoria Park, as was the women's rights activist Annie Besant. But in the 1800s London's people's park never witnessed the kind of crowds it did on 30 April 1978, when as many as eighty thousand young men and women descended on its lawns, many of them carrying flags and banners. The soapbox, too, was much larger than anything the people's park had seen in its history: right in the centre of the park, facing the highrise flats of Tower Hamlets, an enormous stage had shot up from the ground.

At around three o'clock four men walked onto the stage. Two of them had guitars slung over their shoulders: one of them was dressed all in black, wearing a peaked hat which he flung towards the audience as soon as he reached the edge of the stage; the other was sporting a spiky hairdo dyed orange, black trousers and a royal-blue jacket. The last man to walk up to the crowd wore beige skinny trousers, white shoes and a pillarbox-red T-shirt. On the T-shirt, in stencilled letters, were the words *Brigade Rosse*. Between *Brigade* and *Rosse* there was a picture of a Kalashnikov, superimposed on a white star. The machine gun carried the letters 'RAF'.

In *Rude Boy*, a documentary about the Victoria Park concert, a teenager catches the man washing the T-shirt in a sink after the gig.

'What's it say on that T-shirt? Brigade what?' the teenager says.

'Brigade Rosse,' the man says.

'What's that?' the teenager says.

The man says: 'It's the name of a pizza restaurant.'

How many of the eighty thousand knew that, when spelled properly, Brigate Rosse wasn't a pizza restaurant? It's hard to say. What is certain, though, is that at least one person knew. Somewhere in the throng a young woman felt panic rising as she caught sight of the T-shirt with the Kalashnikov logo, though she said nothing to the group of lesbians with whom she had travelled there from Bow to watch the Clash. They knew she was German, but that was all – even at the height of punk, young English people were too polite to ask more than that. Had they asked her what her name was, she would have told them that she was Anna Puttick. She wouldn't have told them that her real name was Astrid Proll, that she had been arrested by German police in 1971, and that she was on the run from the European authorities. She would not have told them that the Brigate Rosse was a radical Italian organisation which had recently kidnapped the former Italian prime minister Aldo Moro (his body was found ten days after the gig, in a car riddled with bullets). Astrid Proll would not have told them that the letters 'RAF' on Joe Strummer's T-shirt stood for Red Army Faction, a German organisation more commonly known as the Baader-Meinhof group, of which she was a founding member.

*

In the forty or so years since its beginning, the Baader-Mein-hof group has been many things to many people. Most called them 'terrorists', but others referred to them as 'class warriors'. The members of the group thought of themselves as 'urban guerrillas'. Some have dismissed them as mere 'style icons with guns'; others thought they posed a genuine threat to security. In a book on the group, the South African journ-alist Jillian Becker refers to them as 'Hitler's children'. Some thought they were cold-hearted killers; others thought their motives were romantic. In retrospect, it's as if even something in their name hints at confusion around the group's motives and intentions. While the press quickly latched onto a name that relied on the gang's two supposed leaders – Andreas Baader and Ulrike Meinhof – the group themselves preferred Red Army Faction or RAF: unfortu-nate choices both, evoking among an older generation either memories of the Royal Air Force's devastating raids on Hamburg or Dresden or the ignominious Soviet Red Army.

Another way to describe the Baader-Meinhof gang would be a group of young people who decided that wearing T-shirts no longer constituted political action, but this requires context. It's hard to understand the Baader-Meinhof group without reference to the events of May 1968, even if the true intentions and achievements of the *Achtundsechziger* continue to be almost as controversial as the RAF. By their own definition, at least, they were the first generation who voiced their frustration with the fact that even twenty years after the end of the Second World War, former National Socialists still seemed to run the country. The poet and former leftwing activist Hans Magnus Enzensberger explained the mindset of his generation to me:

> When you are eighteen or nineteen, you can't stomach silence. Immediately after the war, there was one priority for us: we had to get rid of the bastards. And that was a great nuisance, because you can't change an entire population. Fifty per cent were followers of Hitler, 35 per cent were opportunists and a few others didn't agree. You had all these professors, judges and chiefs of police who were old Nazis, and you had to get rid of them, and a certain violence was necessary to clear up the mess. For a few years we worked in an intellectual sanitation department.

On the one hand the German version of May 1968 was in many ways a quieter, more insular affair than it was in France, where at least nine million French workers downed tools in solidarity with students. In *Kulturnation* Germany, protests were initially confined to university campuses. Theodor Adorno, lecturing at Frankfurt again, voiced vague support for the protests, remarking that 'the students have taken on a bit of the role of the Jews' – but wasn't vocal enough, in the key student leaders' views. *'Die Anti-Faschisten grüssen Teddy den Humanisten'*, 'The anti-fascists greet Teddy the humanist', read a sarcastic banner at the back of the auditorium when Adorno lectured on Goethe's *Iphigenie auf Tauris* in the summer of 1968. 'In my writing I have never provided a model for any sort of action or campaign,' he defended himself; 'I am a theoretical person.' May 1968 looked set to become a rerun of 1848, with Germany pondering and dithering while France took to the streets.

Yet Germany's 1968 was also bloody. There had been street riots in Munich's bohemian quarter, Schwabingen, as early as 1962, after the police had forcibly closed down a student jazz concert – but a decade of intergenerational tension started properly with a gunshot fired from a police Walther PPK on 2 June 1967. The gun belonged to Karl-Heinz Kurras, who was policing a demonstration during the shah of Persia's state visit to West Berlin; the bullet in his gun ended up in the back of the head of a twenty-six-year old student who was attending his first political demonstration. To many young Germans, the killing of Benno Ohnesorg (for which Kurras was never convicted) was an urgent signal that the handover from the war generation to the postwar '68ers wouldn't happen peacefully, but had to be backed up with action. As the crowds dispersed, one female student ended up inside the offices of the social-ist student union, shouting: 'We must organise resistance! Violence is the only way to answer violence! This is the Auschwitz generation – there's no arguing with them!'

The day after the shooting, the same female student was involved in another, smaller protest. Eight young people lined up in the middle of the Kurfürstendamm, one of West Berlin's most exclusive shopping streets, with handpainted letters on their white T-shirts. Viewed from the front, their shirts spelt 'Albertz!' the name of West Berlin's mayor. Viewed from the back, they read 'Resign!' There's a picture of this demonstration which has been reprinted frequently in the German press, perhaps as a deliberate counterweight to the bloody, harrowing picture of Ohnesorg after the shooting. In this picture, the students look cheerful and proud, like a group of scouts who have just managed to build a raft and are now awaiting their badges. Only the blonde student with the blunt fringe stands slightly apart from the group. On her T-shirt is the exclamation mark.

The blonde was Gudrun Ensslin, a pastor's daughter. A few months after the picture was taken, she and her boy-friend Andreas Baader, a former actor, planted a firebomb among the dress fabrics in a department store. On 5 June 1970, Ensslin, Baader, a journalist called Ulrike Meinhof, a young lawyer by the name of Horst Mahler and a group of fellow travellers released a 'communiqué' which announced the need to 'bring about class struggle', 'organise the prolet-ariat', 'start armed resistance' and 'build up the Red Army'.

In previous chapters, we have seen a tendency to romantic, abstract idealism on the one hand, and a talent for rational, efficient organisation on the other as the two trademark traits of the German psyche. Since it's hard to see how such divergent tendencies could ever be combined in practice, it seems like the Baader-Meinhof group was invented purely to prove that that particular ideological circle could be squared. What a uniquely German twist, at any rate, that these terrorists should be headed by a writer: before she joined the group, Meinhof had been one of Germany's leading political journalists, writing for the leftwing, sometime GDR-sponsored weekly *konkret*. Imagine, for comparison, Paul Mason or Polly Toynbee picking up a Beretta and joining the underground struggle against global imperialism.

Most of the columns Meinhof published between 1959 and 1969 displayed not just a sharp eye for social ills glossed over during the 'miracle years', but also a talent for an eye-catching, populist turn of phrase. One of her best columns, a review of the TV programme *File Number XY: Dissolved* from May 1968, slips into political analysis almost by accident. Strange times, Meinhof ponders, when millions of Germans watch real-life crime programmes which fetishise the hunt for petty thieves when Nazi criminals and concentration-camp guards are still unpunished.

We Germans have greater difficulties than others with our suppressed aggression . . . We used to hate the Jews and the Communists. You can't hate the Jews now, it doesn't seem to work any more to hate the Communists; and hating the students is still prohibited by the democratic superstructure. So Zimmermann [the presenter of *File Number XY: Dissolved*] has suggested we hate criminals.

There's an alert, questioning and intelligent mind at work behind these lines, even if ultimately it wasn't a mind intelligent enough to deal with its overflowing aggression. The voice of the Baader-Meinhof group's later statements is more hollow. The communiqués, as they called them, are clogged with set phrases like 'superstructure' and word clusters like *Unterdrückungsapparat*, 'suppression apparatus'.

The name 'Baader-Meinhof group' was so catchy not least because it neatly divided the group into two camps: the brains of the organisation, symbolised by Meinhof, and the brawn, symbolised by the trigger-happy Baader. In fact, almost all the young people associated with the network had artistic aspirations of sorts: the RAF was a *Bildungsbürger* take on terrorism. By the time Ensslin met Baader, she had set up a small publishing house and had worked with Max Brod, Erich Fried and Hans Magnus Enzensberger. Baader was a keen amateur actor at Munich's experimental 'action-theatre', where he had worked with Rainer Werner Fassbinder. During their imprisonment at Stammheim, the core of the group used Melville's *Moby-Dick* to assign code names to one another, with Baader as Captain Ahab and Ensslin as the cook Smutje. Meinhof's alias was even more elevated: Theres, after St Teresa, Carmelite nun and theologian of the contemplative life. It appears merely consistent with this wilful aura of intense intellectualism for Jean-Paul Sartre to accept an invitation from Meinhof and visit members of the gang in prison in October 1974.

Nothing describes the Red Army Faction's curious mix of artistic and political radicalism better than the following anecdote: in December 1971, the sculptor Dierk Hoff got an unexpected visit at his inner-city Frankfurt studio. Two young men were at the door: one of them was Holger Meins, a student at the Berlin Film Academy; the other called himself Lester – his real name was Jan-Carl Raspe. After smoking a few joints and talking about 'hippies and subculture', the two men asked if Hoff could help them build props for a film they were working on. He agreed, in principle. What props? Meins showed him a picture of a hand grenade. Hoff asked what sort of film they were trying to make. '*Eine Art Revolutionsfiktion*,' Meins replied. 'A kind of revolutionary fiction.' By the time Meins (soon to be christened 'Starbuck') and Raspe ('Carpenter') were arrested in June 1972, Hoff's 'props' had been used in five major bomb attacks, leaving six people dead and at least forty-five seriously injured.

This is where ruthless efficiency comes into the equation. At least forty-seven people died as a result of the Red Army Faction's terrorist attacks, including seventeen members of the group itself, and two innocent people who were shot in error by the police. In Britain, meanwhile, the closest comparable movement was a group called the Angry Brigade, to whom police have attributed a total of twenty-five bombings: one person was slightly injured. In the US, five people have been proven to have lost their lives as a direct result of the activities of the Weather Underground collective, all of them members of the group itself – three of them died when a badly constructed nail bomb exploded prematurely. Only Italy beats Germany in this grim competition: a total of seventy-five people are thought to have been killed by the Brigate Rosse, the group who would enter pop culture via Joe Strummer's T-shirt.

A 'faction' of an international whole, inspired by French philosophy and South American guerrilla groups and word-associatively linked with the British air force and the Soviet army, the Baader-Meinhof group tried their best to make it plain they were on an anti-German mission. In their minds, they were the only ones doing anything to stop Germany from tipping back into fascist totalitarianism. They saw themselves as the solution to the German problem. It is therefore not without irony that to most people looking at Germany from abroad, the Baader-Meinhof group was very much part of that German problem. Calling Baader, Ensslin and Meinhof 'Hitler's children' isn't very subtle, and yet there was undeniably something interchangeable about the extreme right and the extreme left in Germany. For all their militant opposition to fascism, the group was quite happy to source their weapons from the far right. Horst Mahler, their in-house lawyer, found it disconcertingly easy to perform an ideological 180-degree turn after he was arrested in 1970, joining the far-right NPD in 2000 and publishing pamphlets which called for a ban on all Jewish organisations in Germany and the expulsion of all asylum seekers. In 2007, he gave an interview to the German Jewish journalist Michel

Friedman, which he opened with the words '*Heil Hitler, Herr Friedman*'. 'You know,' Mahler said in the same interview, 'those terms "right" and "left" are an old story which relates to your position in relation to the parliament, which has a right-hand side and a left-hand side ... that's something that concerns the spectator, but not me.'

*

Germany's Hamlet-like nature – a constant sense of being both too old and too immature – had first been noted in the nineteenth century. But that feeling of having to play catch-up was there to stay. In 1935, the sociologist Helmuth Plessner had described Germany as a *verspätete Nation*, a 'belated nation' which had failed to develop an organic democracy. Even by the 1970s, it looked like it was still wobbling uneasily between the far left and the far right, with an unhealthy affection for authority figures that promised to cure its latent vertigo. This was certainly the British view of Germany. 1971 had seen the re-publication of a book by one of Britain's most influential historians of the Hitler era. In the epilogue of *The Last Days of Hitler*, Hugh Trevor-Roper suggested that 'the despair of politics' was the most discouraging aspect of the German character: 'German history is characterised by a record of political failure so continuous as to have become a tradition – a tradition which in turn perpetuates the record by the appearance of inevitability ... What liberal or popular movements have ever succeeded in Germany?' The wave of terrorist activity in Germany made many international observers think that Trevor-Roper had a point. Would Germany ever manage to gain an inner balance? Could Germans really do democracy? Churchill's adage that 'the Hun is always either at your throat or at your feet' came to mind.

The 1972 Munich Olympics were supposed to show off a new, modern West Germany, but they didn't do much to improve the country's reputation. The local police force had been desperate to project themselves as harmless, peace-loving folk, so they were promptly caught unawares: the Palestinian terrorist commando 'Black September' killed eleven Israeli hostages, having failed to negotiate the release of 234 prisoners from Israeli jail as well as their 'foreign comrades' Ulrike Meinhof and Andreas Baader. An enduring image of the clueless German border police was their arrival in brightly coloured Adidas tracksuits that were quickly picked out by the terrorists watching footage of their siege on the hotel-room TV.

When it came to Baader-Meinhof terror, the German state swung to another extreme. In 1972, the Bundestag issued a special law, the *Radikalenerlass*, which barred members of far-left organisations from taking any public-sector job. Precisely what this law was meant to achieve wasn't clear. Would it stop teachers teaching Mao's little red book at primary school? Would it prevent post-office workers from preparing parcel bombs? Was it designed to avoid extremely leftwing train drivers going off the rails and heading straight for Moscow? In *The Times*, Dan van der Vat noted an uncomfortable parallel to the *Berufsverbot* that had barred Jews from holding public office in 1933. Far from deflating the situation, the officials seemed to inflame it: becoming an outlaw had never appeared easier. In England, suggested van der Vat, few people would have taken Baader seriously, yet in Germany he had the country's entire judiciary in a flap.

Few politicians seemed to believe that the terrorist threat could be dealt with by anything other than brute force. Franz Josef Strauss, the arch-conservative Bavarian defence minister who had become a bête noire for the left, took to wearing a gun holster on his belt at all times and mooted the idea that the state could kidnap members of the Baader-Meinhof group and start shooting them if they weren't prepared to release their hostages. The mood seemed to tip into sheer hysteria. One evening, the police sealed off the centre of Hamburg and a nervous policeman fired an entire round of bullets into a Beetle after the Dutch driver had reached for the glove compartment to show his papers. In June 1972, the police stormed a flat in Stuttgart which had briefly been used as a hideout by the gang and shot at the young man they found inside with sub-machine guns: Ian MacLeod, an innocent Scotsman who had recently moved there but had forgotten to change the name on the door, died on the spot. By law, the German state was not yet allowed to employ the army for anti-terror measures, which meant that a special police unit had to be formed, the GSG9 – another uncomfortable echo of the prominent role of special forces in recent German history.

By June 1972, the core members of the Baader-Meinhof group had all been arrested, yet the fanaticism and hysteria of that era didn't dissipate for several months. When the story of the group reached a climax, it did so in spectacular style. On 5 September, second-generation members of the Red Army Faction kidnapped the high-ranking business executive Hanns Martin Schleyer, formerly an enthusiastic leader of the Nazi student movement, killing two guards and a driver in the process. On 13 October, a linked group of Palestinian terrorists hijacked a Lufthansa plane carrying eighty-six passengers en route from Palma de Mallorca to Frankfurt, diverting the flight to Mogadishu in Somalia. Both acts were intended to force the release of first-generation RAF members from Stammheim prison. Things weren't to work out that way, however. Five days later, around half past midnight, German police stormed the plane as it stood on the runway of Mogadishu airport, shot the kidnappers and released the hostages unharmed. It didn't take long for the news to trickle through to Stammheim prison, and that night Baader, Ensslin and Raspe committed suicide in their cells. The next day Schleyer was found in the boot of a car in the Alsace area, dead.

In Germany, October 1977 is referred to as 'the German Autumn' – a phrase that carries more than an overtone of defeatism. It seems to suggest that there was something uniquely German about the tragic outcome of the situation. After the German spring of 1848, had Germany really not matured? Could foolishness on such a spectacular scale have happened anywhere else?

*

Astrid Proll's role in the German Autumn was relatively minor. Having joined the group in November 1969, she was arrested less than two years later, on 6 May 1971, when a cashier at a petrol station in Hamburg recognised her. Spending the next two and a half years in strict confinement in Cologne's Ossendorf prison, she missed out on the most militant phase of the group. In 1974, after her trial for robbery and attempted murder was adjourned due to poor health, she went underground and eventually ended up in London's East End, knowing no one except for a small group of left-leaning lawyers.

When Proll arrived at Victoria station, one of the first things she saw was an *Evening Standard* poster announcing the hunger strike of the Price sisters, who had been imprisoned for their role in a series of IRA bombings in London in 1973. England, apparently, had terrorism too. But the parallels were mainly superficial. An alliance between the Red Army Faction and the IRA existed only in the minds of the Germans; when the RAF dedicated a 1985 shooting of the industrialist Ernst Zimmermann to the activist and hunger-strike victim Patsy O'Hara, the IRA vehemently rejected any association with the murder. Terrorism in England, it seemed to Proll, was something imported from outside, from abroad, not a product of internal struggles. Few of the people on the British left who helped her questioned the political system as a whole; they identified specific problems and worked on ways to solve them. Political activism here was perhaps less ambitious, but also more practically minded: rather than pen lengthy

manifestos about the global revolution, Proll's new peers organised rent strikes, food co-ops and squats in period buildings that had been neglected by the council. In Germany,
Stefan Aust's definitive account of the gang, *Der Baader-
Meinhof Komplex*, got him in trouble with the militant wing
of the *Sympathisanten*, and he continues to receive death
threats to this day. Yet in London Proll's comrades took a
more common-sense approach to dealing with her enemies:
they ripped out the pages which bore a photograph of Proll
in Jillian Becker's book about the RAF.

For all their talk of motivating the proletariat, the majority of Baader-Meinhof members had had little direct contact
with the working classes. In London, on the other hand,
Proll trained as a car mechanic and worked for a year as a
fitters' mate on the shop floor at Lesney's Matchbox factory in Hackney. On 15 September 1978, a few months after
the gig at Victoria Park, she was working as an instructor for
trainee mechanics at a workshop in West Hampstead when
a group from Special Branch came to arrest her. She tried to
tell them that she hadn't been in contact with the remainder
of the Red Army Faction since she had come to London,
though they didn't listen. Roughly around the same time,
the Clash wrote 'The Guns of Brixton', a song written from
the perspective of a terrorist cornered by the police, ready to
make his last stand.

*

I started listening to the Clash in March 1998. Playing in the
football team had boosted my confidence. If I could man-

age to pass myself off as a football player, I thought, surely it couldn't be all that difficult to pass myself off as a genuine Englishman. One day I found myself sat next to Sam W on the bus home from school, and rather than trying to hide behind my book I just asked him what he was listening to. By the end of the journey he had agreed to swap a mix tape of German punk for a compilation of songs by the Clash, which I listened to on repeat for the next few weeks.

Many of the songs seemed to entertain the idea of armed struggle against the authorities. Apart from 'The Guns of Brixton', there was also 'Guns on the Roof' and 'Tommy Gun', a song that the Clash first played during the Victoria Park gig. Of course, members of the Clash never did take up arms (or at least not in earnest: bassist Simonon and drummer Topper Headon were once arrested for shooting three racing pigeons with an air rifle). 'Tommy Gun' at least gave a slight nod to that inconsistency, being both a song about a terrorist who is 'a hero', and a song about people who worship terrorists like rockstars, buying the same leather jackets to copy their look. That these lyrics would be sung by someone whose Brigate Rosse/Baader-Meinhof T-shirt would effectively coin the term 'terror chic' of course adds another layer of irony.

My favourite Clash song was a cover of a Bobby Fuller song that went 'I fought the law . . . and the law won', because it added a typically English sentiment to the idea of revolt, somehow managing to sound both arrogant *and* self-effacing. The line between irony and seriousness was not always so easy to spot, though. The Clash's 1978 performance in Victoria Park was the highlight of the Rock against Racism festival, which had been conceived in reaction to electoral gains of the British National Party in nearby Bow and the prospective candidacy of the National Front in Hackney South. Yet when the band walked on stage at Victoria Park, the first song they played was 'White Riot' – perhaps not the most appropriate choice for a concert that was meant to make a stand against racism. For 'White Riot', the Clash were joined on stage by Jimmy Pursey, the lead singer of Sham 69, a band who had only two months previously played a gig at the London School of Economics where the audience had chanted '*Sieg Heil*' and posted Nazi stickers all over the concert hall. And it's worth remembering that before the Clash were called the Clash, they went under the terribly witty name of London SS.

In his *Irish Journal*, the novelist Heinrich Böll recalls arriving in Dublin in 1957 and being nearly run over by a bright red car 'whose sole adornment was a distinctive swastika'. After a double-take, he eventually deciphers the smaller letters on the side of the car: 'Swastika Laundry, founded in 1912'. Arriving in England as a German, I would constantly find myself in situations like these. Back at home in Norderstedt, for example, simple items of clothing could have secret meanings: a red shoelace in your boots meant that you were a lefty, while a pair of white laces identified you as a neo-Nazi. Punk was *links*, skinheads were *rechts* – the latter group in particular often wore English labels such as Fred Perry or Lonsdale. A Lonsdale T-shirt was preferably worn underneath a jacket so that the only visible letters were NSDA: the acronym of the National Socialist Workers' Party. In England, though, punks sang songs about white riots and felt-tipped swastikas on their jackets, while skinheads listened to black Caribbean music. Fred Perry polo shirts weren't secret code for a political conviction, just fashion. England in the late 1990s struck me as a strangely apolitical place, where pop stars, footballers and even fashion designers were treated with more respect than politicians.

It would be stupid to say I learnt all this from listening to the Clash, because the Clash were punk, and punk was always more about shock effect than consistency. And yet it felt as if British parliamentary politics in the late 1990s was moving into a post-ideological sphere too. In 1995, Tony Blair had effected a rewriting of Clause IV of the Labour Party Constitution, recasting his party as a more middle-class, pro-free-market organisation, effectively making a claim for the ideological centre. When New Labour won the general election in 1997, it did so less because it had managed to distinguish itself from the Conservative Party on political grounds than because it managed to capitalise on the new wave of cultural patriotism, embodied nowhere better than Noel Gallagher's Union Jack guitar.

I had got a vague picture of British politics from watching the news after school, but in June 1998 Mr C organised a trip to parliament which brought me close up. The Houses of Parliament instantly reminded me of an English pub: it had the same creaky-timbers-and-damp-carpets feel, the same sense of intimacy. Unlike the German Bundestag, in which politicians were sat in the round, British politicians sat on rows of benches directly facing one another, as if in trench warfare. There were no separate seats, and on front benches the men and women (though mostly men) sat squashed together, shoulders touching. It was very noisy, another feature that made parliament more like a pub than the austere Bundestag. When the session began in earnest, the noise levels ratcheted up a notch rather than down: as Blair spoke there was cheering and raucous laughter from the Labour bench and tittering and grimacing from the Conservatives. At one point William Hague made a rather childish joke about the Labour minister for women, Harriet Harman, and the trade secretary Peter Mandelson's recent visit to Disneyworld: 'Peter shook hands with Mickey Mouse and realised he was wearing a Harriet Harman watch.' The Conservative front bench giggled and guffawed so animatedly that they nearly slid off the green leather. The whole thing reminded me of watching the slapstick parliament my philosophy class performed after our teacher had disappeared. But it also seemed less genuine than that, and more rehearsed – like a pantomime in which all the actors knew their lines by heart. Watching this strange performance from the upper balcony of the House of Commons, it seemed very odd to think that this was supposed to be the mother of all democracies.

*

Can countries 'come of age'? And if so, how? The war reporter Martha Gellhorn asked herself these questions when she revisited Germany after the Second World War, in February 1964. In the polemic 'Is There a New Germany?', she suggested that in order to mature, a country needs to undergo an internal change, rather than just a change of government. 'In my opinion there is no New Germany, only another Germany,' she wrote. 'Germany needs a revolution which it has not had and shows no signs of having; not a bloody, old-fashioned, revolution, with firing squads and prisons, ending in one more dictatorship, but an interior revolution of the mind.'

In the same way that the world wars have distracted us from the ongoing exchange between the two countries, the sheer drama of the German Autumn means that much attention has been paid to the old-fashioned revolution, and very little to the revolution of the mind. And that revolution did take place, though some didn't realise it was happening. The vanguard of the *Achtundsechziger* thought of themselves as a minority fighting against a majority that was at best indifferent and at worst deeply reactionary – Böll described the Baader-Meinhof gang as 'six against sixty million'. But that's misleading, because in the late 1960s the majority of the German public was becoming more liberal than ever before. In September 1969, the country even got its first ever Social Democratic chancellor: Herbert Frahm, better known by his assumed name, Willy Brandt, an anti-fascist from Lübeck with dimpled cheeks and melancholy eyes, who had spent the Second World War in enforced exile in Norway and Sweden. Brandt had been mayor of West Berlin from 1957 to 1966 and had witnessed both President

Kennedy's '*Ich bin ein Berliner*' speech and the building of the Berlin Wall: two experiences that directly informed his way of running the country. Under Brandt, West Germany tried to engage with the leaders of the East, rather than shut them out. Trade and cultural exchange with the East was encouraged, and West German security laws were relaxed. '*Wir wollen mehr Demokratie wagen*,' 'We want to dare to be more democratic,' is the motto most closely associated with his reign. Brandt also became the first German chancellor to visit Israel. In 1970, attending a ceremony in honour of the victims of the Warsaw Rising in 1943, he suddenly sank to his knees on the cold concrete, his head bowed in front of the floral wreaths: an authentic apology for the crimes of the Third Reich. For my parents and their generation, Willy Brandt was a German JFK: someone who personified a new idealism in politics, an antidote not just to the reactionary conservatism of past German governments on the right, but also to the cultural pessimism of the Frankfurt School and the political pessimism of the Baader-Meinhof group on the left.

When I interviewed Astrid Proll in 2008, I was initially surprised by how little she seemed to have engaged with, or even just thought about, the liberalisation in mainstream politics in the 1960s. For a start, Proll was convinced that Brandt 'came long after us'. This would be less damning if it were not for the fact that Brandt's attempt to make Germany more liberal was hindered, not helped, by the radical left. Already an easy target for jibes from the right about his exile during the Third Reich ('What did you get up to for twelve years out there?' the Bavarian conservative Franz Josef Strauss once asked him; 'we all know what we got up to in here'), Brandt came increasingly under attack as the Red Army Faction cast the country under their spell. His leniency made it easy for others to paint him as a sympathiser: when Baader was arrested, the CDU politician Carl Damm suggested that the terrorist should call the chancellor for his defence. With pressure from the right mounting, Brandt eventually announced the *Radikalenerlass*, which lost him much of the initial support from the younger generation. He eventually resigned when it emerged that his assistant Günther Guillaume had been a spy for the GDR, a fact that had made the head of the republic even more vulnerable to blackmail than his weakness for alcohol and women.

On 16 May, Brandt was replaced by Helmut Schmidt, another Social Democrat, but a realist who shared little of his predecessor's idealism. Schmidt pursued a much harder line with the RAF. Shortly after the kidnapping of Hanns-Martin Schleyer, a representative of the Bundestag gave an interview to the BBC. 'Do you think Mr Schmidt will give in to the terrorists' demands?' the interviewer asked.

'It is going to be a hard decision for him, but like most people here I believe that he won't give in to any demands.'

'Even if that means that Mr Schleyer is killed?'

'Yes, I believe that giving in is not an option.' The same evening, Schmidt asked a government lawyer to put down in writing that the government was not to enter into any negotiations with the terrorists, even if he himself or his wife were kidnapped.

These days, Schmidt is frequently voted the most popular German politician of all time; according to a 2010 survey by *Der Spiegel* 83 per cent of Germans considered him the highest moral authority in the country. The highbrow weekly *Die Zeit*, where Schmidt is a contributing editor, used to feature a regular series of interviews with the former chancellor called 'A cigarette with Helmut Schmidt'. Brandt, on the other hand, is still admired, but not revered.

*

My interview with Astrid Proll lasted two hours. At six o'clock on the dot she got up from her seat, walked to the other end of the room and switched on the television. 'You can stay if you like, but I'm going to watch this now,' she said over her shoulder. People in the Hesse region were voting in a local election that day, and for the next two hours we sipped cups of Earl Grey and ate squares of rye bread with cheese and gherkins as the first results came through.

It is not easy to get people excited about regional German politics. On 8 May 1949 the country had adopted a parliamentary system closely modelled on American federalism, though this doesn't mean it automatically resembles the drama and pace of *The West Wing*. The German parliament is made up of a lower house, the Bundestag, which is voted for directly every four years, and an upper house, the Bundesrat, made up of locally elected representatives from the sixteen *Länder* or regions. The Bundestag can cook up new laws, the Bundesrat can pass or veto them. Just to make things that bit more complex, there are also not one but two federal law courts which can put laws up for judicial review. All legislation has to be in keeping with the Basic Law of 1949. Because the Bundestag is elected by proportional representation, it's nigh on impossible for any government to gain an absolute majority: since 1949, every German government has been a coalition. Some parties make natural bedfellows: Germany's Conservatives, the Christian Democratic Union (CDU) and Bavaria's Christian Social Union (CSU) are effectively one and the same party. The Free Democratic Party (FDP) has been the Conservatives' traditional coalition partner over the years. The Social Democratic Party (SPD), Germany's Labour, dominated the late 1990s in a coalition with the Greens and they've been holding hands behind everyone's backs ever since. At municipal level, though, it's like suburban swingers' parties: anything goes.

The run-up to the 2008 Hesse elections had been highly controversial. Faced with a poor showing in the pre-election polls, incumbent minister Roland Koch had led an unashamedly populist election campaign in which he promised tough measures against youth crime among the state's migrant minorities. Emphasising the foreign-sounding names of the candidates for the SPD and the Greens, his posters had read 'Stop Ypsilanti, Al Wazir and the communists!' But when the first results came in, Astrid let out a cheer. With the CDU's vote down by 12 per cent, Koch's negativity had been duly punished by the electorate. Voter turnout was at 64.3 per cent, which wasn't out of the ordinary, but still something only seen at a general election in Britain. Hugh Trevor-Roper once claimed that Germany would never have a liberal politician who wasn't remembered as a failure, but if twenty-first-century Germany was still in love with autocrats who promised 'blood and iron', it was certainly doing a good job of hiding its crush.

As usual, none of the main parties had scored an absolute majority. The TV presenter went through the various options. Would Hesse go all red, with a coalition between the Social Democrats and the leftist *Die Linke*? Would there be a 'traffic-light coalition' between the Social Democrats, the Greens and the Liberals? Or could the Conservatives find their way back into power via a 'Jamaica coalition' (after the colours of their flag) with the FDP and the Greens? German politics have a so-called '5 per cent' hurdle which means that very minor parties rarely get representation in local government, and yet I was struck by the long list of small parties who had entered the race. There was a Party for Animal Rights, a Family Party, a Pirate Party (which has since gone on to win fifteen seats at the Berlin state election), a Grey Panther Party for the over-seventies and even a Violet Party which represented 'alternative spiritual politics in a new age'. As the various candidates were dragged in front of the cameras, I was struck by how grown-up and sensible they all sounded – a far cry from the pantomime theatrics of Prime Minister's Questions.

As the broadcast progressed, it became clear that a winner wouldn't be announced this evening and that politicians were only going to give cautious interviews in anticipation of weeks of coalition negotiations. We switched channels to catch the last half hour of a docudrama on RTL. Set in the late 1980s, the film told the story of a group of church-goers in Leipzig who organised a weekly march in peaceful protest against the GDR regime. Eventually, the demonstrations swelled to such numbers that the government can no longer ignore them. For a minute, it looks like the Leipzig protests will end up with gunshots being fired into the crowds, as in Prague. But they don't: in the end the borders open, the regime is toppled and the churchgoers have won. Based on just the last half hour, it's clear the film isn't very good: a TV production with fairly perfunctory acting and simplistic dialogue. There seems to be a major structural problem too, in that the film tries to isolate a young couple as the lead characters, while also making the point that the protest marches are the achievement of collective will, rather than the decision of individuals. And yet, in spite of all this, I am suddenly very moved, simply by the idea that it happened. Astrid is off to the kitchen for more rye bread and gherkins. How odd that something like that could take place in a country like Germany: a revolution in which not a single shot is fired. Not a bloody, old-fashioned revolution, with firing squads and prisons, but a revolution of the mind.

Epilogue

'We don't serve irony here, but we've got all kinds of beer.'
Heinrich Heine, *Journey from Munich to Genoa*

The large public park in the centre of Munich is known as the Englischer Garten, but the name is misleading. Constructed in 1789, its creation was supervised by a certain Sir Benjamin Thompson, a politician, engineer and maverick soup-inventor, whose British knighthood masks the fact that he was born in Massachusetts, had a long spell serving under Kaiser Joseph II in Bavaria and died in Paris. Some sections of the park certainly *look* like a nineteenth-century English landscape garden, with the sudden rise and fall of artificial meadows, unexpected clumps of shrubbery, a Chinese tower in the style of the pagoda at Kew Gardens and none of the geometric pedantry of a *jardin à la française*. But its character is more German than Anglo-Saxon. There's an enormous beer garden beneath the pagoda where you can buy wheat beer, pretzels and white veal sausages, all in grotesquely large portions. With a total area of 1.4 square miles, the park itself is rather large too, and wholly un-English in its ability to swallow up entire afternoons if you dare set a foot in it at lunchtime. There's a stream, the Eisbach, which powers through the park with such force that its choppy waves can accommodate surfers in some spots – a gentle reminder of the Alpine peaks that cast their shadow on Munich like a row of unfriendly bouncers. Instead of the open assembly spaces and 'speakers' corners' that dot London's Victoria Park, the Englischer Garten has hidey holes and cosy corners aplenty, so that one can spend hours here without chancing upon, or being chanced upon by, another human being. In fact, some parts of the park are so secluded that it is ideally suited for another typical German pastime: nudism.

It's the Germanness of Munich's English Garden that draws the English socialite Unity Mitford to the park one scorching August afternoon in 1937. Writing a letter to her sister Jessica, she confides:

> The other day when it was boiling hot I found a secluded spot in the Englischer Garten where I took off all my clothes & sunbathed, luckily no-one came along. While I was lying in the sun I suddenly wondered whether Muv [Mother] *knew* I was sunbathing naked, like when she *knew* that you were bathing naked, & I laughed till I ached, if anyone had come along they would have thought me mad as well as indecent.

Unity, a cousin of Winston Churchill through her sister's

marriage, is not the only member of the Mitford clan with an interest in German matters and manners, with 'Muv' and 'Farve', brother Tom, sisters Diana, Deborah and Jessica and cousin Clementine all visiting Munich in the 1930s. Like her, they're never far from the giggles: they love the language, the landscape, the films you can see in the cinemas ('most heavenly'), and the food ('wonderful'), especially the bread ('wasn't it killing'). Germany is a hoot, and the Mitfords are seemingly in constant stitches – Jessica, who is an out-and-proud lefty, is remembered by the locals as *die lustige Kommunistin*, the jolly communist. It's Unity, however, who has the strongest desire to go native, especially after bumping into a handsome young man (Muv thinks he has 'a very nice face') in one of the local bars. The first time they meet, at the Osteria Bavaria, she is so nervous that she nearly drops her cup of hot chocolate, but soon the twenty-one-year-old Englishwoman and the German are on intimate terms. In December 1935, after another rendezvous in the Osteria, Unity writes to her sister Diana: 'The Führer was *heavenly*, in his best mood, & very gay. There was a choice of two soups & he tossed a coin & he was *so* sweet doing it. [...] He talked a lot about Jews, which was lovely.'

Unity Mitford's adventures in Nazi Germany were documented meticulously in the British press at the time, and she and her sisters are gossip-column gold to this day: as recently as 2007 the *Daily Mail* promised to reveal 'the truth about Hitler's lovechild' with the English society girl (there is no evidence that her relationship with the leader of the National Socialists was ever sexual). Unity is usually portrayed as the black sheep in the Mitford flock. Often, her story is told as that of an isolated aberration, a rare failure of British common sense, which leaves aside some of the more troubling questions arising from this encounter: which other members of English high society would take tea with Hitler if they had the chance? And why did Hitler let an English It girl into his inner circle? Did he see Unity as a symbol of the British ruling class he so admired, especially for its expansive empire?

One popular line, supported by her younger sister Deborah, is that Unity became 'too German' during her stay in Munich, which is to say not just too immersed in Nazi ideology but too serious and po-faced about politics, without that all-important English instinct for the ridiculous. But is someone who can write the words 'poor sweet Führer' really po-faced? Reading Unity's letters from Germany, the impression is of someone who doesn't take politics that seriously at all, or only seriously in the way a young girl might have a serious love of cocker spaniels or a serious addiction to ballet. Shortly after Unity had left England for Germany, her sister Nancy wrote a comic novel in which a thinly disguised Unity figure called Eugenia stands in the middle of a village square on an upturned bathtub, with her 'Reichshund' by her side, recruiting for the 'Union Jackshirts'. Some, including Unity, have read it as a parody of British fascism, even though Nancy didn't think so herself: 'I still maintain that it is far more in favour of Fascism than otherwise. Far the nicest character in the book is a Fascist, the others all become much nicer as soon as they have joined up.' The novel, *Wigs on the Green*, seems to fall into the same category as P. G. Wodehouse's *The Code of the Woosters,* a book which takes a swipe at a crypto-fascist 'Black Shorts' movement and yet cannot be counted as real evidence of its author having grasped the seriousness of the situation (Wodehouse later recorded some ill-judged broadcasts for the German propaganda services while interned in Upper Silesia). In fact, what links Unity and Nancy Mitford and Wodehouse is a unique trait of Britain's non-labouring upper classes in the years between the wars: the tendency to see the build-up to the greatest disaster in European history through a thick film of irony.

Unity's German jolly has an ironic ending, even though it is ironic in that other, tragic sense, and so not that funny. Almost exactly a year after baring it all in the Englischer Garten, Unity once again seeks out a remote spot amid the bushes and branches of that deceptive symbol of Anglo-German affinities. Two days previously, Hitler spoke to the nation: 'I have proposed friendship to England again and again and, when necessary, the closest collaboration. But love cannot be one-sided, it must be reciprocated.' On 3 September 1939, the Second World War begins, and Unity puts a pistol to her head. She survives, and lives, severely disabled, for another nine years, until the bullet in her brain becomes infected and kills her.

*

When I first started writing this book, I made a pact with myself that I would do my best to avoid unnecessary referen-

ces to the Nazis and the Second World War. When it came
to Anglo-German relations, the Nazi era had seemed to me
like a historical black hole, sucking up everything interesting
that happened before or after. 'Why don't you write about
Hitler meeting Churchill?' English friends would say when
I told them that I was writing a book about meetings. 'Why
would you want to read about that?' I'd say to them. 'You
already *know* those stories.' The Third Reich, I felt, was the
only period in German history people were ever told about
in this country: at school, on television, in the newspapers.
There are hundreds of books about Churchill, and thousands about Hitler. Do we really need another one? And yet,
when I chanced across Unity Mitford's letters, I realised that
there was no way I could leave her out of the book. Ignor-
ing the Nazis as a matter of principle suddenly seemed just
as forced as obsessing about them.

One thing in particular fascinates me about the encounter between Unity Mitford and Adolf Hitler: in a way,
it reads like an urgent parable about the uses and abuses of
English irony. If irony used to be the preserve of the English upper classes in the 1930s, it had become inextricably
part of the broader English mindset by the time I arrived
in 1996, and over the years I invested a large amount of
time and effort in becoming more ironic and less serious. I
copied people's gestures until I had mastered the deadpan
face, the Oxford stutter and the 'wanker' hand gesture. I
copied people's speech patterns until I was permanently ambiguous in everything I said: commenting sarcastically that
a friend's dress was 'quite nice' when I thought it was ugly, or

remarking wryly that a film was 'quite good' when I thought it was great. I even copied the fashions, joining the tongue-in-cheek revival of sportswear and haircuts. For our joint eighteenth birthday party, my friend Tom and I sent out invitations that told guests to 'dress with a sense of defeated irony'.

The downside of learning to become more ironic is that it intensifies the tragic teenage condition of never quite feeling yourself. You get so into the habit of copying others that it becomes hard to imagine ever being anything other than a doppelgänger. I kept on copying when everyone started to send off their university applications in the second year of sixth form, and somehow ended up getting into Oxford. I wasn't stupid, I knew that, and yet I couldn't suppress the feeling that I had managed to cheat my way into one of the most prestigious universities in the world merely by being very good at copying the manners and aspirations of young Englishmen.

The positive side of English irony is that it creates a uniquely pleasant sense of national identity. The great thing about being in England, I believed, was that you didn't have to commit 100 per cent to being English in the way you had to be seriously committed to being a German living in Germany. You could 'be English' in an ironic way: slipping in and out of Englishness mode like a well-worn pair of trainers. When my father retired in 2000, and my parents soon after announced that they were selling our house and moving back to Germany, I took it in my stride. Living in one country but having close family ties to another seemed a perfect prelude to that cosmopolitan ideal of always being *in* a country, but never being *of* a country.

It only dawned on me slowly that you can't keep living in quotation marks forever. It started one half-term holiday, when I joined my old schoolmates in Germany for a game of five-a-side in the park: having received a pin-perfect cross from midfield, I had turned a defender and steadied myself, only to then skyrocket my shot over the crossbar. 'Fuck!' I shouted – in English – and immediately checked myself, baffled why I had not sworn in German. '*Der Engländer*', one of my teammates chuckled behind my back, and another started humming 'God Save the Queen' as I walked back to the centre of the pitch.

Every time I went back to Germany to visit my parents, the signs that England had somehow got under my skin became harder to ignore. In the supermarket, I found myself getting easily irritated with the blunt manners of the checkout lady, suddenly missing the how-are-yous, thank-yous and have-a-nice-days that had once struck me as artificial and formulaic. In the pub, I realised that I was drinking on English time, necking back the last dregs while my German friends had barely made headway into the foam. I spent hours in vain trying to convince them that beer could be just as delicious served at room temperature. I even found myself defending English cooking when I overheard yet another German philistine take a cheap shot at baked beans on toast, waxing lyrical about bittersweet marmalade, beef-and-ale pies and rhubarb crumbles. 'And you think they adore us for our dumplings and schnitzels, do you?'

The longer I stayed in Britain, the harder it was to tell whether I was a German in English clothing, or already a fully fledged Englishman who was harbouring pretensions of once having been German. Back at university, I started seeing a girl called Joanna, on whom I had had a crush since the first day of Freshers' Week. On one of our first dates, Joanna said to me: 'Do you know that the other people in our year call you "German Phil"?' I didn't, I said (though I considered myself lucky, given that the other Phils in our year were known as 'Portuguese Phil', 'Neanderthal Phil' and 'Sleazy Phil'). 'The weird thing is,' she continued, 'you're not really that German at all.'

*

What is typically German? What's typically English? To complicate things further, these questions haven't exactly become easier to answer since I moved from one country to the other. You couldn't rely on television or the newspapers to point this out, admittedly. Ever since Theodor Fontane set foot in London, the correspondents of German newspapers have had a habit of describing Britain as an island set in aspic, a world where traditions and institutions remain unchanged through the centuries. Since 1997, I have witnessed a series of clever German journalists be despatched to 'the island', take a year or two to root around the tabloids and get their heads around the workings of parliament, only to then unfailingly conclude that England was still stuck in 1945 and obsessed with the Second World War. 'Dislike of us Germans is a national pastime,' wrote *Der Spiegel*'s Thomas

Hüetlin as recently as 2007, 'which belongs to this island like driving on the left or the assumption that Victoria Beckham has class.' They are not completely wrong – it's hard to deny that Hitler and Churchill play central roles in the founding mythology of modern Britain – but to say that Britain is stuck in the past is to ignore the speed at which the present is changing.

Since the start of the global financial crisis, British economists have turned with a fresh glint in their eyes to the one country in Europe that emerged from the recession not just practically unscathed, but booming. Germany's sound manufacturing base, robust apprenticeship system and consensual industrial relations have been held up as the alternative to the chronic short-termism of Anglo-Saxon 'casino capitalism'. Politicians just took a little bit longer to notice. On the Left, Labour leader Ed Miliband has praised Germany's industrial policy, shadow business secretary Chuka Umunna has hailed 'cultural and institutional lessons from the German experience', while the Labour life peer Maurice Glasman has gone as far as suggesting that Britain should 'bring in German masters, as we did in the fifteenth and sixteenth centuries to renew guilds'. For a while, there was even talk of 'Neue Labour'.

On the surface, relations between British and German conservatives may look more frosty: David Cameron crucially decided to take the Tories out of the European centre-right alliance in 2009, and the British Prime Minister's veto against the EU treaty change in November 2011 seemed to mark a major parting of destinies. But the German line on

Europe may be about the only lead the coalition government is unwilling to follow. It has since emphatically modelled itself as one of 'fiscal conservatives', eager to be shown to be minimising Britain's budget deficit. Chancellor George Osborne has hailed 'a Britain carried aloft by the march of the makers', while Business Secretary Vince Cable has launched a 'Made in Britain' initiative that feels like a late corrective to the nineteenth-century 'Made in Germany' disaster. Tory MP Lynne Truss has published a paper praising Germany's job-market reforms of the early noughties, while the much-trumpeted 'localism' initiative looks like a thinly veiled version of the decentralised federal *Bundesrepublik*, with Eric Pickles declaring in his first major speech as Communities and Local Government Secretary that Germany has 'really got the idea in local government'.

Particularly in the early days of the current government, there was no shortage of commentators pointing out that Britain's first coalition government bore a remarkable similarity to the Conservative–Liberal coalition that has been standard in Germany for years. 'Cameron is a closet Angelaphile', a journalist colleague told me recently. 'His whole cabinet has learnt to speak with a German accent.'

Understanding the grammar may be a bigger challenge. In July 2011, the government announced that it had awarded a £3 billion train deal to German giant Siemens rather than to the British-based Canadian company Bombardier. As usual, politicians claimed that their 'hands were tied' by EU regulation; if Germany and France managed to keep manufacturing within their own borders, they hinted, it must be because they were bending the rules – lending the whole affair the air of an England team that has just lost another quarter-final on penalties. Bombardier's Derby-based works now look set to close once their current order of London Underground trains is completed in 2014. If this is the heralded 'march of the makers', it looks more like a funeral procession.

An expert on German–British business relations recently told me that the German model tends to become fashionable in Westminster every twenty years or so, 'like flared trousers'. It remains to be seen whether the latest version of Germanophilia is anything more than a passing fad. It's worth remembering that at the TUC conference in 1978 a resolution was put forward to adopt 'the German approach to industrial relations' – followed by a defeat so crushing that no one even bothered to count the votes. But only four years earlier, a conservative think tank was founded to draw lessons from the success of German industry. In the end, the Centre for Policy Studies' founder, Margaret Thatcher, instead became more interested in the market liberalism of the Austrian economist Friedrich Hayek. The rest, as they say, is history.

It's not just England that has become more German in the last ten years. Germany has become more English too. There's a new German lightness, irony even, which would have been quite uncharacteristic only a decade ago. The one place where this change is most easily measurable is Berlin, which has grown fast into a global cultural hub to rival London since the German parliament relocated there from Bonn in 1999. As well as the cliché about Britain being stuck in the past, a line repeated again and again in the German press is that telling English people you are German can easily lead to a punch-up. I have never got into trouble for telling people where I am from – once, on the top of a double-decker bus, I was confronted by a gang of menacing teenagers whose faces softened before my eyes when I told them I was from Germany: 'They've got marzipan there, haven't they? I love that shit!' Usually, the response used to be a polite, pitying silence. For the last two years or so, however, 'I'm German' has suddenly started to trigger an entirely different response: 'Germany? Oh, I *love* Berlin.'

In the first five years of the new millennium, it was mainly young people from the provinces of Schleswig-Holstein, Baden-Württemberg and Mecklenburg-Vorpommern who descended on the new capital. When they realised that lecture halls in Berlin were overcrowded and job opportunities rare, they gradually deserted the city again, and their place was taken by young people from all over the world. In the last five years, at least six of my friends have uprooted from London to Berlin. When I ask them why they prefer Berlin to London, the usual answers are either 'It's got so much history' or 'People in Berlin just know how to party', neither of which seems to make much sense, given that London doesn't particularly lag behind in the history department or the party stakes. A rarer, more plausible explanation is that Berlin is simply a cheaper place to live, and more tolerant of creative and bohemian lifestyles. Indeed, whenever I've gone to visit friends there, the people I met were either writing novels, playing in bands, making documentary films or DJing in bars – or all of those at the same time.

Some critics like to maintain that Berlin isn't really a 'proper' metropolis like London or New York, but more of a network of small interconnected villages, each with their own *Kiez*, or neighbourhood community, and the mentality of a provincial outpost. I am not sure I buy that argument: London might have Trafalgar Square or Piccadilly Circus, but they are only centres in the geographical sense and full of tourists at any rate; most Londoners don't cross the river more than once a week. Berlin certainly *thinks* like a worldly wise capital. Like Londoners, arguably more so, Berliners are aware of their own hipness, and love knowing in-jokes that draw attention to their self-awareness. In post-Wall Berlin, there are bars called White Trash Fast Food, Chinese restaurants that have been turned into cocktail lounges, and sausage stalls that sell *Currywurst* with wasabi-flavoured potato salad. Most tellingly of all, you've got cafes that are made to look exactly like the cafes of GDR-era East Berlin, where they sell Club Cola and Bambina chocolates: an ironic reproduction of their former selves.

Those who didn't make it to Berlin in the last ten years just had to watch football to be reminded that Germany isn't quite the place it used to be. Fourteen years after I had recoiled in horror as Andi Möller performed his cockerel strut at Wembley, I sat in a packed front room in a flat in Finsbury Park to watch England play Germany in the quarter-finals of the 2010 World Cup in South Africa. Of course Germany won – nothing new there. What was new was the *way* in which they won, and the reaction among my English friends. The moment that summed up this change best happened in the seventieth minute of the match. Germany had already scored three to England's one, and the team in the red shirts was showing signs of frustration after having a perfectly clear goal disallowed. It's unclear whether it was lion-hearted courage or mere desperation that made England's barrel-chested defender John Terry desert his position and storm upfield to meet a cross from winger Joe Cole. The cross never arrived. Blocked by the German defence, the ball sailed back into the England half, putting defence midfielder Gareth Barry one-on-one with attacking midfielder Mesut Özil. Initially, it looked like the tall, muscular and athletic Barry was certain to reach the bouncing ball before the short and weedy twenty-two-year-old Özil. Two seconds later, Özil was five metres ahead of Barry, with the ball at his feet, making the Englishman look like a retired bobby chasing after a teenage delinquent. Özil passed for twenty-one-year-old Thomas Müller to score, and England found themselves at the receiving end of their highest defeat in World Cup history.

I turned around to look at my English friends, expecting angry faces and clenched fists. There was disappointment, for sure, but also the odd admiring nod of the head and a few sympathetic smiles. England, everyone agreed in the pub afterwards, had looked old, overhyped and overpaid, a collective of individuals without spark or spirit. Germany, on the other hand, looked young, fun, light-footed and confident in their new multicultural identity, with names like Khedira, Boateng, Gomez and Trochowski now among the more familiar Müllers and Friedrichs on the team sheet. By the end of the first round people had decided that this was the first World Cup they were going to support Germany to win, a sentiment I heard echoed in newspapers, online forums and office chats for the rest of the tournament. Even though Mesut Özil and co. in the end failed to lift the cup, they had managed something their parents' and grandparents' generations had repeatedly failed at: to make the English like the Germans again.

*

Just because Germany is more ironic and more lighthearted doesn't also mean it is always much wiser. The BBC's former Europe and North America editor Mark Mardell has called Germany 'the most mature country I know', yet you only have to look at the news to see that it is still perfectly capable of acting like a pre-teen. Just a few months after the phenomenal success of Germany's 'Multi-Kulti' football team, Angela Merkel announced at a meeting of young members of the CDU that multiculturalism had 'utterly failed', sparking a soul-searching debate about migrant integration which looked as tedious from Britain as it looked unnecessary. Other than the fact that the wilfully polemical Social Democrat Thilo Sarrazin had published a book, *Deutschland Schafft Sich Ab* ('Germany Is Digging Its Own Grave'), in which he had suggested that the Muslim population was lowering educational standards, there was no particular reason to reheat the debate at that exact moment. According to *Der Spiegel*, the number of Turkish immigrants entering Germany in 2008 was as low as it had been in 1983, and the number of asylum applications about a sixth of what it was in the mid-1990s. More Turks returned to Turkey in 2009 than came to live in Germany: bad news for a country whose population is forecast to fall by 11.6 million by 2050, and which needs every qualified worker it can get its hands on. Xenophobia is always on the rise when times are rough, yet in Germany this debate kicked off at a time when the economy was buzzing: the whole debate looked in desperate need of a dose of Ayer-esque common sense. But instead of telling the Germans to do their maths, David Cameron all but repeated Merkel's words at a security conference in Munich in February 2011: 'Under the doctrine of state multiculturalism we have encouraged different cultures to live separate lives, apart from each other and the mainstream. We have failed to provide a vision of society to which they feel they want to belong.'

Other recent developments indicate that in spite of its apparent maturity, Germany can still be more of a dreamer than a doer. During the eurozone crisis, as other international leaders cried out for decisive political action the German government was for a long time passive to the point of inactivity. Under the current coalition, Germany has abolished conscription into the military, considerably reduced the size of its army and refused to be drawn into a military conflict in Libya which Britain, France and the US entered with glee: a noble tendency, if the idea of a German military still makes you think about the Wehrmacht; naïvety verging on hypocrisy if you consider that the country is also the world's third largest exporter of major conventional weapons, including to Middle Eastern countries like Saudi Arabia.

I was puzzled by how differently Germany and Britain reacted to the Fukushima Daiichi nuclear disaster caused by the Japanese tsunami in March 2011. In Britain, many concluded that the worst-case scenario had turned out to be not as bad as everyone had feared, and that nuclear power was therefore the safer and cleaner alternative to dirty coal power. In Germany, news from Japan triggered a return of the '*Atomkraft? Nein danke!*' slogans of the 1980s, a soaring Green Party and, eventually, the announcement that the country would shut down all nuclear power stations by 2022. It has led some critics to wonder if the Germany of the second decade of the twenty-first century is living in a childhood dreamworld where there is no war, free money and endless electricity. Being hopelessly idealistic strikes me as a lesser crime than being depressingly cynical, especially if that idealism might eventually translate into a successful renewable energy industry. And yet Germany can surely benefit from some constructive criticism from England, just as England can still learn from Germany. Perhaps that is the real lesson we can take from the encounter between Unity Mitford and Adolf Hitler: that cosying up too closely isn't always a good idea, and that sometimes the value of the meeting isn't in the friendship, but in the criticism friends can give each other.

In June this year, Joanna and I went to Munich on our honeymoon. It was a boiling hot day, so we headed for the shade of the Englischer Garten.

'Where do you think she tried to shoot herself? Do you think it was the same spot she had secretly sunbathed?' I asked her.

'If I went to shoot myself in a park, I would make sure it's somewhere a little bit hidden, so that no one can stop you.'

'Yes, but not that hidden, so that they can still find your body before it starts decomposing.'

'Let's have a look if there's a plaque somewhere.'

An hour later we'd seen a man wearing a red-and-white check shirt, lederhosen and a big felt hat, like on a postcard ('He definitely needs more irony,' Jo said), a 'beer bike' on which up to ten people can drink beer from a bar on wheels while they're cycling along, and a woman followed by a small army of pug dogs, but no sign of Unity Mitford. We decided to stop in the beer garden underneath the pagoda, and I ordered beer, pretzels and white sausages. Just as I was about to take a first swig, an oompah band started to play in the background. I rolled my eyes.

'You know what? You're definitely more English than you are German,' Jo said. 'Me, on the other hand,' peeling a white sausage to dunk in sweet mustard, 'I could get into this.'

London, July 2011

Acknowledgements

Not all of those who have been bored by me droning on about this book over the last four years can be named, for they are legion. But some deserve a special mention. Kate Bucknell and Peter Parker were enthusiastic in sharing research and page references on the work and life of Christopher Isherwood. Julian Reid patiently let me leaf through Merton's college archives. Without Gretel Hinrichsen, Ian Hunter, Gwendolen Webster, and Jasia Reichardt and Nick Wadley at the Themerson Archive, my account of Kurt Schwitters's time in England would be riddled with mistakes. Daniel Gustav Cramer, David Foot, Noel Kingsbury, George Peterken, Heinrich Spiecker, Jan Woudstra and Andrea Wulf have taught me enough on gardening and forestry history to fill another book. Rebecca Baxter, David Buckle, Bill Heine and Andrew Lorenz have given me an exhaustive account of the industrial and corporate history of the Mini. Alex Clark and Ellah Alfrey first commissioned and edited the car chapter for Granta and have inadvertently shaped the rest of this book. Audrey Maye, Nora Harding and Mike Frinton generously shared memories of their parents, and

Acknowledgements

Barry Band drove and talked me around Blackpool. Graham Agg, Peter Ahrens, Klaus Christ, Stefan Hermann and Ed van Opzeeland have made me understand the magic of Borussia Mönchengladbach and Liverpool FC, even if I will go on supporting Arsenal for now. Astrid Proll could easily have batted away my approach but turned out to be a diligent and helpful interviewee. Dan van der Vat and Paul Hubert plugged the holes in my account of the German Autumn, and Aditya Chakrabortty, David Gow and Daniel Siemens all provided invaluable feedback at various stages.

Rüdiger Görner and Kevin Hilliard have been inspirations with their academic rigour and love of German literature from the start. Charlie English, Tom Gatti, Tobias Jones, Simon Kuper, Paul Laity and Craig Taylor have all given invaluable advice on the undercurrents and slipstreams of the publishing process. Walter Donohue has been a fantastically patient and inspiring editor, and Peter Straus the kind of supportive agent writers imagine in their dreams. Finally, there's not a chance in the world that this book would have happened without Jo, who has been my fiercest critic and my closest friend over the last four years. I owe you weekends.

Sources

Preface

Blur lyrics from 'Girls and Boys'. Words and Music by Graham Coxon, Steven Alexander James, David Rowntree and Damon Albarn. ©1994. Reproduced by permission of EMI Music Publishing Limited, London W8 5SW.

Jill Rutter from the Institute of Public Policy Research first drew my attention to the influx of German migrants in the 1990s; Danny Dorling has an interesting interpretation of those figures in *So You Think You Know About Britain* (Constable, 2011), pp. 111–12.

The anecdote about Thatcher and Kohl's meeting is related in beautifully chatty detail in Charles Powell's talk at the Witness Seminar on German Unification, 1989–90, which took place at Lancaster House on 16 October 2009 – a transcript has been published by the German embassy in London and is freely available online.

1. Heinrich Heine Can't Bear William Cobbett's Swearing

G. K. Chesterton: *William Cobbett* (Project Gutenberg Australia eBook) http://gutenberg.net.au/ebooks09/0900441.txt
William Cobbett: *Cottage Economy* (John Doyle, 1833)
William Cobbett: *Rural Rides* (T. Nelson & Sons, 1830)
G. D. H. Cole and Margaret Cole (eds): *The Opinions of William Cobbett* (Cobbett Publishing Company, 1944)

Sources

Peter Edgerly Firchow: *The Death of the German Cousin: Variations on a Literary Stereotype* (Associated University Press, 1986)

Theodor Fontane: *Glückliche Fahrt: Impressionen aus England und Schottland* (Aufbau Verlag, 2003)

Heinrich Heine: 'Englische Fragmente', in *Reisebilder* (Insel Verlag, 1980)

Richard Ingrams: *The Life and Adventures of William Cobbett* (Harper-Collins, 2005)

Siegfried Kracauer: *From Caligari to Hitler: A Psychological History of the German Film* (Princeton University Press, second edition, 2004)

Adolf Loos: 'Die englischen Schulen im Österreichischen Museum', in *Ins Leere gesprochen* (G. Prachner, 1981)

Keith Lowe: Inferno: *The Devastation of Hamburg* (Penguin, 2007)

Gerhard Müller-Schwefe: *Deutsche erfahren England: Englandbilder der Deutschen im 19. Jahrhundert* (Gunter Narr Verlag, 2007)

Siegbert Salomon Prawer: *Frankenstein's Island: England and the English in the Writings of Heinrich Heine* (Cambridge University Press, 1986)

Fritz J. Raddatz: *Taubenherz und Geierschnabel: Heine Heine – Eine Biographie* (Beltz Quadriga, 1997)

Jerry White: *London in the Nineteenth Century* (Jonathan Cape, 2007)

The two quotations from Goethe are my own translations of sections from the essay 'Zum Schäkespear-Tag' ('I am often ashamed . . .') and the memoir *Dichtung und Wahrheit* ('Hamlet and his monologues are ghosts . . .'). The various quotations from Heine too are my own translations, mainly from the essay 'Englische Fragmente' (EF): 'The German language makes my ears explode . . .' (Letter to Christian Sethe, quoted in Raddatz, p. 41); 'a secret consensus' (EF, in *Reisebilder*, p. 518); 'Land of freedom . . .' (EF, p. 501); 'the new religion . . .' (EF, p. 501); 'a husband and his long-term wife . . .' / ' like an old grandmother . . .' (EF, p. 504); 'The German censors . . .' ('Das Buch Le Grand', in *Reisebilder*, p. 193); 'Poor old Cobbett! . . .' (EF, p. 548); 'These people have no ear . . .' / 'They neither have accurate . . .' (*Lutetia*, chapter XV); 'a grey, yawning monster . . .' / 'the most repulsive people . . .' / 'a country which would have been swallowed up . . .' / 'the island of the damned . . .' ('Shakespeares Mädchen und Frauen'); 'Don't send poets to London!' (EF, p. 507); 'Let us praise the French!' ('Reise von München nach Genua', in *Reisebilder*, p. 308).

My portrayal of Cobbett is largely indebted to Richard Ingrams's excellent biography and Chesterton's immensely readable description of Cobbett's style. Various short quotations have been taken from a variety of sources: 'real insufficiency of the food . . .' (*Cottage Economy* (*CE*), p. 6); 'the land, the trees . . .' (*CE*, p. 28); 'A terrible evil' (*The Opinions of William Cobbett* (*OWC*), p. 258); 'Swarms of locusts . . .' (*OWC*, p. 127); 'loan-mongers, tax-gatherers . . .' ('Twopenny Trash', January 1832, pp. 145–6); 'dens of dunces' (*Rural Rides* (*RR*), p. 93); 'Scotch feelosofers' (*RR*, p. 568); 'mercenary villains' (*RR*, p. 559); 'an old eat' / 'a dirty dog' (quoted in Chesterton); 'a destroyer of health . . .' (*CE*, p. 19).

The quotations from Fontane's travel writing and Freiligrath's poem 'Hamlet' too are my own translations: 'awesome and incomparable' (*Glückliche Fahrt* (*GF*), p. 29); 'Music, as many have pointed out . . .' (*GF*, p. 76); 'The great tyrants . . .' (*GF*, p. 88).

2. Christopher Isherwood Listens to Marlene Dietrich

Katherine Bucknell and Nicholas Jenkins (eds): *W. H. Auden: 'The Map of All My Youth': Early Works, Friends and Influences* (Clarendon Press, 1990)

Gordon A. Craig: *Germany 1866–1945* (Oxford University Press, 1981)

Peter Edgerly Firchow: *Strange Meetings: Anglo-German Literary Encounters from 1910 to 1960* (The Catholic University of America Press, 2008)

Hugo von Hofmannsthal: *The Lord Chandos Letters and Other Writings*, trans. Joel Rotenberg (New York Review of Books, 2005), pp. 117–28

Christopher Isherwood: *The Berlin Novels: Mr Norris Changes Trains & Goodbye to Berlin* (Vintage, 1992)

Christopher Isherwood: *Christopher and His Kind* (University of Minnesota Press, 2001)

Sources

Christopher Isherwood: *The Sixties: Diaries, Volume Two: 1960–1969*, ed. Katherine Bucknell (HarperCollins, 2010), pp. 211–12

Wolfgang Kemp: *Foreign Affairs: Die Abenteuer einiger Engländer in Deutschland 1900–1947* (Carl Hanser Verlag, 2010)

Heinrich Mann: *Professor Unrat* (S. Fischer, 2nd edition, 2005)

Peter Parker: *Isherwood* (Picador, 2nd edition, 2005)

S. S. Prawer: *The Blue Angel* (BFI Publishing, 2002)

Maria Riva: *Marlene Dietrich* (Alfred A. Knopf, 1993)

Werner Sombart: *Händler und Helden: Patriotische Besinnungen* (Duncker & Humbolt, 1915)

Josef von Sternberg: *Fun in a Chinese Laundry* (Secker & Warburg, 1966)

Stefan Ullrich: *Der Weimar Komplex* (Wallstein Verlag, 2009)

Frank Wedekind: *Lulu: Die Büchse der Pandora* (Deutsches Schauspielhaus, 1988)

Eric D. Weitz: *Weimar Germany: Promise and Tragedy* (Princeton, 2007)

The quotation from Kurt Tucholsky ('You can imagine a Frenchman speaking English . . .') is my own translation of a section from 'Die Weltbühne', 20/48, November 1924 (Verlag der Weltbühne, 1924), p. 804. Firchow and Kemp helped shape the account of the English taking in Berlin's 'decadence': 'pervert's paradise . . .' (Firchow, p. 117). Auden's series of brilliantly filthy poems hasn't made it into most collections of his poems, surprisingly; the lines from 'Chorale' I quote can be found, eloquently rendered into English by David Constantine, in Bucknell and Jenkins' *The Map of All My Youth*', p. 15. Citations from the 'Lord Chandos Letter' are from Joel Rotenberg's translation of Hofmannsthal's short writings, p. 125. The quotation from Charlotte Roche is from my own interview with the author, which appeared on *Granta* Online on 10 May 2008.

Excerpts from *Mr Norris Changes Trains* (1935), *Goodbye to Berlin* (1939) and *Christopher and His Kind* by Christopher Isherwood (1976). Copyright © 1935, 1939 and 1976, Christopher Isherwood, used by permission of The Wylie Agency (UK) Limited. Quotations from *Chris-*

topher and His Kind: ('Christopher was suffering from . . .'), the Vintage collection of the Berlin stories (The word *Liebe* . . .', p. 108; 'What in the world can he have been eating . . .', pp. 246–7; 'nude fleshy arms ripple unappetisingly', p. 253; 'nervous, veined and very thin', p. 277; 'do you find German girls . . .', p. 262; 'I am a camera', p. 243). Isherwood's account of the Dietrich concert, and the non-meeting backstage, is taken from his diaries: *The Sixties: Diaries, Volume Two: 1960–1969*, ed. Bucknell, p. 511–12. Dietrich's struggle with the English language is rendered in cruel detail in Josef von Sternberg's biography, pp. 245–51.

3. Theodor Adorno Doesn't Do the Jitterbug with A. J. Ayer

Theodor Adorno: *Briefe und Briefwechsel* (Suhrkamp, 1994)

Theodor Adorno: *Briefwechsel Adorno/Krenek* (Suhrkamp, 2003)

Theodor Adorno: *The Culture Industry: Selected Essays on Mass Culture* (Routledge, 1991)

Theodor Adorno: *Gesammelte Schriften* (Suhrkamp, 1997)

Theodor Adorno: *Minima Moralia*, trans. E. F. N. Jephco (Verso, 2005)

Theodor Adorno: *Versuch, das Endspiel zu verstehen* (Suhrkamp, 1978)

Theodor Adorno and Max Horkheimer: *Dialectic of Enlightenment* (Allen Lane, 1973)

A. J. Ayer: *Language, Truth and Logic* (Penguin, 2001)

A. J. Ayer: *Part of My Life* (Collins, 1977)

Detlev Claussen: *Theodor Adorno: One Last Genius*, trans. Rodney Livingstone (Harvard University Press, 2008)

Wolfram Ette: 'Adorno in England', in *Musik & Ästhetik*, vol. 4 (1997), pp. 36–51

John Harris: *The Last Party: Britpop, Blair and the Demise of English Rock* (Fourth Estate, 2003)

Michael Ignatieff: *Isaiah Berlin: A Life* (Chatto & Windus, 1998)

Stefan Müller-Doohm: *Adorno – Eine Biographie* (Suhrkamp, 2003)

Ben Rogers: *A. J. Ayer: A Life* (Verso, 1999)

Heinz Steinert: *Die Entdeckung der Kulturindustrie, oder: Warum Professor Adorno Jazz-Musik nicht ausstehen konnte* (Westfälisches Dampfboot, 2nd edition, 2003)

Sources

Evelyn Wilcock: 'Adorno, Jazz and Racism: "Über Jazz" and the 1934–7 British Jazz Debate', in *Telos* 107 (Spring 1996), pp. 63–81

Kevin Hilliard first pointed me in the direction of the Merton JCR register, which has previously been written about by Malte Herwig in a short article in the *Süddeutsche Zeitung* ('Minima Marginalia', 12 April 2002). Evelyn Wilcock's article on Adorno's jazz writing and the 'British jazz debate' provided invaluable background reading for the German philosopher's time in Oxford.

Adorno's aphorisms quoted here are mainly from E. F. N. Jephco's translation of *Minima Moralia* (*MM*): 'Life has become the ideology . . .' (*MM*, p. 122); 'Art is magic . . .' (*MM*, p. 222); 'The splinter in your eye . . .' (*MM*, p. 50); 'Intelligence is a moral category' (*MM*, p. 197); 'The joke of our time . . .' (*MM*, p. 141). All other quotations from Adorno are my own translations: 'All reification is a kind of forgetting' (Walter Benjamin, 29 February 1940, in *Briefe und Briefwechsel*, vol. 1, p. 417); 'oldest and one of the most exclusive colleges . . .' / 'true basics of my philosophy . . .' (*Briefwechsel Adorno/Krenek*, p. 18); 'like going back to school . . .' / 'a fear-filled nightmare' (Letter to Max Horkheimer, 2 November 1934, *Gesammelte Schriften* vol. 15, p. 262).

Ben Rogers's biography and Ayer's autobiography were the main sources for my account of the English philosopher's life and times; the line about the 'Emperor of Manchukuo' is from *Language, Truth and Logic*, p. 167. Methuen's *The Complete Beyond the Fringe* is the place to go for a transcript of Alan Bennett's sketch about Oxford philosophers – once you've watched a clip of the real thing.

4. Kurt Schwitters Reinvents Dada by Grasmere Lake

David Blackbourn: *The Conquest of Nature: Water, Landscape, and the Making of Modern Germany* (Pimlico, 2007)

Paul Cronin: *Herzog on Herzog* (Faber and Faber, 2002)

E. M. Forster: *Howards End* (Penguin, 2000)

Hermann Hesse: *Wanderung* (Suhrkamp, 1975)

Sources

Federico Hindermann (ed.): *Sag' ich's euch, geliebte Bäume* (Manesse, 1999)

Hermon Ould (ed.): *Freedom of Expression: A Symposium* (Kennikat Press, 1944)

Simon Schama: *Landscape and Memory* (Vintage, 1995)

Kurt Schwitters: *Wir spielen, bis uns der Tod abholt: Briefe aus fünf Jahrzehnten*, ed. Ernst Nündel (Ullstein, 1975)

Stephen Spender: *European Witness* (Hamish Hamilton, 1946)

Stefan Themerson: *Kurt Schwitters in England* (Gaberbocchus Press, 1958)

Fred Uhlman: *The Making of an Englishman* (Gollancz, 1960)

Evelyn Waugh: *Scoop* (Penguin, 2000)

Gwendolen Webster: *Kurt Merz Schwitters: A Biographical Study* (University of Wales Press, 1997)

Stefan Zweig: 'Die Gärten im Kriege', in *Auf Reisen* (Fischer, 2004)

The story of Schwitters's appearance at the International PEN Conference and the varying reactions to Forster's speech are a mosaic of accounts in Themerson, p. 10, Ould, pp. 7–8, and George Orwell's review of *Freedom of Expression*, 12 October 1945. The Dadaist manifestos are quoted in Uhlman, p. 233. The account of Schwitters's life in England is indebted to Gwendolen Webster's exhaustive biography (GW), Stefan Themerson's book (ST), Ernst Nündel's edition of letters (EN) and the collected letters in the Schwitters Archive (SA) in Hanover: 'We Germans . . .' (Letter to L. Gleichmann, 17 July 1946, SA); 'The English people are . . .' (EN, p. 204); 'You always talk . . .' (Letter to C. Spengemann, 3 April 1946, SA); 'I am working three hours a day . . .' (Letter to M. Hagenbach, 2 September 1947, EN, p. 286); 'Thanks to England . . .' (Letter to C. Spengemann, EN, p. 261); 'Whenever you are standing . . .' (ST, p. 45).

Evelyn Waugh's 'the kind of place . . .' is from *Scoop*, p. 27. Stephen Spender's 'Germany has not the cultivated look . . .' is from the unjustly forgotten work *European Witness*, p. 15. Werner Herzog's 'When I am walking . . .' is from Paul Cronin's fascinating long interview in *Herzog on Herzog*, p. 281. The Robert Walser line is from his short essay/story

'Der Wald'. Hermann Hesse's aphorisms on the forest are from *Wanderung* (both author's own translation), Stefan Zweig's essay 'Die Gärten im Kriege' from *Auf Reisen*, p. 144 (author's own translation) and Heine's travel essay 'Die Harzreise' from *Reisebilder*, p. 64. Harry Pierce's description of the look and philosophy of Cylinders Farm is from an unpublished manuscript, which was kindly loaned to me by Ian Hunter.

5. The Beetle Overtakes the Mini

Werner Abelshauser: *The Dynamics of German Industry* (Berghahn, 2005)

Gillian Bardsley: *Issigonis: The Official Biography* (Icon Books, 2006)

Chris Brady and Andrew Lorenz: *End of the Road: The True Story of the Downfall of Rover* (Pearson, second edition, 2005)

Roy Church: *The Rise and Decline of the British Motor Industry* (Cambridge University Press, 1995)

Simon Garfield: *Mini: The True and Secret History of the Making of a Motor Car* (Faber and Faber, 2010)

Frank Grube and Gerhard Richter: *Das Wirtschaftswunder* (Hoffmann & Campe, 1983)

Erica Jong: *Fear of Flying* (Vintage, 1998)

Markus Lupa: *The British and Their Works: The Volkswagenwerk and the occupying power 1945–1949* (Volkswagen AG, second edition, 2005)

Hermann Muthesius: *The English House*, ed. Dennis Sharp, trans. Janet Seligman and Stewart Spencer (Frances Lincoln, 2007)

Andrew Nahum: *Alec Issigonis* (Design Council, 1988)

Simon Reich: *The Fruits of Fascism: Postwar Prosperity in Historical Perspective* (Cornell University, 1990)

Ralf Richter: *Ivan Hirst: British Officer and Manager of Volkswagen's Postwar Recovery* (Volkswagen AG, 2nd edition, 2004)

Max Weber: *The Protestant Work Ethic and the 'Spirit' of Capitalism*, trans. Peter Baehr and Gordon C. Wells (Penguin, 2002)

Martin J. Wiener: English Culture and the Decline of the Industrial Spirit, 1850–1980 (Cambridge University Press, second edition, 2004)

Jonathan Wood: *Alec Issigonis: The Man Who Made the Mini* (Breedon Books, 2005)

The story about Rover workers' trips to Germany was relayed to me by the former Cowley worker David Buckle in an interview. A detailed account of Issigonis's life, including the Davos anecdote, can be found in Gillian Bardsley's biography, while most of the section on the BMW/Rover takeover is sourced from Chris Brady and Andrew Lorenz's *End of the Road* (including the quotation from Bernd Pischetsrieder, p. 133), as well as an interview with Lorenz. Erica Jong's theory about German toilets is from *Fear of Flying*, p. 24. Road death statistics published by Statistisches Bundesamt Deutschland, www.destatis.de.

6. Freddy Frinton Teaches the Germans to Laugh

Theodor Adorno: *Versuch, das Endspiel zu verstehen* (Suhrkamp, 1973)
Arnold Blumer: *Das dokumentarische Theater der sechziger Jahre in der Bundesrepublik Deutschland* (Verlag Anton Hain, 1977)
Karl Heinz Bohrer: 'Individualismus, Realismus, Freiheitlichkeit – Elemente des englischen Humors', in *Merkur*, Sept./Oct. 2002 (9/10)
Peter Frankenfeld: *Das war mein Leben* (Herbig, 1982)
Sigmund Freud: *Jokes and Their Relation to the Unconscious* (Routledge, 1966)
Hans-Dieter Gelftert: *Max und Monty – Kleine Geschichte des deutschen & englischen Humors* (Beck, 1998)
Wend Kässens: *Der Spielmacher: Gespräche mit George Tabori* (Verlag Klaus Wagenbach, 2004)
Stefan Mayr: *Dinner for One von A–Z: Das Lexikon zum Kult-Vergnügen* (Eichborn, 2002)
George Orwell: 'The Art of Donald McGill', in *Essays* (Penguin, 2000)
Manfred Pfister (ed.): *A History of English Laughter* (Rodopi, 2002)
Thorsten Unger: *Differente Lachkulturen: Fremde Komik und ihre Über-setzung* (Gunter Nart, 1995)

The account of the meetings between Frankenfeld, Dunkhase, Frinton and Ward is a compound of details from Frankenfeld's autobiography,

Sources

Stefan Mayr's encyclopaedic history of the sketch, and interviews with Audrey Maye, Nora Harding and Mike Frinton, as well as Blackpool historian Barry Band.

Frinton, 'I have played the drunk as long as I can remember,' is quoted in Mayr, p. 43, the review from the *Berliner Stimme* in Unger's *Differente Lachkulturen*, p. 257. The Adorno quotation is my translation of a line from *Versuch, das Endspiel zu verstehen*, p. 188; and 'a sort of saturnalia . . .' is from Orwell's 'The Art of Donald McGill', which is in the Penguin collection of his essays. George Tabori's anecdote about Thomas Mann in Hollywood was told me by the late playwright in person when I interviewed him in 2006, later published as 'The Banality of Comedy' in *The Believer* (October 2007).

7. Kevin Keegan Runs Past Berti Vogts

Jorge Luis Borges: 'The Lottery in Babylon', in *Collected Fictions*, trans. Andrew Hurley (Penguin, 1998)

David Downing: *The Best of Enemies: England v Germany* (Bloomsbury, 2000)

Christiane Eisenberg: *English sports und deutsche Bürger. Eine Gesellschaftsgeschichte 1800–1939* (Schöningh, 1999)

Clifford Geertz: 'Deep Play: Notes on the Balinese Cockfight', in *The Interpretation of Cultures: Selected Essays* (Basic Books, 1973)

Brian Glanville: *Kevin Keegan* (Hamish Hamilton, 1981)

Ulrich Hesse-Lichtenberger: *Tor! The Story of German Football* (WSC Books, 2002)

Rafael Honigstein: *Englischer Fussball: A German View of Our Beautiful Game* (Yellow Jersey, 2008)

Kevin Keegan with Mike Langley: *Against the World* (Sidgwick & Jackson, 1979)

Kevin Keegan: *My Autobiography* (Little, Brown, 1997)

Karl Planck: *Fusslümmelei: Über Stauchballspiel und englische Krankheit* (Lit-Verlag, 1988)

Alan Tomlinson and Christopher Young (eds): *German Football: History, Culture, Society* (Routledge, 2006)

Sources

The account of the 1977 European Cup final draws on DVDs of the BBC's and Westdeutscher Rundfunk's recordings of the match, interviews with numerous fans, in particular Graham Agg and Klaus Christ, and an interview with the Dutch journalist Ed van Opzeeland, as well as Keegan's autobiography.

Keegan's description of his own qualities is quoted in Brian Glanville's biography, *Kevin Keegan*, p. 42, while the Sepp Herberger quotation ('a good footballer . . .') is from Jürgen Leinemann's *Sepp Herberger: Ein Leben, eine Legende* (Rowohlt, 2004), pp. 192–3. The translation of Borges's Babylonian lottery I quote from is Andrew Hurley's for Penguin's *Collected Fictions*, pp. 101–6, while the Isherwood quotation here is from *Christopher and His Kind*. The match reports I quote are from *The Times* ('a cross between Russian roulette and the OK Corral', 28 June 1996; 'innocently lost not a football match but a lottery', 5 July 1990; 'a bizarre form of punishment . . .', 6 July 1990) and the *Sun* ('never lost to Germany – at soccer neither', quoted in David Downing, *The Best of Enemies*, p. 110). Tim Adams's article 'The best chance you'll get?' in the *Observer* on 7 January 2007 offers a very good analysis of changing attitudes to gambling regulation under Labour. Roger Willemsen's line about Berti Vogts is from his documentary portrait from 1996, in the ZDF 'Zeitgenossen' series. Both the Lineker and the Mussolini quotations are part of football folklore and have been endlessly quoted in articles, but are hard to verify, and should thus be taken with a pinch of salt.

8. Astrid Proll Wishes She Wasn't on Joe Strummer's T-shirt

Stefan Aust: *Der Baader-Meinhof Komplex* (Hoffmann und Campe, 2nd edition, 1986)

Jillian Becker: *Hitler's Children: The Story of the Baader-Meinhof Terrorist Gang* (Michael Joseph, 1977)

Heinrich Böll: *Irisches Tagebuch* (Deutscher Taschenbuch Verlag, 51st edition, 2001)

'Die Rote Armee aufbauen!', *Agit* 883 (5 June 1970)

Sources

Ulrike Edschmid: *Frau mit Waffe – Zwei Geschichten aus terroristischen Zeiten* (Rowohlt, 1996)

Martha Gellhorn: 'Is There a New Germany?', February 1964, from *The View from the Ground*

Johnny Green: *A Riot of Our Own: Night and Day with the Clash* (Orion, 2003)

Ulrike Meinhof: *Everybody Talks About the Weather . . . We Don't: The Writings of Ulrike Meinhof*, translated by Karin Bauer (Seven Stories Press, 2008)

Jon Savage: *England's Dreaming: Sex Pistols and Punk Rock* (Faber and Faber, 2001)

Kay Schiller and Chris Young: *The 1972 Munich Olympics and the Making of Modern Germany* (University of California Press, 2nd edition, 2010)

Hugh Trevor-Roper: *The Last Days of Hitler* (Heron Books, 4th edition, 1971)

The account of the Victoria Park gig is based on reviews in the *NME* and *Melody Maker* archive, as well as the Clash tour manager Johnny Green's memoir. Stefan Aust's *Der Baader-Meinhof Komplex* is still unsurpassed as the definitive account of the origins of the Baader-Meinhof group and is one of the main sources for the detail in this chapter, including the anecdote about the sculptor Dierk Hoff's brush with the Red Army Faction. Adorno's reaction to the student protests is quoted in Becker's *Hitler's Children*, p. 73; the quotation from Ulrike Meinhof, 'We Germans have greater difficulties . . .' is from Karin Bauer's translation of the *konkret* article 'File Number XY: Dissolved' (1968), in *Everybody Talks About the Weather . . . We Don't: The Writings of Ulrike Meinhof*, p. 227; Michel Friedman's interview with Horst Mahler was published in *Vanity Fair Deutschland*, 11 September 2007; Hugh Trevor-Roper's assessment of German politics is from the afterword to *The Last Days of Hitler*, pp. 262–3; Martha Gellhorn's 'Is There a New Germany?' (February 1964) is quoted in *Granta 42: Krauts!*, p. 205.

The quotation from Hans Magnus Enzensberger is from my interview with the author in February 2010, published in the *Guardian* on 15 May 2010. The account of Astrid Proll's time in England is based on several interviews with Proll, with additional material from Ulrike Edschmid's *Frau mit Waffe*.

Epilogue

Quotations from the Mitford sisters are copyright of the Mitford Estate and are reproduced by permission of The Estate, care of Rogers, Coleridge and White Ltd, 20 Powis Mews, London W11 1JN. They are taken from *The Mitfords: Letters between Six Sisters*, ed. Charlotte Mosley (Harper Perennial, 2008): 'The other day . . .', p. 113; 'The Führer was *heavenly* . . .', p. 68; 'I still maintain that it is far more in favour . . .', pp. 59–60. Hitler's speech starting 'I have proposed friendship . . .' is my translation of a section quoted in 'Die Opfer schuldig?', *Die Zeit*, 22 November 1956.

The quotation from Thomas Hüetlin is my translation of a line from an article that appeared in *Der Spiegel* on 14 May 2007; Martin Kettle, 'It is not irrational . . .', is from the *Guardian* on 21 August 2009; Maurice Glasman floated the idea of importing German masters in an interview with Mary Riddell in the *Daily Telegraph* on 18 July 2011; Eric Pickles's speech on German local government is quoted in Tim Montgomerie's blogpost 'Eric Pickles urges councils to axe "non-jobs" and share back office functions' on the Conservative Home website on 6 July 2010; Grant Shapps praised German housing policy in an interview with Anushka Asthana in the *Observer* on 2 January 2011, while the statistic of Turkish immigrants entering and leaving Germany is quoted in the article 'Deutschland ist Auswanderungsland', *Spiegel Online*, 15 October 2010.

Index

Index

Index

Index